THE REFERENCE SHELF

DRUGS AND AMERICAN SOCIETY

edited by ROBERT EMMET LONG

THE REFERENCE SHELF

Volume 57 Number 6

THE H. W. WILSON COMPANY

New York 1986

THE REFERENCE SHELF

The books in this series contain reprints of articles, excerpts from books, and addresses on current issues and social trends in the United States and other countries. There are six separately bound numbers in each volume, all of which are generally published in the same calendar year. One number is a collection of recent speeches; each of the others is devoted to a single subject and gives background information and discussion from various points of view, concluding with a comprehensive bibliography. Books in the series may be purchased individually or on subscription.

Library of Congress Cataloging in Publication Data

Main entry under title:

Drugs and American society.

(The Reference shelf ; v. 57, no. 6)
Bibliography: p.
Summary: A collection of reprinted articles from various sources discussing drug trafficking and drug abuse in the United States today.
1. Drug abuse—United States—Addresses, essays, lectures. 2. Narcotics, Control of—Addresses, essays, lectures. 3. Cocaine—Addresses, essays, lectures. 4. Marihuana—Addresses, essays, lectures. [1. Drug abuse—Addresses, essays, lectures. 2. Narcotics, Control of—Addresses, essays, lectures] I. Long, Robert Emmet. II. Series.
HV5825.D786 1985 362.2'932'0973 85-26604
ISBN 0-8242-0714-9

Printed in the United States of America

CONTENTS

PREFACE

Although drug use has been part of American life since the mid 19th century, it did not come into great prominence until the 1960s, when it was embraced by students and young people protesting what was regarded as the sterile conformity of the past decade. LSD was touted as "mind-expanding," and the cry was to "turn on" to the exotic realms of experience that lay hidden in the human mind. This hallucinogenic experience was available not only through a variety of hard drugs but also through a milder one, marijuana, which became the most fashionable choice among the young and disaffected. The Vietnam war dramatized this conflict, and it contributed to the rising use of drugs among young people as a form of affiliation with protest and defiance. By the early 1980s, drug use was no longer limited to a single group of people but had become part of the mainstream of American life. Today drugs are used commonly by the rich and successful as well as by the disadvantaged and, perhaps most startlingly of all, have been accepted by the middle class. America has become a drug culture, the marketplace of an international flow of drugs on an unprecedented scale.

The disruption of American life due to trafficking in illegal drugs has been enormous, affecting small towns as well as large metropolitan areas. Fortunes are made suddenly and illicitly, and lives are ruined by drug dependence and drug overdoses. A criminal empire has risen that dwarfs the activities of the Mafia during the days of Prohibition. Moreover, those who become addicted to drugs often turn to crime to support their habits, thus creating a second major social problem. In the present epidemic of drug use, the U. S. government has acted to stem the flow of narcotics from foreign countries, and President Reagan has called the battle against drug use a chief priority of his administration. Yet this concerted effort to halt or at least to contain the flow of drugs into the country has produced only limited results, and it seems clear that this will be a problem not easily resolved.

In this survey of drugs and American society, Section I is devoted to international drug trafficking—the overseas sources and distribution network that depends on the United States as its prime market. Section II focuses upon cocaine, which has become the "drug of the eighties," overshadowing all other narcotics in its adoption by Americans. Section III takes up the subject of marijuana, and particularly the debate now taking place over whether or not it should be legalized. Finally, Section IV takes a brief look at the widespread use of drugs by celebrities and poses the question: Is drug use a symbol of success in American life?

The editor is indebted to the authors and publishers who have granted permission to reprint the materials in this compilation. Special thanks are due to Ellen Morin and the Fulton Public Library, and to the staff of the Penfield Library, State University of New York at Oswego.

ROBERT EMMET LONG

June 1985

I. INTERNATIONAL DRUG TRAFFICKING

EDITOR'S INTRODUCTION

The production and distribution of illegal drugs exists on a global scale that extends from the Middle East and Asia to South America and the Caribbean. The U. S. Drug Enforcement Administration has charted its activities and has made efforts to halt the introduction of drugs into the country. But combatting the flow of drugs into the United States is a task so formidable that to do it effectively would take most of the federal budget. Drug smuggling is sophisticated and complex, defying the efforts of the most vigilant agents. When one source is closed down, through cooperation with a foreign government, another will simply spring up in a different country. Such huge sums of money are involved that corruption of officials almost inevitably results, and, in fact, the banking communities of American cities have themselves become implicated in the "laundering" of drug money so that its sources cannot be traced. Despite all of its resources and its dedication to curbing the influx of drugs into the country, the U. S. government itself seems hardly equal to the power, wealth, and determination of those who profiteer in the drug trade. This dilemma is reflected in the articles that appear in this section.

Mathea Falco's article, "The Big Business of Illicit Drugs," which appeared in the *New York Times Magazine*, provides an important overview of the international narcotics trade. It traces sources of production in Asia and South America, particularly in Colombia, the foremost supplier of cocaine and marijuana in the Southern hemisphere, and concludes that even with the federal government's best efforts to contain smuggling, the flow of drugs into the country has increased rather than diminished during the last few years. Susanna McBee's report, "Flood of Drugs—A Losing Battle," from *U. S. News & World Report*, discusses the situation in Colombia in further detail, as well as that in the drug-supplying nations in Asia. Penny Lernoux's revealing investigation, "The Miami Connection," which appeared in *The Nation*, focuses upon Miami as the drug-importing capital of America and particularly upon the complicity of Miami banks in "laundering" illicit drug money. Harry Anderson's "Drug Wars: Murder in Mexico," from *Newsweek*, discusses the brutal murder of U. S. Drug Enforcement Administration agent Enrique Camarena Salazar—an instance of the aggressive defiance of enforcement efforts in many parts of Central and South America. The section concludes with the statement by Jon R. Thomas, Assistant Secretary of State for International Narcotics Matters, which appeared in the *Department of State Bulletin*. Thomas's paper argues for closer international cooperation in containing drug traffic and reviews present enforcement policies in South American countries. It does not, however, hold out the hope of any immediate or easy solutions to the drug dilemma.

THE BIG BUSINESS OF ILLICIT DRUGS[1]

The international drug trade is no longer a haphazard or even a particularly shady undertaking. In the last 10 years, illicit drugs have become one of the world's most lucrative and dynamic industries, with revenues so enormous and so dispersed over the surface of the globe that they can only be guessed at.

In the United States, Exxon is the sole corporation with annual revenues in excess of the $79 billion that, according to the Drug Enforcement Administration's last estimate, is generated every year by the sale of illicit drugs. And, the National Organization to Reform Marijuana Laws reports, marijuana is currently our second-largest cash crop nationally, after corn and just ahead of soybeans.

Like any other growth industry, this is one run by men of ambition and vision, by executives and entrepreneurs, often from the

[1]Excerpted from an article by Mathea Falco, formerly Assistant Secretary of State for International Narcotics Matters. *New York Times Magazine*. p. 108–12. D. 11, '83. Copyright © 1983 by the New York Times Company. Reprinted by permission.

middle class, backed up by a full complement of bankers, lawyers and financiers. Stimulated by their enormous, and untaxed, profits, they keep a sharp eye on growth rate, territorial expansion and market share.

In many less-developed countries of the third world, drug trafficking, which has provided a new way to earn vast sums of hard currency, is transforming whole economies. In Colombia, according to its National Institution of Financial Associations, marijuana and cocaine, together, produce more foreign exchange than coffee and cut flowers, that nation's chief lawful exports. As a result, Colombia has the healthiest balance of payments in Latin America. In Jamaica, says the United States Drug Enforcement Administration, the annual $1.2 billion marijuana trade accounts for more revenue than all other exports combined.

The driving force behind the world's escalating drug traffic is, simply, escalating demand. The National Institute of Drug Abuse estimates that 56 million Americans have smoked marijuana, and 22 million have ingested cocaine. And, for the first time in half a decade, heroin use in the United States, particularly in its big cities, is on the rise.

At home, the explosion in the demand for drugs has overwhelmed the already painfully limited budgets of the social-welfare, public-health and law-enforcement organizations charged with combatting the problem. These agencies can deal with only a small fraction of the millions of Americans who use illicit drugs daily.

Abroad, the international drug traffic is having an even greater impact, eroding the stability of fragile social and political institutions ranging from banks to courts to governments. In many of the countries where drug trafficking has become a major economic force, most notably Bolivia and Peru, the traffickers openly use money—and violence—to intimidate government officials, thereby challenging the viability of democracy itself.

In July 1980, Bolivia—a prime producer of coca, the shrub from whose leaves cocaine is refined—underwent yet another military coup, this one led by Gen. Luis García Meza. García Meza, according to officials of the Drug Enforcement Administration, had bought the support of key military commanders with money supplied by cocaine dealers. Indeed, his regime was rife with cocaine connections: The new Interior Minister, Col. Luis Arce Gómez, responsible for, among other things, state security, provided protection to traffickers in return for a share of the profits. The Minister of Education, Col. Ariel Coca, also was deeply involved in the cocaine trade.

In October 1982, the generals turned over power to a democratically elected President, Hernán Siles Zuazo.

The Siles administration is highly unstable, however, weakened by a slumping economy—and by domestic criticism that, despite its dismissal of dozens of officials implicated in cocaine traffic, it is ineffective at curtailing that movement.

Ironically, the problems of cocaine traffic and money are inextricably linked: While Bolivia's lawful foreign-exchange earnings, derived primarily from the export of tin, account for $800 million a year, cocaine is estimated to generate as much as 10 times that amount. Consequently, the drug traffickers in Bolivia are at least as powerful as the government. What's more, they have more money than—and weapons and equipment as good as—the armed forces or the police.

Elsewhere, drugs provide the principal source of income for insurgent and terrorist groups. In Burma, the struggle by dissidents for control of the northeastern portion of the country, which has its roots in decades of ethnic and political tension, is financed largely by drug traffic. One of the insurgent groups, the Burmese Communist Party, formerly received its most substantial assistance, in the form of money and arms, from China. Now, according to State Department intelligence sources, the Burmese Communist Party, with approximately 10,000 armed men, and with control of half of Burma's opium cultivation, uses drug money to buy black-market weaponry and equipment in neighboring Thailand.

The Shan United Army, the most important of the Southeast Asian trafficking groups, operating along the Burma-Thiland border, is a vertically integrated organization that oversees everything from the cultivation of a vast acreage of opium poppies to the refining and shipment of heroin. Although well-publicized raids by irregular Thai forces during the last year have forced the Shan United Army to relocate its main headquarters from Ban Hin Taek on the Thai side of the border to Mong Kan, 20 kilometers inside Burma, the impact of these forays has been negligible on the drug problem.

Countries do not have to be producers or refiners of drugs to be able to make money from the drug traffic—or to use that money to political advantage. Bulgaria no longer grows opium poppies for medicinal morphine and codeine. However, its Government, motivated apparently both by a desire to exacerbate the drug-addiction crisis in the West and by the need to obtain hard currency, openly tolerates the transit of heroin across its borders. With five million tourists a year, Bulgaria provides and ideal site for the movement—and purchase—of drugs enroute from the "Golden Crescent" of Afghanistan, Iran and Pakistan to Western Europe and the United States.

The Turkish terrorist Mehmet Ali Agca, who shot Pope John Paul II in May 1981, maintains that he was financed by Turkish drug smugglers with close ties to Bulgaria's security police. In addition, there is credible evidence, according to the State Department, that officials from the Bulgarian state export corporation, KINTEX, have been involved in trading guns for drugs with both left- and right-wing terrorist groups in Turkey.

The massive sums of money generated by the traffic in illicit drugs have greatly distorted the economies of those drug-producing countries. In Colombia, Bolivia and Peru, many farmers have turned from growing food crops to growing marijuana and coca, from which they routinely make three to four times as much money a year. In the mountainous Sierra Nevada de Santa Marta region of Colombia, for instance, where 45,000 acres are given over to the cultivation of marijuana, 82 exporters make $700 million in annual profits, according to Colombia's National Association of Financial Institutions.

But the producing countries retain only a fraction of the drug-trade profits. Moreover, the profits that are spent locally tend to go for luxury consumables, most of which are imported, rather than long-term investment in industry and agriculture. In Bolivia, for example, only about $300 million of the billions earned from sales of coca and cocaine remains there; in Colombia, less than a third of the estimated $3 billion generated annually by the cocaine and marijuana traffic stays in the country.

At the same time, some American financial institutions are also reaping enormous profits from the billions of dollars generated by international drug dealing, principally by assisting traffickers in moving large numbers of dollars from one country to another and in "laundering" those dollars through legitimate investment.

A joint investigation by the United States Treasury and Justice Departments, begun in 1980 and dubbed Operation Greenback, identified several Florida banks, among others, that had actively solicited traffickers' accounts. These banks provided the traffickers with such services as wiring "drug" money to offshore banks that were set up specifically for that purpose and providing letters of credit for the purchase of legitimate businesses. Operation Greenback resulted in the arrest of 61 major narcotics traffickers and the seizure of $20 million in drug assets.

In March 1983, after a two-year study, the Permanent Subcommittee on Investigations of the United States Senate's Committee on Governmental Affairs reported that Panama, the Bahamas and the Cayman Islands, as well as other Caribbean countries have become major havens for drug money, laundering as much as $43 billion a year. Because of these countries' strict financial-secrecy laws and their lack of exchange controls, the money is almost impossible to trace when it returns to the United States whether for investment or for other purposes.

The criminal use of these off-shore banks has become so pervasive, the subcommittee wrote, that it "undermines the integrity of American banks . . . threatens the integrity of our tax system . . . and feeds the coffers of criminal enterprises." The report concluded that the proliferation of accounts opened by criminals and drug traffickers, and "not the failure of repayment of a loan from a sovereign nation, could be the backbreaking straw to the banking system."

The most cost-effective way to reduce the quantity of illicit drugs coming into the United States, drug-enforcement officials argue, is to destroy those drugs at their source, rather than try to stop them at our borders or search for them once they are already here. As a result, our international drug policy has, since the early 1970's, been focused on working with foreign governments to help them strengthen their own narcotics-control efforts. But, while the logic of this policy is appealing, it has been only marginally successful.

In 1975, the Mexican Government, with American assistance, initiated a program to eliminate its marijuana crop by spraying it from the air with the herbicide paraquat. Mexico, then a major supplier of relatively cheap, low-potency marijuana to the United States market, effectively destroyed much of that crop. But what survived the paraquat spraying still flowed north, where it caused widespread concern among marijuana smokers and public-health officials. As a result, though not exactly according to plan, imports of Mexican marijuana began to plummet.

Jamaica and Colombia, previously only minor suppliers of marijuana, quickly stepped up production. Unfortunately, their marijuana, with a much higher potency, only increased the hazards for American users. At the same time, American domestic production of marijuana began to boom. Indeed, it was in the wake of the Mexican spraying that it became such a prominent cash crop domestically.

When, in 1980, the United States urged Colombia to suppress rapidly expanding marijuana cultivation in its remote Guajira peninsula, officials in Bogotá, responding privately to State Department representatives, said that the United States only wanted to protect its own burgeoning marijuana industry from foreign competition. Recently, Colombia has received a proposal from the Reagan Administration that it undertake, with American aid, a multimillion-dollar marijuana-eradication program, based on the aerial spraying of paraquat—even though, as Colombians like to observe, marijuana eradication in the United States is effected with the much slower cutting-and-burning method. Even if President Belisario Betancur Cuartas agrees to defy the powerful economic and political forces arrayed against him at home and to authorize the herbicidal eradication, it is unlikely that marijuana availability in the United States would be substantially reduced. American marijuana growers are, as the Colombians alleged, ready and able to take up the slack.

What's worse, Colombian traffickers might compensate for losing marijuana profits by further expanding their production of coca. Colombia currently receives 95 percent of the coca leaf and coca paste that it refines into cocaine from Bolivia and Peru. But several Colombian states are ideal for large-scale coca cultivation, and the trafficking organizations already in place could move rapidly to complete the vertical integration of their operations by providing their refining and distribution capabilities with an agricultural base.

At the same time, the Peruvian and Bolivian traffickers, faced with the loss of the Colombian market for their raw materials, would themselves probably expand into large-scale cocaine refining, then undertake direct exporting to the United States. Although it would take these two countries time to locate their own sources for the chemicals used in the refining of cocaine and to set up an international transportation network, the United States would still, eventually, find itself contending against three fully integrated Latin American cocaine sources, where only one—Colombia—exists at present.

Already, an oversupply of Bolivian and Peruvian coca, supplemented by the burgeoning Colombian production, has driven down the price of coca paste from $600 to $350 a kilogram. In turn, a kilogram of cocaine, which a year ago sold for $60,000, can now be purchased for $30,000. If there is vigorous three-way competition for the United States cocaine market, prices will drop even further, making cocaine affordable to that many more users.

During the last 10 years, four American Presidents have declared that our international drug-control program is the key to reducing domestic drug abuse. Yet, during this decade, the funds allocated for the international program have remained a fairly constant $38 million a year since the mid-1970's, a minuscule figure next to the billion dollars that constitutes the domestic drug-abuse budget.

Today, more drugs are entering the country than were five years ago, the General Accounting Office has reported. And only about 10 percent of the more than 5 tons of heroin, 75 tons of cocaine and 15,000 tons of marijuana that are estimated to cross American borders annually is being intercepted. To stop three-quarters of the marijuana entering the United States from the Caribbean alone, the Coast Guard projects that an additional $2 billion is required. To reduce the world-wide flow of cocaine and heroin by the same amount would, according to the G.A.O., require billions of dollars more.

In the last 10 years, we have learned from successful narcotics-control experiences with both Turkey and Mexico that heroin availability can be controlled—if still not permanently curtailed—by a major commitment of our own financial and diplomatic power. But today we face much higher levels both of international production and of domestic demand of cocaine and marijuana than we have ever faced with heroin.

Moreover, narcotics-control efforts have tended to be successful in direct proportion to the national consensus on the relative dangers of the drug at issue. An overwhelming majority of Americans favor the total suppression of heroin and support Government action to that end; therefore, heroin-control efforts, until recently, have been relatively successful.

Conversely, it is in part because the American people are divided over whether cocaine and marijuana should be high-enforcement priorities that efforts to reduce their availability have not succeeded. William Webster, director of the Federal Bureau of Investigation, describes the current situation as "an inundation of drugs . . . that is eroding public confidence and corrupting police officials." Public authorities cannot deal effectively with criminal violations, such as the possession and sale of cocaine and marijuana, when more than a third of our total population are committing them.

Beyond that, it is very difficult to convince a foreign government to take the serious political and economic risks that are entailed by an all-out campaign against, say, cocaine production when the American public's predilection for cocaine is so well-known. And it is virtually impossible to persuade foreign growers of marijuana to stop producing when one American in four has tired the drug—and billions of dollars in profits are being made by marijuana growers in the United States.

What little progress *has* been made in reducing cocaine and marijuana use in the United States has been the result not so much of law enforcement as of education and rehabilitation. A statewide poll in California last July reported that the number of adult marijuana users had dropped 5 percent since 1979, the result, the poll found, not of fear of prosecution but of concern about health. Even so, the Reagan Administration has cut Federal dollars for prevention and treatment programs by more than half.

Indeed, at the highest levels of the Federal Government, the lack of a clear strategy and overall policy direction encourages the dozen Federal agencies involved in the drug-control effort to set competing priorities. Earlier this year, the President also vetoed legislation passed overwhelmingly by both houses of Congress that would have centralized in a single Cabinet-level office the responsibility for directing all foreign and domestic narcotics-control activities. Publicly, the Administration objected to the establishment of yet another bureaucracy. But White House staffers confirmed that the real reason for the President's veto was Attorney General William French Smith's concern that Justice Department prerogatives would be compromised by the new "Drug Czar."

The drug problem that this nation faces shows no signs of going away. Cocaine traffic is increasing and, given the likelihood of a significant street-price reduction, will probably continue to do so. Marijuana consumption is predicted at least to hold steady. Heroin use is beginning to show an upturn.

Still, the multinational, multibillion-dollar drug traffic has not yet become the subject of open public debate in this country. Many people have an interest in not focusing public attention on it too closely: Government officials and politicians have the fear of being held responsible for the magnitude of the problem, bankers the need to shore up confidence in the integrity of banking. The cumulative effect of this uncoordinated conspiracy of silence has been to conceal the real dimensions of the problem from public view.

Meanwhile, two things seem clear. The first is that the most fundamental aspect of the problem is, and will continue to be, demand. Until users of marijuana, cocaine and heroin are ready to give up their accustomed "highs" and to recognize the health hazards those highs entail, marijuana, cocaine and heroin will continue to be sold and used in violation of the law.

The second is that it is time for the American people to think clearly about drug use in general—and about the nature of individual drugs. Ultimately, what is needed is a national debate—and a political consensus—on the scope of the problem and the amount of money to be spent fighting those drugs that the public wants stopped. As one veteran Drug Enforcement Administration agent put it: "The D.E.A. is not the answer. The answers are going to be found in your wallets and your conscience." Until now, Americans have refused to commit enough of either to a war on illicit drugs.

FLOOD OF DRUGS—A LOSING BATTLE[2]

The mighty United States government, despite exposing its agents to hair-raising personal risks and spending millions of dollars, is losing an uphill battle to throttle production of narcotics around the globe.

In Colombia and other drug-growing countries, every thrust by Washington and cooperating governments is parried by ruthless and elusive traffickers who wield incredible power and money. So far, they have been able to keep flowing a stream of narcotics that costs thousands of lives and inflicts immeasurable social damage in America.

Overwhelming odds. Economic realities, corruption, threats, politics and nature itself combine time after time to foil the best efforts of local and U.S. drug busters in Latin America, Asia and the Middle East.

[2]Reprinted from *U. S. News & World Report* issue of M. 25, '85. Copyright © 1985, U. S. News & World Report, Inc.

Shock waves from the narcotics conflict in Colombia—which has tried harder than most nations to stifle dope producers—are felt with stunning impact in the United States. Colombia provides 59 percent of the marijuana to 20 million American smokers and 75 percent of the cocaine supply for 5 million habitual U.S. users.

Declares one Washington official: "Colombia is the key to whether we'll be able to do anything effective to stop drug production overseas."

Right now, the outlook is gloomy. Last year, seven of 13 major drug-producing nations boosted their output of marijuana, coca (cocaine) and opium-poppy crops. In Colombia, marijuana production dropped by a third but cocaine output edged up. This year, despite an American expenditure of 1.2 billion dollars to combat the drug trade, marijuana and heroin imports are expected to jump 10 percent and cocaine 4 percent.

Adm. Daniel Murphy, who heads efforts of the Reagan administration to halt the drug flow, concedes a feeling of disappointment. "We've doubled our efforts since 1982," he says. Yet we're facing a greatly enlarged cocaine supply on the world market. It has increased by a third."

Bogatá, Colombia's gleaming capital of 4 million people, is on the front lines in the drug war. A seige mentality prevails among U.S. officials hunkering down to avoid retaliation for their anti-drug efforts.

The U.S. Embassy is heavily guarded. Nearby streets are barricaded, and only police-checked cars may enter. Embassy employes arrive and depart in armored vans with guards in backup cars. Their job hours change daily. Their school-age children are out of the country. Some also have sent their spouses abroad.

The current alert began in March of 1984. Colombia's elite Special Anti-Narcotics Unit (SANU), machine guns blazing, raided 10 cocaine-processing labs in the jungle area of Tranquilandia some 275 miles southeast of Bogotá.

The narcocops arrested 44 workers. More important, they seized 10 metric tons of cocaine—about a seventh of the volume that entered the U.S. in 1984 and four times the amount they had taken in all of 1983.

Counterpunch. The operation was a mighty blow to the "cocaine cowboys," whose fabulous wealth had made them politically powerful in several parts of the country. The drug dealers reacted in characteristically brutal fashion in late April by assassinating Colombia's Minister of Justice, Rodrigo Lara Bonilla, who had vowed to defeat them.

Lara Bonilla's assassination was a major turning point. Colombians who had either regarded the drug trade as beneficial to the nation's economy or as a worry only for the North Americans now saw it as their own problem. President Belisario Betancur, who had supported Lara Bonilla but had opposed on philosophical grounds U.S. demands for extradition of drug traffickers, wore a bulletproof vest to Lara Bonilla's funeral and emotionally declared "war without quarter" on the drug kings.

Since then, Bentancur has approved extradition of 12 Colombians wanted on U.S. drug charges. He plans a state visit to the United States in early April, and narcotics will top the agenda for his talks with President Reagan.

The *traficantes'* response to the extraditions was to accelerate their violence. Last November, they set off a car bomb outside the U.S. Embassy. It killed a Colombian woman and shattered heavy glass windows for blocks around.

The drug kings also threaten to kill five Americans for every Colombian extradited. They are believed to have dispatched a hit squad to attack anti-drug officials in the U.S.

The violence reflects the high economic stakes involved in drug trafficking. Farm workers in Colombia make about $3.50 a day on traditional crops and about $25 a day in the coca fields. "That makes it tough for the government to try to stop them from growing coca," notes Diego Pizano, economic adviser to Betancur.

Colombia, at least, has other crops—beans, potatoes, cacao—that might be substituted. In countries such as Bolivia, many farmers depend on narcotics as their only cash crop. Ready-for-export cocaine costs $8,000 to $9,000 wholesale here for a kilo (2.2 pounds) and sells for $200,000 per pound on the street in the U.S.

High-speed career. Pizano says many well-educated young men of Medellín, a textile—and drug—center northeast of Bogotá, are opting for the fast-buck *narcotráfico.* He explains:

"They tell their fathers, 'You worked all your life for a small fortune. With drugs, I can have 20 million dollars in six months.'

"We're losing too many young people who could form a strong entrepreneurial class in legitimate business," the Colombian official adds. "They'll end up either dead or in an American jail."

Cocaine and marijuana together form Colombia's second-largest export crop, trailing only coffee. In Peru, the world's largest coca-leaf producer, drugs are the biggest export crop, hauling in a billion dollars a year.

The taint of drug money has permeated many levels of Colombian society. Hundreds of local judges are under investigation, and some 75 SANU policemen and 10 Air Force officers have been dismissed for drug connections. A dozen members of Congress "are either druggers or front men for druggers," says a diplomat. Hernán Botero Moreno, one of the Colombians extradited to the U.S. on drug charges, owns a soccer team.

Persuasive pitch. American officials caution against making snap judgments on corruption. Says one: "A local judge is going to think twice when a *narcotraficante* tells him, 'You either cooperate or I'm going to kill your wife, your child, your mother, your maid, your dog and your parakeet.'"

Politics, too, is a potent factor hindering the war on drugs. Colombian drug czar Pablo Escobar—reportedly worth up to 4 billion dollars—was elected in 1982 as an alternate deputy in the lower house of Congress. He is regarded locally as a kind of Robin Hood, having provided education, housing and even a public zoo for the people of Medellín.

Last year, Escobar and some other drug chieftains boldly offered Betancur a deal: Drop charges and extradition orders, and the drug czars would give up smuggling and bring into the country enough assets to help pay off Colombia's 11-billion-dollar foreign debt. Betancur refused.

Still, Escobar and another major drug dealer, Carlos Lehder, are rich and powerful enough to defy Betancur's government. In February, Lehder appeared on national television from a jungle hideaway—praising Adolf Hitler, attacking Betancur and "American imperialism" and threatening to raise a 500,000-man army to defeat both.

Colombia's fight against drugs is often diluted because authorities also must cope with several leftist guerrilla organizations. Betancur signed a truce with some but not all of them last year. While a tenuous peace still holds, government forces face additional dangers when they try to destroy drug crops in guerrilla-held territory.

Trouble elsewhere. The fight against narcotics runs up against even more formidable obstacles in other countries.

Despite heavy U.S. pressure and 2.7 million dollars in antidrug aid, Bolivia did not eradicate a single coca plant last year. The State Department called the failure "a major disappointment."

The *Miami Herald* called the Bahamas "a nation for sale" as a key transshipment point for South American drugs on their way to the U.S.

Three top officials of the Turks and Caicos Islands, a British protectorate in the West Indies, were arrested by U.S. undercover agents in Miami in early March after being filmed taking bribes to shield drug smugglers.

The State Department sees corruption in Mexico as "the major obstacle to effective [drug] enforcement." In mid-March, Mexican authorities arrested several police commanders and others in connection with the kidnap-murder of DEA agent Enrique Camarena Salazar—but only after vehement protests from President Reagan and other U.S. officials at what they saw as Mexico's slowness to react.

Peru's antidrug campaign came to an abrupt halt last fall when a nihilistic terror group called Sendero Luminoso, or Shining Path, killed 19 members of a crew sent into the jungles to eradicate coca plants. Peru did not resume its drug war until February.

Pakistan only recently has started to extend its forces into tribal areas where opium poppies grow. The government has banned cultivation and smashed several big laboratories. Even so, Pakistan and Afghanistan combined still produce at least 6 metric tons of heroin a year, sending most of it to India, Africa and Europe and providing America's 500,000 addicts with 2 metric tons, or about half their annual supply.

Unimpeded operations. Burma, the world's largest illicit opium producer, has moved forcefully to halt growth and traffic. It has even tested aerial sprays with U.S. aid. But success has been limited because most of the opium fields and refineries are in remote areas controlled not by the government but by the Communist Party.

Some Reagan administration officials, including Secretary of State George Shultz, charge that the Marxist governments of Cuba and Nicaragua are engaged in the drug trade to make money and to undermine the United States. Others suspect that the rightist regime of Paraguay's Alfredo Stroessner is involved in narcotics. Even Dr. Josef Mengele, the world's most wanted Nazi war criminal, is reputed to have financed drug dealings in South America in the 1970s. So far, not one of these allegations has been proved.

Nature itself can be a significant factor in any drive against drugs.

Afghanistan's opium-poppy yield was down by perhaps a third last year, partly because of bad weather. It can work the other way: Pakistan plans to eradicate many fields this year, but heavy rains still could produce a bumper crop throughout the Golden Crescent, the Southwest Asia area that includes Iran as well as Pakistan and Afghanistan.

As Colombia has found after several long efforts, coca bushes are particularly hard to wipe out. Explains one U.S. official: "Coca is a weed. You have to chop it down, burn it, then poison the stump." Such work takes a lot of time and a lot of people. So, in several parts of the world, from Colombia to Burma, the U.S. is helping countries test herbicides to find an effective spray.

Shifting sources. Stamping out illicit drugs is like trying to control a glob of mercury: Press it, and it squirts off in all directions.

Turkey, for instance, once was a major source of opium. No longer. Since 1975, it has rigorously controlled poppy growing. However, with its strategic location astride two continents, Turkey has become a major transit country for drugs moving from the East to the West.

When the Italian government successfully knocked out heroin laboratories in Sicily in 1982, drug traffickers in Pakistan and Afghanistan started their own labs and by the end of that year were making high-quality heroin. Now, both Italy and India are accused of being major transfer points for drugs from producing countries to the U.S.

Colombian officials say that the same kind of transformation is taking place in the cocaine and marijuana trades. As police raid coke labs and burn bales of pot in this country, production springs up elsewhere. Neighboring Venezuela and Brazil now have widespread marijuana cultivation, and Colombian coke dealers have been moving into western Brazil.

In the United States, cocaine-conversion labs are sprouting up in southern Florida. Marijuana farming has blossomed into a major underground business in such states as California and Hawaii.

Users blamed. Many officials of drug-producing countries insist that the fault lies largely with the insatiable demand of consumers in the U.S. and Europe. Colombia's Pizano says of cocaine: "As long as large numbers of people are willing to pay any price for this horrible drug, it won't go away."

Many Washington officials refuse to believe nothing can be done. Senator Dennis DeConcini (D-Ariz.) is pushing a bill to spend 100 million dollars to create a special air command equipped with sophisticated radar to spot smugglers flying dope into the country.

Senator Paula Hawkins (R-Fla.), who calls narcotics "the single most threatening menace to civilization today," demands that Reagan enforce a 1983 law that suspends foreign aid to countries that fail to cooperate in the war against drugs.

"What will it take for us to uphold the law?" Hawkins asks. "Another kidnaping? Another death?"

Infected countries. The threat of narcotics addiction is spreading from the United States and Europe to the less developed nations where the drugs are produced.

Colombia, for instance, is worried because many of its young people are smoking the mind-bending *basuco*, a cheap mixture of coca base and tobacco. Pakistan estimates that it has some 150,000 heroine addicts and 313,000 opium addicts, a crisis the State Department says "has had a more profound effect on the attitudes and actions of Pakistani officials than external pressures from any source."

A recent United Nations study said that the problem has grown to the point where it endangers "the very security of some states."

With all the setbacks, U.S. officials could well be expected to give up hope that the threat of illegal narcotics may yet be conquered.

However, Assistant Secretary of State Jon Thomas argues: "We haven't run the traffickers into the ground yet, but they are running. That's why they are fighting back.

"Sure, 1985 and 1986 are going to be years of violence. But we're not going to be intimidated."

THE MIAMI CONNECTION[3]

A Drug Economy

The high visibility of Cubans and other Latins in Miami's drug traffic enables Anglos to blame them for all of it. But Miami would not be the nation's gateway for drugs without the acquiescence of the city's civic and business leaders. "We bankers are always saying how Miami has become an international banking center like London or New York," observed the chairman of a Florida bank. "But that's a lot of hogwash. The reason so many banks have opened offices here is because of the hot money, particularly drug money."

A prominent lawyer decries civic apathy. "There is no real interest here in preserving the quality of life," he told *Time*. "I don't think there is any real community outrage about the drug trade. When I urge the junior lawyers here to join civic groups instead of playing racquetball, they say they're not interested."

[3]Excerpted from article by Penny Lernoux, the magazine's Latin American correspondent. *The Nation*. p 186–98. F. 18 '84.

Miamians who do speak out, like insurance executive Arthur Patten, a former City Comissioner, are vilified by their fellow citizens. Muncipal leaders called Patten a coward and told him to shut up after he made negative comments about the city to the press. He lost business from hotel owners, who were annoyed by the bad publicity he generated, and eventually he moved to North Carolina. But playing ostrich won't solve the problem. As *The Miami Herald* has repeatedly said, "Reality, not image, is South Florida's problem."

A Florida grand jury that studied crime in Miami agreed:

> We recommend that the hard issues begin to be addressed. We find that we have not fully committed ourselves as a society to eradicate narcotics, and perhaps we never will. Our local economy apparently has benefited enormously and our culture has become tolerant of marijuana and even of cocaine. Yet we ask the small numbers of law enforcement personnel assigned to narcotics interdiction to stop a supply for which we create a demand. That is clearly a costly hypocrisy.

Charles Kimball, a real estate economist who watches foreign purchases of South Florida property closely, estimates that nearly half the $1.5 billion that foreign companies invest annually in Miami real estate comes from illegal sources: drug dealers, organized-crime syndicates, foreign criminals and international swindlers. The construction industry in Miami would be on the rocks were it not for shady investors. The same can be said of retailers of luxury items such as yachts and airplanes, and of accountants, lawyers and other professionals who have fattened on the narcotics traffic. In an article in *Inquiry*, a spokesman for the U.S. Customs Service, one of five Federal agencies trying to stop the drug traffic, said: "You know what would happen if we really did our job here? If we were 100 percent effective we would so drastically affect the economy that *we* would become the villains."

Dodge City South

Crime is a major concern among Miamians. Instead of talking about the weather or last night's TV program, neighbors discuss the latest robbery or murder on their street. Everyone has a personal horror story—getting caught in the crossfire of a gangland shooting at the local shopping center, watching in terror as the occupants of two cars spray each other with machine-gun bullets at a stoplight. Perhaps the most bitter reaction was that of a Colombian banker. During his first week in Miami, the banker's briefcase was stolen from under his legs while he was paying his bill at the luxurious Omni Hotel. Then the hubcaps on his car were stolen. One night he and his wife went out to dinner, leaving their newborn son with their Colombian maid, who had been with the family for years. Their house had two different alarm systems, one of which was connected to the local police station. Upon returning home, the couple discovered the maid's body floating in the swimming pool; their baby was safe in his crib, but his clothing was drenched, as if he had been in the pool. The banker swore that if one more thing happened to him or his family, they would pack up and return to Bogotá, once considered the most dangerous city of its size in the hemisphere.

The Miami Herald is full of such stories from people who want to know why "the city of my dreams" has become Dodge City South. In the last decade, the homicide rate in South Florida has jumped more than 400 percent, making Miami one of the most dangerous cities in the United States. "When you see a helicopter, you know they've found another body," said a college professor, whose backyard was used as a murderer's dumping ground several years ago. The corpse was of a young Colombian man who had attended the birthday party of a neighbor's daughter. Like most crimes in Miami, the murder was never solved, and to this day the professor and his neighbors have no idea why the man was killed, "except that he was a Colombian."

Since 1980 the Miami police force has been enlarged, and there are more judges on the criminal circuit; even so the city cannot cope. "In an average month we file 2,000 felony cases after screening," said George Ray Havens, head of the Miami Criminal Investigative Division of the State Attorney's office. "If every individual charged was granted a jury trial, we wouldn't be able to file another case for at least three years." The Criminal Investigative Division has twenty-two agents and receives nearly 500 requests for investigations every month. "If the case is complicated—say, a financial racket—we just can't handle it," said Havens. A lawyer in the U.S. Attorney's office cited in *Harper's* said that even if no cases were added, it would take the sixty-three full-time lawyers under him nine years to finish those already filed.

The Miami police are reluctant to accept drug cases because they have no more room to store the evidence, even after burning tons of marijuana in the Florida Power and Light Company's furnaces. The Key West sheriff's office finds itself most days with a stash worth $4 million on its hands; the sheriff's men spend most of their time protecting it from thieves. Convicted drug dealers are jamming Florida prisons: between 1978 and 1980 paroles jumped 50 percent as burglars, armed robbers and other criminals were turned loose to make room for them. Still most drug traffickers, even the biggest fry, serve only a short time: the average sentence is less than two years, with eligibility for parole after a year.

About all the overburdened authorities can do about the murder rate is to keep a body count, and that is a challenge. So many corpses pile up at the Miami morgue that since 1981 the Dade County medical examiner has had to rent a refrigerated hamburger van to house the overflow. "If you stay here, you arm yourself to the teeth, put bars on the windows and stay at home at all times," Arthur Patten told reporters. "I've been through two wars and no combat zone is as dangerous as Dade County."

Gun sales are rising, as are purchases of security devices—alarms, locks, floodlights, guard dogs, surveillance systems. In 1981, gun sales in Dade County were up approximately 46 percent over the previous year. "Most customers are people like your mother," said the owner of a gun shop in *Time*. "They're just average, everyday folk who want to continue to live." Even those who favor stricter gun-control laws doubt they would have much effect in South Florida. "If you take guns away, they'll use knives, they'll use a hammer. Hammer, saw. Saw, machete. Pretty soon we'll be back to hands."

No one is immune from crime. The regional commissioner for the Customs Service was mugged and robbed outside a Miami disco. A Federal judge's life was threatened by drug defendants. A Florida drug gang let out a $200,000 contract to hit men: their job, to kill all the State's witnessess before the gang's upcoming trial.

Governor Robert Graham told me that after he visited Colombia seeking the cooperation of local authorities to stop the cocaine trade, a Columbian mob dispatched an assassin to Tallahassee to kill him.

The Colombian Brethren

The Colombian mafias are much like the Sicilian original, tightly knit organizations based on blood ties. The penalty for betraying one's family is death; the sentence is usually carried out by a Colombian-based hit man who takes the morning flight from Bogotá to Miami and returns that night. Long the world's leaders in counterfeiting U.S. dollars, Colombian racketeers have become more sophisticated in recent years, mingling drugs, stolen securities and counterfeit bills in giant money-cycling operations which span three continents. They entered the U.S. cocaine market as suppliers, but since the mid-1970s they have taken control of most of the distribution. (Cubans still dominate the marijuana traffic.) The Latin mafias are organized like multinational corporations, with separate divisions for imports, transport, distribution and finance. A major smuggling operation has 100 to 200 employees in Miami, usually illegal aliens carrying false passports. The Florida organizations are supported by larger ones in the producing countries, where complaisant politicians are often paid to look the other way. Some 200,000 peasant families in four countries depend on the traffic for their livelihood.

Given the international scope of the traffic and the huge sums of money involved, it is ridiculous to believe that any police force can interdict the flow. No matter how many tons of narcotics are seized or how many people are arrested, there will always be more where they came from. Federal District Judge Alcee Hastings, who is frequently criticized for the lenient sentences he gives in drug convictions, explains that most of the people who come before him are low-level traffickers. "Drugs are tearing the hell out of the social fabric of America, but we're not catching the right people," he told *The Herald*. "They're arresting a mule a minute, an offender an hour. When they start catching bankers, judges, senators . . . you'll see who's tough. The ringleaders are in a lot of trouble if they come before me."

The D.E.A.'s Numbers Game

In 1981 *The Miami Herald* printed the results of its four-month study of the Drug Enforcement Administration; it went a long way toward explaining the basis of Hastings's complaint. In addition to finding the usual bureaucratic infighting, the study showed that the agency's principal weakness is its obsession with statistics. To make the D.E.A. look good, agents are ordered to concentrate on quick seizures and arrests. They are often occupied for days, setting up relatively small buys that yield no new information and no important indictments. "All of us in law enforcement have got to get away from this attitude that our sterling successes involve the number of tons of marijuana and cocaine we can seize," James York, commissioner of the Florida Department of Law Enforcement, told *The Herald* "A ton of cocaine isn't worth a damn. You've got to penetrate the organizations." Assistant U.S. Attorney Robert Perry added, "Street operations are dangerous, disruptive, labor-intensive, expensive and frequently unsuccessful."

Getting the high-level traffickers entails long, tedious investigations for which few D.E.A. agents are trained and on which they receive little support. Example: In 1981 a two-month investigation by Operation Greenback, an interagency task force, led to the arrest of Isaac Kattan, a Colombian and the biggest drug-money launderer ever caught in Florida. Kattan was an impressive catch, but he was only a middleman. Others in the task force, particularly Internal Revenue Service agents, wanted to delay his arrest, hoping he would lead them to his bosses, but the D.E.A. insisted on nabbing him for dealing in cocaine. "They got twenty kilos of coke but not much else," said a member of the task force. "We found that chopping off Kattan's head didn't kill off the organization; another head popped up to do the same things. If the D. E.LA. hadn't been in such a hurry to make an arrest, maybe we would have got the organization."

The Government Accounting Office criticizes the Justice Department, which oversees the D.E.A., for not "taking the profit out of drug trafficking." In a 1981 report, the G.A.O. pointed out that although Congress passed a law in 1970 enabling the government to seize the financial assets of criminals, the D.E.A. "simply has not exercised the kind of leadership and management necessary to make asset forfeiture a widely used law enforcement technique." As of 1980, the Justice Department had obtained a mere $2 million in forfeited assets, the G.A.O. found, and most of those were items that drug traffickers consider expendable, like boats and airplanes.

Congress passed the forfeiture law, expecting the Justice Department to seize the U.S. and foreign bank accounts of the top-level dealers. But that requires an entirely new approach by the D.E.A., which continues to see narcotics enforcement in simplistic cops-and-robbers terms. Observed George Havens, "The attitude of the average bureaucrat is: big cases, big problems; little cases, little problems; no cases, no problems. People don't want problems."

It is also unhappily true that with so many narcobucks floating around Miami, corruption among police agents, judges and others is inevitable. One-fifth of an entire division of the Dade County police force was indicted for taking payoffs and enaging in drug trafficking. Two officers were charged with working with a known drug racketeer. Jeffrey Scharlatt, a former group supervisor of the D.E.A.'s Miami office, pleaded guilty after being indicted by a Federal grand jury on corruption charges. Florida's Attorney General, Jim Smith, said in an interview on *60 Minutes*, "Frankly, I lie in bed sometimes at night and it . . . just scares me, the level of corruption we may have in Florida."

Terrorists and Politics

What role does drug money play in South Florida politics? The evidence is inconclusive, but the clout of Cuban exile terrorists, some of them having narcotics connections, suggests at least an indirect influence. However, their anticommunist cover, President Reagan's support for exile causes and local politicians' awareness of the importance of the Hispanic vote (38 percent of the electorate in Miami) have obscured the extent of the terrorists' penetration.

That Reagan is perceived as the Cuban exiles' friend in Washington came up in a rather odd context in the recent Miami mayoral race. The Democratic candidate, incumbent Maurice Ferre, appealed to blacks and Anglos by telling them that a vote for his opponent, Xavier Suarez, would enable Reagan to "take control" of Miami. Suarez is a Cuban exile.

Ferre is of Puerto Rican descent and is supposedly unsympathetic to the Cubans, but even he finds it expedient to appeal to the Cuban terrorists who wield power in Little Havana. Reelected to his sixth term, Ferre calls the influence of terrorists in Miami politics "unavoidable." "It just happens to be part of political life," he told *The Herald*.

Last year, the Mayor led a delegation to Venezuela to request the release of Orlando Bosch, who was being held in a Caracas jail, charged with participating in the Air Cubana bombing in which Monkey Morales was involved. Although Bosch is probably the most notorious terrorist in the Cuban exile community, Ferre reasoned that associating with him would be popular with the exiles.

Nor did Ferre have any compunction about associating with Letelier hit-squad member Guillermo Novo in a campaign to raise funds for Bosch's release. Novo was one of eight terrorists listed on the campaign's official letterhead; all have been indicted and some, like Novo, have drug connections. Not to be outdone, Suarez dipped into his campaign treasury to contribute to the legal defense fund of Eduardo Arocena, the alleged leader of Omega 7. In providing such support, said Arthur Nehrbass, head of the Dade County Organized Crime Bureau, politicians enhance the terrorists' stature in Miami, "Respectability is an important weapon in the terrorists' arsenal," he told *The Herald*.

Last year, Miami City Comissioner Demetrio Perez proposed a plan to honor a Cuban terrorist who was killed in Paris when a bomb he was assembling exploded. In 1982 the terrorist organization Alpha 66 gained respectability when the Miami City Commission gave it a $10,000 grant to arrange temporary housing for the Mariel refugees. Ferre defended the grant, saying that Alpha 66 had "never been accused of terrorist activities inside the United States." Former Acting Chief of Police Adam Klimkowski said in

The Herald that Ferre told him he had heard "quite a bit [about] bombings coming up" in the Miami area but refused to provide any details. "I was flat irritated," Klimkowski said. "Here the Mayor was saying he had information [on terrorism], and he wouldn't divulge it to me."

The career of former City Commissioner Manolo Reboso illustrates the shadowy line between politics and crime in Miami. The son of Batista's military attaché in Washington, Reboso was an intelligence officer in the Bay of Pigs operation and later represented the Miami interests of Nicaragua's Somoza dictatorship. He also had business ties with the Miami-based World Finance Corporation (W.F.C.), which laundered proceeds from drug sales. One of his principal campaign fund-raisers was later indicted for embezzling from a Texas bank that was a subsidiary of W.F.C. In 1981 Reboso ran for mayor amid accusations by Monkey Morales—never proved—that drug traffickers were financing his campaign. Like Ferre, Reboso defended the City's patriot terrorists when he was City Commissioner.

In late 1983 officials of a Venezuelan government bank charged that Reboso had failed to account for more than $9 million of the $36.5 million it had loaned him to construct a Miami high-rise which was to have housed the bank's offices. The deal had all the markings of a Miami scam, including offshore front companies and a cooperative banker, who actively pushed Reboso's requests for unsecured loans. The claim was eventually settled out of court.

Bank Laundromats

If the role of drug money in politics is murky, it is well documented in the banking industry. Miami is the Wall Street of the United States' $80 billion drug traffic. There are more than a hundred banks in the city representing two dozen countries. The most prestigious banking address is Brickwell Avenue, a block from Biscayne Bay, where gold-and-black skyscrapers rise incongruously above the palm trees. Coral Gables, where a hundred multinational corporations have their Latin America headquarters, is also considered a chic location. Architecture tends to reflect management style: Citibank's Miami headquarters is housed in a sleek glass building embellished with ultramodern chandeliers; Credit Suisse's offices gleam with chrome and mirrors. In contrast, the Republic National Bank, which is owned by Cuban exiles, operates out of an old-fashioned structure decorated with middlebrow Latin American art. Then there are the fly-by-night operations, some of which look like converted hamburger stands. The initial capitalization needed to obtain a bank charter in Miami is only $1.5 million (in a similar-size Ohio city, say, it can be as much as $5 million). If a bank attracts even a small fraction of the $4 billion deposited by Latin Americans each year, the profits are enormous.

When bankers know that money is hot, they accept it only for deposit in non-interest-bearing accounts, or change it into cashier's checks, which usually aren't returned to the bank for collection for months, providing another pool of interest-free funds. Some banks launder drug money on a regular basis, earning up to 3 percent in commissions on it and lending it out at a fat profit as well.

Unprofitable banks are easily sold; buyers, usually foreigners, are willing to pay two to three times the real value of a bank simply because it has a Florida charter. The smaller the bank, the more dubious the buyers it is likely to attract. "In Miami they have a saying in Spanish: 'The sharks are on the streets, not in the sea,'" said Richard H. Dailey, president of the small Dadeland Bank, who started his career in California. "You wouldn't believe how many people come in here to ask if the bank is for sale. This would never happen in San Francisco."

"We used to have the same problem," agreed Aristides Sastre, president of Republic National Bank, "but it's become less prevalent because we've grown so much. I don't know anywhere else in the United States where people just walk in off the street and offer to buy the bank."

In addition to foreign and locally controlled banks, Miami has forty-two Edge Act corporations (foreign and out-of-state bank subsidiaries that deal exclusively in overseas transactions) and another forty-eight foreign bank agencies and representatives. Indeed, banks in Miami are more plentiful than supermarkets—one to a block. The out-of-state and foreign bankers claim that their institutions have been attracted to South Florida by the area's explosive growth, its Latin American trade or the need to service customers like the multinational corporations in Coral Gables. But according to a Treasury Department report, at least a third of the banks in Miami are drawn by the huge profits to be made from laundering drug money. As many as forty banks have neglected to report cash deposits of $10,000 or more, as required by law. The majority of those are small banks, known to cops and crooks as Coin-O-Washers. At least four such banks are controlled by drug dealers, according to local and Federal law enforcement officials. The advent in 1981 of international banking facilities in Florida, subsidiaries which operate under less stringent controls than their parent bank, has contributed to the free-for-all. Predicted a senior bank official in New York City at the time: "It's going to be the biggest laundering game in history."

Because retail sales of marijuana, heroin and cocaine are made on the street, dealers amass large numbers of small bills. The banks feed bales of them into high-speed money counters or simply weigh them (300 pounds of $20 bills equals $3.6 million). A common sight in Miami banks is a Latin lugging several shopping bags crammed with cash to a teller's window. Professional middlemen prefer to deliver cardboard boxes of cash to a bank's back door. If there are any questions, the courier will often abandon the money. When a Miami teller asked a woman why the money she carried in a shopping bag had a fishy odor, she dropped it and fled, leaving behind $200,000.

While the Federal government has tightened bank reporting regulations for large cash transactions and has arrested a half-dozen Miami bankers, laundering operations still flourish. Since the drug boom began, the Florida banking system has consistently registered staggering annual surpluses of cash—on average, $6 billion to $8 billion a year—more than twice the surplus cash reported by banks in the rest of the country. Financial experts calculate that more than half the Florida surplus is hot money.

Customs officials say the banks have been more cooperative in recent years. But William von Raab, U.S. Commissioner of Customs, told *The New York Times* that in 1981, Florida banks did not report $3.2 billion in cash transactions, evidence of "flagrant violations by some of the employees of many of the institutions and even by some of the institutions themselves." The practice declined briefly in 1980, after Senator William Proxmire came down hard on the banks during hearings that summer on drug-money laundering before his Committee on Banking, Housing and Urban Affairs. "But now we're back to pre-Proxmire levels," claimed an undercover agent who worked on a Miami F.B.I. sting in which the agents posed as middlemen in a laundering operation. "The bankers were delighted to deal with me when I was 'dirty,'" she continued. "Bank guards were always willing to carry crates of money into a back room with counting machines. Cash reporting requirements never hindered banks, since they could afford to pay the fines if caught."

Every Florida banker will swear his bank is clean, but as Miami banker Anthony Infante told Proxmire's committee, "Without banks . . . it would be almost impossible that these transactions would continue to happen." Infante said, "It is extremely difficult for a professional banker not to be aware of the way in which drug traffickers try to use our institutions to facilitate their illegal transactions. In twenty years as a bank officer in Florida, I have seen very few cases in which cash deposits of any substantial amount are necessary in the normal transactions of a customer."

Infante said that bankers must go beyond "the letter of the law" to solicit information about customers. In his testimony Rudolph Giuliani, a former U.S. Associate Attorney General who helped Chemical Bank stop drug-money laundering at its branches, agreed: "The law places the responsibility on banks to obtain and report [information] concerning domestic and foreign transactions." Giuliani said he found that many bank employees were ignorant of cash reporting regulations and that ignorance led to negligence—or worse. He urged closer scrutiny of customers. "Among the problems I've seen is that there were accounts maintained for drug traffickers and for others who were engaged in illegal activities under phony corporate names, and a simple visit to the business entity, the address that was given when the account was opened, would have revealed the fact that there was no such business in that location."

But many Miami bankers assert that it's none of their business where the money comes from. They apparently do not realize how seriously connections with criminals can damage an institution's reputation. "There is no doubt . . . that if the drug situation continues, the decent and respectable members of our community will eventually leave the area," Infante warned, "thereby damaging the image that Miami has been for so long trying to build as an international banking center." Alexander McW. Wolfe Jr., vice chairman of Florida's giant Southeast Bank, told me, "People will not take this place seriously as an international banking center until this hanky-panky stops."

Southeast ought to know. When confronted by the committee's evidence that a major Columbian drug-money launderer kept large deposits in his bank, president David A. Wollard sheepishly admitted that he had no information on the man. "I honestly read more about it in the paper than anyplace else," he explained. When asked whether putting some bankers behind bars would encourage their brethren to obey the law, he replied, "I can see where that would greatly stiffen the resolve of all banking officials to comply."

But no Florida banker has received a prison sentence, possibly because, as one frustrated bank regulator told me, juries "always seem to think that if the guy wears a three-piece suit, he can't be guilty of any serious crime." The Proxmire hearings and studies by the G.A.O. show that most bankers believe they risk a slap on the wrist, at worst, since regulatory agencies are unable or unwilling to stop the banks from laundering drug money.

The Absent Regulators

The Bank Secrecy Act of 1970 gave regulators a powerful tool for uncovering illegal banking transactions, but according to the G.A.O., they have not used it. The act requires banks to provide the Treasury Department with information on the depositor for cash transactions of $10,000 or more, except in the case of a customer that has a large cash flow, for example, a big department store. The information is supposed to be filed within fifteen days of the deposit. Transfers of $10,000 or more to foreign banks must also be reported. The G.A.O. found that a significant number of banks ignore those requirements. Some that do comply delay their reports for as long as two months after the transaction; by that time it is too late to take action. Few of the banks surveyed by the G.A.O. claimed that the reporting requirements were onerous, so excessive paperwork is no excuse for their failure to follow the law.

According to an employee of the state banking regulatory agency, most of the reports that are filed gather dust at the Treasury Department because "nobody know what to do with them." The G.A.O. confirmed that few law enforcement agencies use the reports and blamed Treasury for failing to encourage their distribution. The Proxmire hearings revealed that divisions of the Treasury Department, including the I.R.S. and the Office of the Comptroller of the Currency, hide information from one another and from state banking regulators, the Customs Service and the D.E.A. Robert Serino, director of enforcement in the Comptroller's office, told the committee that "bank secrecy" prevents regulators from disclosing suspicious information, no matter how general, to any other agency. Given the regulators' "dismal" record on reporting cash transactions, said Senator Proxmire, it looks as though the regulators use bank secrecy to protect violators. Paul Homan, then deputy comptroller in the Comptroller's office, told the Proxmire committee that regulators are not zealous in cracking down on laundering by the banks because drug-money deposits have no effect on a bank's "financial safety and soundness." According to Homan, "So long as the bank invests those deposits in overnight money and is able to cover when the deposits are withdrawn, there is no financial threat to the bank other than the peripheral one of perhaps affecting the confidence that people have in it, because of known associations with criminals." In other words, the fact that a bank does business with criminals, or is owned by them, is of minor importance to the overseers of the nation's banks.

Unable to prod bank regulators into action, the enforcement division of the Treasury Department has initiated a series of joint task forces in conjunction with the Justice Department, using reports filed in accordance with the Bank Secrecy Act to identify individuals and organizations involved in laundering drug money. Modest in scope and relatively new, those operations mark the first succesful attempt to take the profits out of drug trafficking. They have also provided an education in how money is laundered.

Isaac Kattan, the Colombian drug-money launderer apprehended by Operation Greenback, ran a sizable operation in Miami. (Kattan was given thirty years in prison for cocaine trafficking, one of the few harsh sentences received by a Florida dealer.) Although he dealt in hundreds of millions of dollars, Kattan's methods were crude compared with those of the top dealers. As go-between for Colombian drug suppliers and U.S. buyers, Kattan received instructions, usually by telephone, to pick up payments for drugs in Miami parking lots, restaurants, alleys and even on busy Biscayne Boulevard. He and his Latin helpers lugged the cash to his apartment, which was equipped with five counting machines, a computer and a telex. When the money had been sorted and stacked neatly in cardboard boxes, Kattan took it to one of his friendly Miami banks for deposit, using a currency-exchange business run by his Miami travel agency as a cover. The money was either telexed from the bank to a Colombian currency-exchange house or was sent on a more roundabout route through a brokerage firm or real estate operation. When the dollars arrived in Colombia, the exchange house converted them to pesos, usually on the black market. For those services Kattan, like other middlemen in the drug trade, collected a stiff fee. Task force agents estimated that Kattan's Swiss bank account stash was worth more than $100 million.

Since it is the source of three-quarters of the cocaine and marijuana entering the United States, Colombia plays a key role in laundering. The principal exchange houses used for that purpose there are located in Barranquilla (marijuana), a coastal town on the Caribbean, and Medellín (cocaine), the second largest city. The more sophisticated operations include a network of offshore banks in Panama, the Bahamas and the Cayman Islands, as well as dummy companies incorporated in Panama and the Netherlands Antilles. The idea is to create so many zigs and zags of intermediary stops that it is virtually impossible to trace the paper trail out of, and often back into, the United States. Kattan got caught because he made only perfunctory attempts to hide his trail. He often carried boxes of cash to the bank, and he broke a cardinal rule of money launderers by dealing dope. But he made his biggest mistake by relying on the discretion of the Miami office of the brokerage firm Donaldson, Lufkin and Jenrette, which alerted the D.E.A. that suspiciously large amounts of money were moving through one of its accounts.

Smelly Money

That firm's scruples contrasted sharply with those of four Miami banks with which Kattan also did business: Great American Bank, the Bank of Miami, Northside Bank of Miami and the Popular Bank and Trust Company. When Federal agents raided the Bank of Miami in 1981, they found that bank employees had been switching funds from one of Kattan's accounts to another. According to the investigators, Kattan and members of his organization regularly hauled huge sums of money to the Bank of Miami and the Great American Bank ($60 million to the latter in just over a year). In an affidavit, an agent testified that he once heard Kattan apologize to Great American Bank official Carlos Nuñez for a suspicious-looking transaction. "Don't worry—the main thing now is to count the money," Nuñez assured him.

During a concurrent raid on the Great American Bank, agents found a number of other irregularities, according to court documents. An article in the July 20, 1981, *Newsweek* summed up their discoveries:

> Large cash deposits were sometimes taken to the bank's installment-loan department . . . and the depositors would be given a cashier's check; the cash was then logged in as the bank's own money. Pages of the cash-deposit log and some cashier's checks were missing. When questioned about the practice, Nuñez said that a bank vice president, Lionel Paytuby, had approved the procedure as a favor to special customers. One bank employee told authorities that Latins bearing cardboard boxes arrived almost daily at the bank. Agents said that bank employees assigned to count the money sometimes complained that the bills were wet or smelly—as if they had been buried.

While bank officials complained that the task force raiders had "descended on the bank en masse like storm troopers," there was a hollowness to the complaint. Before the raid, the Bank of Miami had been identified by a Treasury Department report as an institution frequently used by drug dealers to launder their cash. As for the Great American Bank, it was again in the news in late 1982 when Paytuby and three other bankers were arrested by the D.E.A. on charges of operating a giant laundering operation, which involved forty-one domestic and five foreign bank accounts. The bank was charged with laundering $94 million in dope profits over a fourteen-month period. The twenty-one-count indictment marks the first time a South Florida bank has been charged with laundering; if convicted the bank could be fined up to $6.1 million. John Walker, the Treasury Department's chief of enforcement, told reporters the Great American Bank was indicted because it had consistently failed to fulfill currency reporting requirements and that this failure "wasn't due to the actions of an isolated employee but was, in fact, a bank practice."

Cashier's checks are probably used most commonly in money-laundering transactions. They are safer to carry than cash and harder to trace than ordinary checks, because they do not have to bear the payee's name and address. The checks frequently change hands eight or nine times before returning to the bank, and they are common currency on the black markets of drug-producing countries. According to bankers, any bank that has more than 3 percent of its deposit in such checks is likely to be engaged in a laundering operation. In 1980, according to the Proxmire committee's report, two dozen Miami banks held a higher percentage.

Not coincidentally, many Florida banks implicated in the drug traffic are controlled by Latins. While some have unblemished reputations more than a third of the twenty-one South Florida banks owned by Latins have been suspected of laundering by U.S. authorities. One such is Continental National Bank, founded in 1974, the first Miami bank to be owned and managed entirely by Cuban exiles.

The first indication that Continental was accepting large dope-money deposits came in 1978, when the Customs Service and the Treasury Department uncovered a laundering opearation run by a well-known Colombian narcotics dealer, Arturo Fernández, who worked with Isaa Kattan. Eight banks were involved, but the largest portion of the money—$95 million—had been deposited in Continental. Fernández had made most of his early transactions with the Bank of Miami and the Canadian Royal Trust Bank of Miami, but when Orlando Arrebola, a Bank of Miami official who knew Fernández, moved to Continental as a vice president, Fernández switched most of his accounts to that bank. There, according to government investigators, he usually dealt with Arrebola. The banker was charged with laundering drug money but was acquitted when a Miami jury ruled that tape recordings of Arrebola's conversations with undercover F.B.I. agents were insufficient proof of his involvement in a conspiracy. The undercover agents claimed that Arrebola had helped them open an account at Continental and had counseled them on laundering money. According to Arrebola's attorney, the banker may have had reason to suspect that drugs were the source of the money pouring into Continental, but the government's case fell far short of proving anything more than that. "His intent was merely to do his job well at his bank; his intent was to further the business of the bank," the lawyer claimed in *The Herald*, although he admitted that Arrebola'a actions might have "helped the conspiracy along."

There appears to be some truth in the lawyer's contention that Arrebola was just doing his job. In a 1978 report to the Comptroller of the Currency, a Florida bank examiner said he had informed Continental's management that even if the bank " is in compliance with the reporting regulations, some of the transactions may involve the laundering of illicit moneys," and he went on to cite thirty-four such cases. But, said the examiner, Continental's management "does not intend to discourage" such transactions "since a fee is levied for the handling of these deposits."

As any banker will point out, it is management's responsibility to see that employees comply with the law. Bankers also admit that compliance involves more than filling out forms; it means that the banks must not engage in activities that the law is intended to prevent. But Continental's vice chairman, Bernardo Benes, told NBC News that it is enough to fulfill the letter of the law: "It's not really up to bankers to become investigators of customers."

More than carelessness or complacency is to blame for that attitude. Senator Proxmire'statement four years ago still holds true: "Many banks are addicted to drug money, just as millions of Americans are addicted to drugs."

A Mirror of the United States

Driving northwest through the Everglades on Highway 41, one feels a great sense of relief at having escaped the gaudy, violent world of Miami. Midway to Naples, there's a gas station with a ham-and-eggs joint that caters to the redneck trade and identifies itself as a checkpoint on the border between alien South Florida and the rest of the country. A sign on the wall announces, "Will the last American leaving South Florida please bring the flag!"

But Miami is as much a reflection of the United States as it is an extension of Latin America. Without the social acceptance that has made organized crime the biggest industry in the United States, gangsters like Lansky and Trafficante could not have flourished in Miami. Unfortunately, there is no quick fix for the evils generated by the Miami connection. Moral leadership is lacking in a nation that accepts and even admires Mafia godfathers, and whose President has unleashed C.I.A.-backed *contras* against Nicaragua's revolution just as the Kennedy Administration encouraged anti-Castro *contras* in the early 1960's—some of whom sit atop Miami's big candy mountain of drug money.

Remedial action can be taken in certain areas—enforcing the laws aginst bank laundering of drug money, for example. But the C.I.A.-mob-narcotics connection will not be broken by this Administration.

Would a Democratic Administration change things? Not likely. The party has proved itself as myopic as the Republicans when it comes to understanding the social and economic roots of pervasive drug use in America. Latin Americans, at least, are less hypocritical about it. As the Colombians say, cocaine is good for the economy. Many Miamians would agree, in private.

The response from Washington has been and will probably continue to be "political posturing," in the words of Lester Wolff, former chairman of the House Select Committee on Narcotics

Abuse and Control. The Federal government has "declared so many wars on drugs," Wolff said, "that if we lost that many wars the United States wouldn't be around." Perhaps the loss of all those wars against drugs has deeper implications than we realize. Have so many principles been sacrificed to greed and *Realpolitik* that the nation is in spiritual ruin? It is a question few Americans care to ask.

DRUG WARS: MURDER IN MEXICO[4]

A bricklayer walking down a road near the Mexican town of Villahermosa discovered the two plastic bags half buried in the dirt. Inside were two bodies decomposed beyond recognition. It was not until two days later that a positive identification could be made. The corpses were those of U.S. narcotics agent Enrique Camarena Salazar and Alfredo Zavala Avelar, a Mexican pilot who had flown occasional missions for the U.S. Drug Enforcement Administration. Both had been kidnapped a month earlier in Guadalajara; their brutally tortured bodies confirmed American law-enforcement officials' most disheartening fears. "Now is the time to honor and mourn our dead," said Attorney General Edwin Meese in his first public statement since becoming head of the Justice Department. "But the drug traffickers who committed these crimes will have no rest."

A military transport plane brought Camarena's body back to the North Island Naval Air Station near San Diego. "It was a very sad journey," John Gavin, U.S. ambassador to Mexico, told Geneva Camarena, who stood by her husband's flag-draped coffin with her young son. Camarena had spent five years in the hot drug wars of Guadalajara. He had been due for reassignment to the DEA's San Diego field office this week. Feelings over the case ran high in Washington. Nancy Reagan, who has taken a personal interest in the administration's war against nacotics, was distraught.

[4]Reprint of an article by Harry Anderson, staff writer *Newsweek*. p 28–32. Mr. 18, '85.

And Secretary of State George Shultz told the Senate Appropriations Committee, "Our level of tolerance has been exceeded by these events."

Even so, the administration's response was diplomatically calibrated. In most matters, Mexico officially remains a good friend to the United States. And it is very much a friend in need. The country's economy is still recovering from the dual blows of declining oil revenues and the developing world's second highest foreign debt. Shultz specifically rejected the notion of using economic sanctions to prod the Mexicans into a more vigorous attack on official corruption and drugs. "What does bringing down the Mexican economy accomplish?" asked a State Department official. "it just creates a mess."

Instead, the administration turned up the heat of its rhetoric. Ambassador Gavin has spoken with increasing forcefulness on the subject of official Mexican corruption, and the State Department has made no attempt to censor his remarks. There was a good cop, bad cop side to Gavin's approach. Washington officials have considered warning Americans travelers to avoid Mexico and disrupting border commerce through increased cargo searches. But Gavin argued that it would be better to threaten such sanctions through press leaks and official statements than to put them into effect.

Meanwhile, the DEA pressed ahead with its investigation. *Newsweek* has learned that U.S. agents are focusing on a reputed drug dealer and hit man who uses the name Manuel Salcido, but is known around Guadalajara as "Cochiloco" (Crazy Pig). DEA officials have received reports from several sources that before the kidnappings, Cochiloco had complained that Camarena, who was investigating Mexican cocaine smuggling, had been harassing his operation. He allegedly threatened to kill the DEA agent if the pressure continued. Cochiloco is also said to have boasted that he had murdered a DEA informant, and officials in Washington confirmed that one of Camarena's informants had been killed. U.S. officials did not believe, however that Cochiloco had planned the kidnapping-murder on his own. According to DEA sources, he worked for a cocaine syndicate run by Rafael Caro Quintero, said by the DEA to be one of the biggest traffickers in Mexico. The

DEA also suspects the involvement of two other alleged kingpins: Juan Matta Ballesteros and Miguel Angel Felix Gallardo.

Snapshot: Additional evidence that top traffickers may have been involved emerged when Mexican police belatedly raided Gallardo's ranch a few days after the kidnapping. Gallardo had disappeared by then, but a photograph of Camarena was discovered at the ranch. The snapshot had been taken at the headquarters of the Mexican Federal Judicial Police (MFJP). As of last week, Mexican police had not yet explained how the picture had fallen into Gallardo's hands.

American officicals could point to one victory in the drug war. DEA agents in Miami arrested Norman Saunders, chief minister of the Turks and Caicos islands in the West Indies, and charged him with conspiring to provide a "safe haven" for drug traffickers in the British territory. If convicted, Suanders could become the first head of a foreign land to be sent to prison in the United States on drug charges. The arrest was the culmination of an operation that began in January when a DEA informant indicated that top island officials might be involved in the narcotics business. Posing as traffickers, undercover DEA agent Gary Sloboda and the informant met with Suanders both in the islands and in Miami. In their final, secretly videotaped meeting, the informant paid Saunders $20,000, allegedly for having protected the movement of cocaine. The men also discussed the possibility of smuggling 800 kilograms of cocaine a week into the United States. Then DEA agents moved in for the arrest. Altogether, Saunders was accused of having accepted $50,000 to allow drugs to move freely through the islands.

But American investigators were chiefly concerned about solving the murder of their agent—and they were deeply disturbed by the apparent eagerness of the Mexican authorities to close the case once the two bodies were found. On the Saturday before the discovery, Mexican police received an anonymous letter saying the remains were located on the ranch of Manuel Bravo Cervantes, a small-time criminal with a past record of homicide. When police arrived at the ranch, gunfire erupted from the small main house. One policeman was killed, as were Manuel Bravo, his wife and sons. Three days later, the bodies were found on the outskirts of the ranch.

But U.S. officials quickly rejected the implication that the Bravo family was behind the deaths of Camarena and Zavala. Police had searched the ranch immediately after the shoot-out—and no bodies were found at the time. They went back with DEA agents the following Tuesday, but again they found no trace of the victims. It was only around 6 o'clock that evening that the young Mexican man came upon the suspicious bags. He ran to inform the chief of his village, and according to DEA officials, when he returned with the chief, the bags had been moved a short way. There was additional evidence that the bodies has recently been planted on the site. Ambassadore Gavin noted, for example, that the dirt found on the bodies did not match the soil of the ranch. "This thing smells," said one U.S. agent involved in the search. The real killers, he argued, were trying to frame the Bravo family.

Cops: It was not the first time that an apparent breakthrough seemed to have been manufactured for U.S. consumption. When the Americans complained that Mexico was not doing enough to root out its corrupt cops, the MFJP promptly trotted out former policeman Thomás Morlett Bórquez and announced that he was a "prime suspect" in the kidnappings. He was later released for lack of evidence, and U.S. officials now believe his arrest was a charade. According to confidential documents, when Morlett was stopped on Feb. 24 on the Tecate-Tijuana Highway, he apparently failed to notice that the Mexican police were accompanied by agents of the DEA. "I thought you were going to stop me in Tijuana," Morlett told his captors. According to the DEA officials on the scene, the MFJP agents apologized and told Morlett they were only carrying out orders from Mexico City. Morlett reportedly responded by saying that he hoped what the cops had told him was true, or else the MFJP agents would be in a lot of trouble.

Newsweek has learned that Ambassador Gavin asked the DEA to draw up a list of everything that is known or suspected about drug-related corruption in Mexico. Numerous allegations have already been compiled. One of the most serious is that Mexico's opium- and marijuana-eradication program, which U.S. officials had long hailed as a model, may in fact be tainted with corruption. Among other things, DEA officials have been told that some Mexican eradication pilots had substituted water for the herbicides they were supposed to spray. "They weren't killing the fields, they were watering them," says a frustrated U.S. official. The allegation has yet to be confirmed. But Mexico's share of the U.S. market for heroin, marijuana and cocaine is increasing sharply, leading some American officials to conclude that the eradication program is verging on failure.

Shoot-Out: And the violence continues to grow. Last week marijuana traffickers massacred half the police force of San Fernando, 30 miles from the Texas border. Four policemen and a civilian were apparently tailing a suspicious tank truck when their car was rammed off the road by a Mercury Grand Marquis. As one officer radioed for help, the occupants of the Mercury opened fire with machine guns, shotguns and pistols. The four officers and the civilian were killed without firing a shot. When three more police arrived at the scene they also were shot, but survived. When still more state policemen arrived, they discovered 1,700 pounds of marijuana in the abandoned tank truck. By Mexican standards it was a relatively insignificant haul. There was no indication that San Fernando police had stepped up their drug-enforcement efforts in response to U.S. pressure. They had just met some unusually nasty traffickers on a bad day.

The U.S. Customs Service closed nine isolated border stations after an informant warned that an inspector would be kidnapped or killed. "The developments in Mexico emphasize the reality of the threats," said Charles Conroy, public-affairs officer for the southwest customs region. The threats were also being taken seriously at the DEA, where coldly furious agents insisted they would continue the fight. "We are willing to accept our losses," said deputy administrator Jack Lawn. "What we will not accept is terrorism, and this has only strengthened our resolve." That was not just bluster. The DEA now had its martyrs, and despite their previously comfortable position in Mexico, the traffickers could expect to be hit hard.

INTERNATIONAL CAMPAIGN AGAINST DRUG TRAFFICKING[5]

I will address today a very special kind of global menace—a problem so complex that many thoughtful people do not believe it can be resolved, a problem so staggering in its implications for all our nations that we have no choice but to succeed. That problem is narcotics production, trafficking, and abuse. I will address the continuing problems we face and share with you an appraisal of our common future, emphasizing the new opportunities I see for more effective action.

I especially want to comment on the new spirit of improved bilateral and multilateral cooperation that increasingly justifies an optimistic appraisal of our prospects.

It has often been said that there is no greater force than an idea whose time has come. Narcotics control is certainly not a new idea; yet, I submit there is a more intensive worldwide declaration of a need for action being expressed at this time by more nations, with a greater sense of urgency, than during any previous period. Today, drug abuse is rampant throughout the community of nations. It affects producer as well as consumer nations, and it is this mutual concern that has resulted in an expanded opportunity for concentrated action. I believe that the greatest force we can harness to combat international narcotics trafficking is this collective desire to rescue our societies, our institutions and especially our children from this dread phenomenon. Joint actions, especially multilateral actions within geographic regions and spheres of interest, can enhance and make more effective the best of our national and bilateral efforts.

Granted, there will continue to be an expanding need for nationally initiated control programs and bilateral assistance projects. But the evidence is compelling that we need something more than individual initiative. No nation can cope with drug abuse by

[5]Reprint of a statement by Jon R. Thomas, Assistant Secretary of State for International Narcotics Matters, delivered in the Third Committee at the UN General Assembly on November 15, 1984. *Department of State Bulletin*. p 50–53. Ja. '85.

relying only on its own treatment, prevention, and domestic enforcement. No single nation can resolve the international production or trafficking problems.

The demand for drugs is so widespread and the supply of illicit drugs so great, that only a truly comprehensive, rigorously pursued international strategy will suffice.

Progress in Control Efforts

Because of the severity and complexity of the narcotics problems, some people say that the situation is hopeless. Nothing could be further from the truth. Recent events give reason to be optimistic that the current approaches of the international community are making significant progress in establishing the base for potential control of production and distribution of major illicit substances. I choose these words carefully; we do not have control, but we have improved the possibility that we will gain control.

We have been encouraged in recent years with many signs of progress in Latin America, Southwest and Southeast Asia.

It would be appropriate to begin with Turkey, where a crop control program enforced by a strong government, with support from the international community, led to a complete suppression of illicit cultivation. That ban continues to be effective today because of that same strong dedication. And, when the problem spread to Mexico, there was an equally strong response. The Mexican Government's successful aerial herbicide eradication program has reduced the production of heroin from about 6.5 metric tons in 1975 to an estimated 1.4 metric tons in 1983, and also dramatically reduced marijuana cultivation. The Mexicans call their efforts the "permanent campaign," recognizing that fighting narcotics requires a constant readiness and long-term sustained efforts.

The Mexican Government has also supported interregional activities, providing helicopters and crews to assist the Goverment of Belize with the herbicidal eradiction of marijuana and providing the Colombian Government with technical assistance on aerial marijuana eradiction.

Latin American Antinarcotics Campaign

The very impressive Colombian campaign against narcotics, which has been increasingly effective over the past 3 years, moved into a decisive new phase on July 5 when the national police began to test the aerial eradication of marijuana with the herbicide glyphosate. More than 5,000 acres have been sprayed, and the Colombians, who anticipated an even more comprehensive program in 1985, are well on their way toward achieving control of cannabis production. They are continuing their strong effort to control cocaine production as well. The Colombians have paid a tragic price for this campaign. On April 30, Minister of Justice [Bonilla] Lara, an outspoken advocate of strong antinarcotics controls, was machine-gunned to death on a residential street in Bogota in a contract murder apparently financed by narcotics traffickers. But the killing did not deter President [Cuartas] Betancur and his ministers. Since the assassination, Colombian police have staged more than 1,500 raids resulting in 1,425 arrests and the destruction of about 50 cocaine laboratories. President Betancur has also declared that Colombia will extradite traffickers.

In August, President Siles ordered Bolivian military as well as police units into the Chapare region, where coca cultivation and narcotics trafficking have expanded dramatically in recent years. These security measures are the prerequisite for future coca control and eradication efforts in that area. The Bolivian Government has also mounted raids against traffickers in the Beni, another important narcotics trafficking center. By mid-year, Peru had increased its eradication of coca bushes in the Upper Huallaga Valley to nearly 4,900 acres, compared to 1,700 acres eradicated in all of 1983. This program is continuing despite increased violence in the valley by terrorists as well as by narcotic traffickers.

A great deal more needs to be done in Bolivia and in Peru to begin to deal adequately with the many narcotics related problems, but clearly movement in the right direction has begun. We and the UN Fund for Drug Abuse Control have responded to requests to assist projects to extend both coca control programs and rural development assistance to the other major growing areas of Peru and Bolivia. While events in Colombia have given rise to hopes that major progress is being made against narcotics trafficking in Latin America, they have also generated well-founded concerns that drug traffickers will seek new bases in other countries.

Panamanian Defense Forces this past May discovered and destroyed a large cocaine complex, which had been constructed by Colombian traffickers in Darien Province, and also destroyed some large plantings of coca in that area, which is adjacent to the Colombian border. Panamanian authorities intercepted large quantities of ether used to refine cocaine, which was bound for that laboratory complex as well as laboratories in Colombia.

Brazilian National Police have had to step up their activities in the Amazonas regions, where traffickers are encouraging tribal groups to expand their traditional plantings of coca and are establishing cocaine laboratories. Similarly, Argentina has been obliged to devote increasing resources to deal with the rising number of cocaine laboratories which have been established within its borders during the past 2 years.

Venezuela has adopted stronger antinarcotics laws, and the government has increased its cooperation with the Colombian National Police on narcotics trafficking and related problems in their common border region. Last year, Venezuela destroyed close to 500 acres of marijuana in its western provinces and, among its narcotics seizures, was a near record 667-kilogram shipment of cocaine, which was being transshipped through Caracas International Airport. This government has recognized the narcotics problem and stands ready to confront it.

A variety of programs have been launched in the Caribbean and Central America, including efforts to improve radar surveillance and interdiction capabilities in the Bahamas and to improve on interdiction in Jamaica.

Asian Narcotics Efforts

As enforcement activities have improved in certain Latin American countries, we have seen a shifting in the smuggling routes and tactics of narcotics trafficking organizations. A similar pattern of shifting sources has been seen in Southwest Asia, where the substantial reductions in opium poppy cultivation in Pakistan are being, unfortunately, overshadowed by uncontrolled production in Afghanistan. In Pakistan, narcotics production has dropped dramatically from 800 metric tons in 1979 to an estimated 45 tons in 1983. Narcotics control programs are operating in the Malakand, Gadoon-Amazai, and Buner areas with assistance from the United States and the United Nations, and the government has embarked on a Special Development and Enforcement Plan under the auspices of the UN Fund for Drug Abuse Control to extend its ban on opium cultivation into the remaining areas of the Northwest Frontier Province. We were especially encouraged by the response of international donors to this program.

The Thai Government increased its commitment this year to controlling opium cultivation in civilian-police-military command villages in return for development assistance and eradicated 800 acres in what we hope was a demonstration of future Thai intentions. The army has disrupted trafficking and refining activities along the border with Burma through military operations against trafficking groups.

Earlier this year, the Government of Burma conducted effective military operations against narcotics traffickers in the Shan and Kachin States which resulted in the seizure of quantities of narcotics, chemicals, refining equipment, and weapons. The Burmese also eradicated more than 10,000 acres of opium poppy cultivation this past season.

A key element in worldwide advances in narcotics control has been the expanding role of the UN Fund for Drug Abuse Control under the effective leadership of Dr. Guiseppe DiGennaro. The Fund is now developing projects in support of coca control in South America, marking a long needed involvement by the United Nations and indirectly by European donors in a problem which effects Europe as well as the United States. This UN activity was largely made possible by a pledge of $40 million over 5 years by the Government of Italy. The Fund has also received pledges of more than $11 million from Italy, the United States and United Kingdom, with other pledges in the offing for the Special Development and Enforcement Program in Pakistan. Other key donors to source country programs include the Federal Republic of Germany, Saudi Arabia, Sweden, and Norway. The major donors support the Fund's leadership in the policy that all UN drug development projects will contain drug enforcement provisions and agree that economic assistance should be linked to commitments by recipient governments to eliminate illicit narcotic crops by specified dates.

A Worldwide Challenge

However, while progress is being made, we are faced with numerous challenges.

Worldwide production of illicit opium, coca leaf, and cannabis is many times the amount currently consumed by drug abusers. Some governments do not have control of the narcotics growing regions, and prospects in several countries are dampened by corruption, even government involvement in the narcotics trade. Markets shift and new production sources emerge even as we achieve success in eradicating current crops, most prominently evidenced by the transitions from country to country of the centers of heroin and cocaine production. To meet these challenges and others, we need to forge a true international alliance of concerned nations.

The world requires narcotics control programs in all the significant producer countries supported by increased assistance from the international community. But we also need more nations to apply their political resources to this problem. All nations have a vested interest in a successful solution, and when finally allied, their combined political and economic resources will make that successful resolution possible. The forging of this alliance is more urgent than ever before. We must capitalize on today's opportunities to expand and improve narcotics control. There are greater incentives on the part of drug exporting countries to act and to move quickly. Virtually every source country has suffered the problems of economic dislocations, institutional instability, and crime related to narcotics trafficking. Several have also been besieged by political problems, including armed insurgencies supported by profits from the drug trade. These source countries increasingly understand that they are the first beneficiaries of successful narcotics control programs.

In a major address on narcotics on September 14, Secretary of State George Shultz noted that the growing narcotics network was part of a trend toward international lawlessness that has been increasing ominously over the past two decades. He called narcotics trafficking, terrorism, and similar kinds of outlaw behavior "the modern versions of piracy." The Secretary noted there is ample evidence showing that these different types of lawlessness are linked. Money from drug smuggling supports terrorists. Terrorists provide assistance to drug traffickers. Organized crime works hand in hand with these other outlaws for their own profit. What may be most disturbing is the mounting evidence that some governments are involved in both narcotics trafficking and in terrorism. As Secretary Shultz went on to say, the world has good reason to suspect that narcotics smugglers are being aided by certain governments, that they are getting protection and are being provided with safe havens and support in shipping drugs to the United States and other countries.

Clearly the complicity of these governments in the drug trade, and government complicity in terrorist acts, are matters of grave concern; and I believe the increasing awareness of these adverse and other effects is improving the prospects for narcotics control.

One of the more encouraging signs in the battle against the narcotics plague is the increased attention governments are placing on the need for bilateral and regional cooperation in antinarcotics activities. Underlying this trend is the realization by governments that first, no country is immune from the political, economic, and social problems associated with narcotics trafficking and second, it can be countered only if nations work together to bridge the legal and physical boundaries which divide them.

In August, several leaders from Latin America, including Argentine President Alfonsin, Bolivian President Siles, Colombian President Betancur, Panamanian President Barletta and Venezuelan President Lusinchi traveled to Quito for the inauguration of President Febres-Cordero of Ecuador. It is very noteworthy that, in meetings among themselves and with Vice President Bush, the first topic was not the issue of financial debt or regional military security, but narcotics control. That this occasion turned into an unprecedented summit meeting on narcotics attests to the awesome challenges narcotics production and trafficking present to the well-being of Latin American nations. What emerged from these meetings is what we might refer to as the "Spirit of Quito"—that is, the recognition among many Latin American nations that they must now stand together and work together to wipe out this scourge which threatens their societies.

The United States believes that strong regional, cooperative efforts are the key to lasting progress against narcotics trafficking in Latin America, throughout our hemisphere, and in the world at large. Thus, we strongly support the spirit coming from the meetings at Quito and Mar del Plata which called attention to the need for increased international action to deal with the multiple political, economic, and social problems caused by narcotics trafficking. This spirit has been reflected in remarks to the General Assembly. For example, President Lusinchi emphasized the need for strong international action and cooperation to support the domestic activities of the individual governments when he addressed the General Assembly on September 24. He said: "The narcotraffickers cross frontiers every day and there is not a government in the world working alone which can eliminate the serious political and social threat which drugs represent."

Leaders of Latin American governments have recognized that drugs constitute a threat not only to the health of their citizens, but also to their societies and democratic systems. Now they say, "We have had enough." The vigor with which these leaders are collectively approaching this problem is reflected in several resolutions, which have been proposed and still others being discussed by national delegations.

We welcome the personal leadership taken by many Latin American leaders, and we support the strengthened commitment against narcotics trafficking and production, as underscored by the resolution drafted by the Government of Venezuela requesting that the Commission on Narcotic Drugs give priority to consideration of a draft convention against drug trafficking. We look forward to working jointly in February, at the Commission meeting, building on the framework of existing conventions to strengthen the international resolve against narcotics trafficking, and we compliment President Lusinchi and his government on this thoughtful initiative.

Similarly, this emerging spirit is reflected in the suggestions of our colleagues from Argentina, Bolivia, Brazil, Colombia, Ecuador, Peru, and Venzuela to strengthen existing international institutions and encourage governments to improve national legal and social frameworks to deal more effectively with drug trafficking. We look to existing institutions, like the UN Fund for Drug Abuse Control, to achieve an immediate impact in meeting the narcotics challenge. The Fund is an established institution with expanding activities. Let us support it financially and politically so that it can pursue the goals which the international community has endorsed.

Conclusion

We believe there is need for improved coordination in the UN system and hope that the designation of the Under Secretary General for Political and General Assembly Affairs will lead to that coordination of the important work of the Fund, the Division for Narcotic Drugs, and the International Narcotics Control Board. We agree with the recently published findings of the Joint Inspection Unit that the specialized agencies should develop specific drug control programs for consideration by their member governments, and that governments should use their own resources whenever possible. We also concur with the recommendation that drug abuse projects should have specific conditions requiring governments to enforce narcotics control objectives.

It is our hope that we can vote for and speak in support of several such initiatives. We have some differences with sponsors on some language in drafts, and we welcome their assurances that we can discuss our respective viewpoints in a manner conducive to agreement, as was noted in my discussions just last week with Venezuelan Foreign Minister Morales Paul.

While I have focused at length today on Latin America, in part because many of the resolutions of interest to this meeting have emanated from that area, our concern is, of course, for the worldwide effort. The United States stands ready to help the governments and people of Latin America, Southwest and Southeast Asia to work together for the common good. This task is spurred by President Reagan's pledge to a foreign policy that vigorously seeks to ensure effective international narcotics control. We believe that national and bilateral efforts must be complemented by strengthened regional cooperation in all global sectors. Recently, we have offered to provide appropriate financial and technical support to improve regional narcotics enforcement information exchanges in Latin America, as well as to develop regional programs to create heightened public awareness of the personal dangers of drug consumption and the social and economic costs of the illicit drug trade. For several years now, we have supported the special drug abuse initiatives of the Association of Southeast Asian Nations, or ASEAN, and encourage the work of the Pompidou Group and others who approach this problem on a multinational basis. We are also proud of our efforts these past 4 years to reduce drug demand in the United States, where a very effective national awareness program led by Mrs. Reagan has dramatically heightened community responsiveness. We are encouraged by the spread of the parents movement, so vital in our country, to other societies. In all of these endeavors, we enjoy a spirit of cooperation with our Congress, which has been most unequivocal in seeking a linkage between narcotics control and development assistance.

Therefore, let us consider these Latin American initiatives as part of the growing worldwide expression of concern about the narcotics problem. The issues these resolutions address and the remedies they seek have implications for all of our international efforts, and my government asks that all nations join together in this new alliance for our common good. And when we have agreed on these resolutions, let us proceed with development of common strategies. Experience dictates the cooperative program of work that is needed.

The grower-to-user chains which stretch across five continents must be broken through a comprehensive program of international control. We must apply pressure at all points in the chain—through crop control, through increased seizures of both drug products and financial assets, through intensified investigation and prosecution of traffickers, and through effective treatment and prevention of drug abuse. International strategies should give top priority to crop control—bans on cultivation and production, enforced when necessary by eradication and by interdiction and other enforcement programs operating as close to the source as possible.

An effective international strategy should offer financial and technical assistance for narcotic control projects. We must improve our knowledge of all aspects of the problem and exchange information to improve coordination of policy and effort. The people and governments of illicit drug producing countries must become more aware of the problems they export to other countries—and the domestic problems they are creating within their own societies. There is a need to raise the foreign policy priority assigned to narcotics control, to integrate narcotics into bilateral relations, and to upgrade the level at which narcotics matters are considered in foreign ministries.

Assistance should be sought by drug producing nations and provided by donor countries with clearly defined crop control objectives if we are to achieve success. We should recognize the need to link this assistance with crop control agreements. Governments of producing nations must have and demonstrate the political will to undertake effective crop contol and interdiction programs. Part of that demonstration of will must be the commitment of social and political as well as material resources, and promulgation and adoption of laws which facilitate control objectives. We need a higher level of awareness throughout the international community. We need to communicate through the world press the kind of intensive efforts that are being made. Awareness is increasing, and it shows in many programs, including not just improved interdiction and eradication, but in the decisions of governments to consult with their people on solutions.

Above all, we must work together, in an alliance at the national, regional and international levels through bilateral and multilateral programs. The agreements which we make here, which will manifest mutual respect and an understanding of individual and collective needs, must send a signal to the international community that we have made common cause in a more vigorous, more widespread, and more united effort to control international narcotics production and trafficking.

II. COCAINE

EDITOR'S INTRODUCTION

By far the most popular and prevalent drug in the United States today, cocaine is the object of intense concern of drug enforcement officials. Cocaine has exercised a tremendous allure as a "recreational" drug that is supposedly non-addictive; that stimulates and excites the brain, rather than dulling it as many other drugs do. It also enjoys a reputation as an aphrodisiac and is said to release inhibitions and give a feeling of power and confidence. Its users include both men and women, many of them young and upwardly mobile, and frequent use is regarded by some as an important status symbol. Yet cocaine, as some of the following articles point out, is not harmless. Nor is it nonaddictive psychologically. Habitual use, moreover, is an expensive habit that few can afford for long, and, just as in the case of heroin, heavy cocaine users are turning increasingly to drug clinics for help. But even if their well-being were not imperiled, cocaine users would still be underwriting the brutal business of international drug trafficking, which could not exist without their complicity or the demand for their commodity.

Section II begins with "Cocaine," a fairly detailed, technical article by Craig Van Dyke and Robert Byck from *Scientific American,* which discusses the social and physiological consequences of cocaine use. The following article, "The Cocaine Society," from *World Press Review,* is by Guy Sitbon, a French leftist, who takes a condemnatory view of American society as a corrupt cocaine marketplace. "Cocaine Spreads Its Deadly Net," an article by John Lang in *U. S. News & World Report,* is an overview of trafficking in cocaine today. Dominick DiCarlo's article, "International Initiatives to Control Coca Production and Cocaine Trafficking," from *Drug Enforcement,* explains the federal government's position in reducing the flow of cocaine from South America and focuses particularly upon the problems faced in Colombia, Bolivia, and Peru. Finally, Gina Maranto's "Coke: The Random Killer," from *Discover,* is a chilling account of drug psychosis and overdose deaths that may result from the use of the "champagne of drugs."

COCAINE[1]

A few hundredths of a gram of cocaine hydrochloride, chopped finely and arranged on a smooth surface into several lines, or rows of powder, can be snorted into the nose through a rolled piece of paper in a few seconds. The inhalation shortly gives rise to feelings of elation and a sense of clarity or power of thought, feelings that pass away for most people in about half an hour. Although the growing interest in cocaine in the U.S. and Western Europe is in part a consequence of this simple, hedonistic experience, the real importance of the drug derives from the interaction of social, economic and political factors: the current status of cocaine as a fashionable drug for "recreational" use, its artificially inflated price, the control of its distribution by criminal organizations, the stresses its barter and untaxed trade impose on the monetary and taxation systems, the strains it places on the resources of law enforcement, and the potential of the cocaine trade for corrupting officials and undermining respect for the law.

Estimates of the cost and consumption of cocaine are subject to the biases of the reporting source and should therefore be viewed with skepticism. According to a 1979 report by the White House Strategy Council on Drug Abuse, some 10 million Americans had taken cocaine within the preceding 12 months, compared with 10,000 people 20 years before. The National Narcotics Intelligence Consumers Committee (NNICC) has estimated that in 1979 between 25,000 and 31,000 kilograms of cocaine entered the

[1]Reprint of an article, incorporating corrections by the authors, by Dr. Craig Van Dyke, Veterans Administration Medical Center and Associate Professor of Psychiatry, Langley Porter Neuropsychiatric Institute, University of California, San Francisco, and Dr. Robert Byck, Department of Pharmacology and Psychology, School of Medicine, Yale University. *Scientific American.* 246:128–141. Copyright © 1982 Dr. Byck and Dr. Van Dyke.

U.S. illegally. During 1980 U.S. cocaine imports are estimated to have been between 40,000 and 48,000 kilograms. These quantities are based on estimates of the refining capacity of clandestine laboratories, on estimates of the proportions of the refined product that are sold in the domestic and foreign markets and particularly on estimates of the production yields of raw coca leaves in the source countries. Perhaps not surprisingly, the estimates of crop yield made in the source countries are in many cases smaller than U.S. estimates by a factor of two or more.

The illicit retail dealer can sell a white, crystalline substance consisting of from 10 to 85 percent cocaine and various other substances for between $100 and $140 per gram. The NNICC, from its estimate of 1980 cocaine imports, puts the retail value of the industry at between $27 and $32 billion. If the cocaine trade were included by *Fortune* in its list of the 500 largest industrial corporations, cocaine would rank seventh in volume of domestic sales, between the Ford Motor Company and the Gulf Oil Corporation. Based on U.S. estimates, the monetary value of Bolivia's cocaine exports may now surpass the value of the country's largest legal industry, tin. Colombia's more highly refined cocaine exports total about $1 billion annually, half the value of the coffee crop.

It is all too easy to suppose the physiological and social consequences of the use of cocaine are commensurate with its popularity and economic importance. Actually the assessment of the medical and psychological implications of short- and long-term cocaine usage has only recently begun. In 1975 the National Institute on Drug Abuse began a research project intended to define the pharmacology of cocaine in man. A number of investigators have since been engaged in various aspects of cocaine-related research, including a detailed description of the effects of the drug in man, its distribution and metabolism in the body, its reinforcing properties and its potential for abuse.

After six years of work on the problem our group at the Yale University School of Medicine has been able to describe with reasonable confidence the time course of the basic pharmacological effects that follow the introduction of single doses of cocaine into the body by various routes. We have also been able to associate the time course of cocaine concentration in the blood with replicatable measures of its psychological effects. Although cocaine is intensely pleasurable to some people, we have found that its ability to produce a unique "high" may be overrated: our subjects, all experienced cocaine users, could not distinguish a single small dose of cocaine taken intranasally from the same quantity of the synthetic local anesthetic lidocaine. Investigators at the University of Chicago School of Medicine found that their subjects could not distinguish the immediate effects of intravenous cocaine from those of amphetamine, although at later times the differences between the drugs are apparent. Such results are the first steps toward distinguishing the almost overwhelming mythology that surrounds cocaine from reliable information about its effects.

At the same time there has been renewed interest in understanding the history of cocaine consumption as well as its significance to the Indian cultures of the Andes, including parts of present-day Colombia, Ecuador, Peru, Bolivia and Chile. Of course, the Andean social and pharmacological experience with the coca leaf cannot be compared directly with the current social experience with the more potent substance cocaine hydrochloride, but one can still hope to gain a cultural perspective on the drug. Such a perspective is at least as important to informed public policy as knowledge of the biochemical and pharmacological action of cocaine is.

Cocaine is an alkaloid, a member of a broad group of plant substances that also includes nicotine, caffeine and morphine. In nature cocaine is found in significant quantities only in the leaves of two species of the coca shrub. *Erythroxylum coca* requires a moist, tropical climate. According to Timothy Plowman of the Field Museum of Natural History in Chicago, *E. coca* may be native to the Peruvian Andes, although it now grows throughout the eastern highlands of the Andes in Ecuador, Peru and Bolivia. The concentration of alkaloidal cocaine in its leaves can be as high as 1.8 percent. *E. coca* was cultivated by the Incas, and it remains the primary source of cocaine for the illicit world trade.

E. novogranatense, the other cocaine-rich species of *Erythroxylum,* is cultivated in drier, mountanious regions of Colombia and along the Caribbean coast of South America. The *truxillense,* or "Trujillo," variety of the latter species is now grown on the northern coast of Peru and in the dry valley of the Marañón River, a tributary of the Amazon in northeastern Peru. Its leaves are harvested for legal export to the Stepan Chemical Company in Maywood, N.J., where the cocaine is extracted for controlled pharmaceutical purposes and the remaining leaf material is prepared as a flavoring for Coca-Cola.

Recent archaeological findings in Ecuador indicate that human experience with cocaine dates back at least 5,000 years, long before the Inca empire was established. To the Incas coca was a plant of divine origin and a symbol of high social or political rank. According to one myth, the god Inti created coca to alleviate the hunger and thirst of the Incas, who believed themselves to be descendants of the gods. The Incas state controlled virtually every aspect of daily life, including the cultivation and use of coca. Coca was chewed primarily by the ruling classes, although on occasion it was disbursed to soldiers, workers or runners. Casual chewing of the leaves was considered a sacrilege.

The first reports of coca chewing to reach Europe were almost coincident with the discovery of the new World. The letters of Amerigo Vespucci, published in 1507, mention the Indian practice of chewing leaves and adding ashes to the cud. A major component of the ash is carbonate of lime, or calcium carbonate ($CaCO_3$), which intensifies the subjective effects of the coca leaves; among the Andean Indians the practice of adding lime continues today. Other European observers were first mystified, then repulsed and finally impressed by the Indian's use of coca. A manuscript completed in 1613 by Don Felipe Guaman Poma de Ayala represents coca chewing as an unauthorized social activity engaged in by the Indians when they were expected to be working.

Other accounts of coca chewing from explorers and chroniclers were more enthusiastic. Coca was reported to cause a striking increase in endurance, enabling men to do hard work with little food at high altitudes. By 1569 the Spanish entrepreneurs in South America had recognized the utility of coca in recruiting Indians for labor, and Philip II of Spain gave their practice official approval by declaring coca necessary to the well-being of the Indians.

If coca leaves retained their potency after drying and long travel as successfully as tobacco leaves and coffee beans do, the role of coca in European and North American society might be quite different from what it is today. Botanical specimens of coca arrived in Europe soon after the Spanish exploration, and coca leaves continued to be exported to Europe in small qunatities throughout the 17th, 18th and early 19th centuries. In spite of the glowing descriptions of the effects of coca among the Indians, however, Europeans did not adopt the practice of chewing coca. In terms of its cultural importance the real crossing of the Atlantic by coca had to await the development of 19th-century methods for isolating chemical compounds. When the pure alkaloid and related substances were made available by these means, it was in a social context quite different from the one that prevailed when tobacco and coffee were taken up in the 16th century. The modern social history of cocaine has been determined in large part by the attitudes that formed in the late 19th century and by the reactions to those attitudes.

The German chemist Friedrich Gaedke was probably the first to isolate alkaloidal cocaine from the coca leaf in 1855, when he prepared an oily substance and small crystals from the distilled residue of coca extract. Albert Niemann of the University of Göttingen was the first to characterize the substance chemically in 1859. Niemann reported that cocaine had a bitter taste and that, after a short time, it numbed the tongue. By 1880 Vassili von Anrep, a Russian nobleman and physician at the University of Würzburg, noted he could not feel a pinprick after he administered cocaine subcutaneously. Meanwhile, because cocaine seemed to have actions opposite to those of drugs that depress the central nervous system, it was studied by American physicians as a possible antidote to the habits engendered by morphine and alcohol.

In 1884 enthusiastic reports about cocaine came to the attention of Sigmund Freud, who was then a young house physician in the neurology section of a Viennese hospital. Although von Anrep was one of his instructors, Freud took an interest in cocaine not primarily as a local anesthetic but rather as a stimulant of the central nervous system and as an aid to overcoming morphine addiction. He ingested cocaine himself and published *On Coca,* a review of the literature on coca and cocaine.

On Coca stirred a ferment of interest in cocaine. The review expressed a highly favorable opinion of the drug, and in letters of the same period Freud rhapsodically described how "a small dose lifted me to the heights in a wonderful fashion." Although he suggested the therapeutically useful possibility that cocaine could reduce the pain of inflammation, it remained for his friend and associate Carl Koller to recognize the full implications of the properties of cocaine as a local anesthetic. Koller applied it to the eye during surgery and so established the critical link between local anesthetic properties and surgical procedure.

The attempt to show that cocaine and morphine could be employed antagonistically, so as to counter each other's effects, did not work out as well. The American surgeon William Stewart Halsted became one of the first victims of cocaine dependence as a result of experiments he carried out on himself to show that the drug could act as a "nerve blocker." Isolation aboard a schooner failed to control the habit, and Halsted was treated with morphine in the hope that its apparently opposite pharmacological effects would cancel his desire for cocaine. Unfortunately, to his dependence on cocaine Halsted simply added a dependence on morphine, which lasted to the end of his life.

As the ineffectiveness of cocaine in treating morphine addiction came to be recognized and reports of serious preoccupation with cocaine began to circulate, Freud's enthusiasm for the drug began to wane. Although he continued to enjoy his own ingestion of the drug, he was shaken when , three years after he had begun his first investigations into cocaine, Albrecht Erlenmeyer accused him of having unleashed "the third scourge of humanity" (after alcohol and the opiates).

The descriptions of the effects of cocaine in man given by Freud and his associates were not superseded for nearly 90 years. Most subsequent scientific work on the topic has been concerned with establishing biochemical mechanisms that might account for

Freud's observations; there has also been much hearsay, anecdote and invective. Interest in cocaine was sustained chiefly because of its properties as a local anesthetic, and as a result of this interest cocaine was one of the first alkaloids to be chemically synthesized. Richard Willstätter and his colleagues at the University of Munich achieved the synthesis in 1923, but the spatial structure of the cocaine molecule remained unknown until E. von Hardeggar and Hans Ott worked it out in 1955.

A local anesthetic blocks the conduction of a sensory nerve impulse when the drug is applied directly to the nerve. Whereas many substances can block nerve conduction by injuring or permanently destroying nervous tissue, a local anesthetic is unusual in that its effect is temporary and reversible. Many of the drugs with local anesthetic properties that have been synthesized since the turn of the century, such as procaine (Novocain) and lidocaine (Xylocaine), are structurally similar to cocaine and work by a similar mechanism.

A local anesthetic inhibits a nerve impulse by altering the membrane of the nerve cell. When the cell is in its resting state, there is an electric-potential difference of from 60 to 70 millivolts between the inside of the axon (the impulse-conducting filament that emerges from the body of the cell) and the fluid surrounding the axon. The axoplasm inside the axon is electrically negative with respect to the fluid outside the cell membrane. When the cell is stimulated, the signal called the action potential travels down the axon as a wave of electrical depolarization. A slight depolarization of the axon membrane usually cause a large transient increase in the permeability of the membrane to positively charged sodium ions outside the cell. As the ions pass through channels in the membrane into the axoplasm, the potential difference between the axoplasm and the surrounding fluid is reduced. The movement of charge is a self-limiting process, and soon after the action potential is initiated potassium, calcium and other positively charged ions leak out of the axon and restore the electrochemical equilibrium of the cell.

It is not known precisely how a local anesthetic changes the axon membrane, but it is now thought that molecules of the anesthetic dissolve in the lipid matrix that composes the membrane and bind to receptor sites within the sodium channels. The presence of the anesthetic molecule at the receptor site probably interferes with the opening of the channel, thereby inhibiting the transfer of sodium ions across the membrane. Thus the depolarization of the axon is prevented and the nerve impulse is blocked. The action of the anesthetic is terminated by the breakdown of the anesthetic molecules and by their diffusion into the bloodstream.

Another property of cocaine that has been valued in clinical medicine is its tendency to constrict blood vessels when it is applied topically. Cocaine is the only local anesthetic that has this effect, and at one time, it was the anesthetic of choice in eye surgery because it limits the flow of blood. It has since been found, however, that the reduced flow can damage the surface of the eye, and so cocaine is no longer recommended for use by opthalmologists. It retains a role in surgery of the mucous membranes, such as those of the ear, nose and throat, as well as in procedures that require the passage of a tube through the nose or throat.

The constriction of blood vessels is one of several peripheral effects caused by the stimulation of the sympathetic nervous system. Drugs that act on sympathetic nerves to mimic such effects are called sympathomimetic drugs. Cocaine is a typical sympathomimetic agent in that it increases the heart rate, raises the blood pressure and, in large doses, increases the body temperature and dilates the pupils of the eyes.

The continual transmission of signals along the sympathetic nerve pathways is essential to life. In the axon the signal takes the form of an action potential, but when the action potential reaches the end of an axon, the signal is conveyed to the next nerve cell by a different mechanism, namely the release of a neurotransmitter such as dopamine or norepinephrine. The neurotransmitter is stored in vesicles in the axon near the synapse, the junction between the axon of one nerve cell and the dendrites of the next. When the axon fires, the vesicles fuse with the cell membrane, releasing the neurotransmitter into the synaptic cleft between the cells. The released molecules stimulate the succeeding nerve by attaching themselves to receptor sites on its dendrites.

Ordinarily the neurotransmitter molecules that do not stimulate the succeeding nerve cell are broken down by enzymes, diffuse into adjoining tissues or are pumped back into the cell terminal that released them. The pumping action is called reuptake. When cocaine molecules are present in the synaptic cleft, however, they inhibit the reuptake mechanism and so mimic the effects of the release of more neurotransmitter molecules. The neurotransmitter tends to remain in the cleft where it can continue to stimulate the receptors in the dendrites of the succeeding nerve cell.

It was once thought the psychologically stimulating effects of cocaine could be attributed solely to its ability to block the reuptake of norepinephrine. It is now known this is not the case. Other neurotransmitters such as serotonin and dopamine may well be involved. Many of the antidepressant drugs employed in psychiatry, such as amitriptyline (Elavil), block the reuptake of neurotransmitters, but they are not stimulants and they do not induce euphoria. On the other hand, there would seem to be little reason to suppose a local anesthetic such as lidocaine would induce euphoria either, although our investigations have shown that it does. A small single dose of lidocaine, when administered into the nose, cannot be distinguished from the same quantity of cocaine. In larger doses lidocaine, unlike cocaine, produces sleepiness. Moreover, other groups have shown that animals will work at a task to get injections of procaine just as they will for injections of cocaine. Since the molecules of cocaine, lidocaine and procaine are structurally similar, such findings may suggest merely that similar drugs cause similar experiences. They may also suggest, however, that certain kinds of drug-induced euphoria are generalized interpretations by the drug user of a rather wide range of unusual sensations caused by the interaction of a number of physiological and environmental factors.

The effects of a drug depend on the dosage, the form in which the drug is taken and the route by which it enters the body. Many effects also vary with the frequency with which the drug is taken: the body may accumulate the drug or develop a tolerance to it. The effects of psychoactive drugs also differ according to the expectations of the user, the setting or circumstances in which the drug is taken and the history and personality of the user. The strength of the last three variables in determining the overall effects of a drug makes it difficult to estimate just what portion of the cocaine experience should be attributed to the substance itself and what portion to ambience or expectation.

When cocaine is taken, expectation and mythology about the drug may generate subjective impressions that overwhelm any effects not consonant with the expectations. Moreover, the cocaine that is available on the street is likely to be adulterated, which complicates the pharmacology of the drug. The adulterant might be a cheaper stimulant such as amphetamine, a simple carbohydrate such as mannitol or lactose, a local anesthetic such as procaine or lidocaine or almost any other substance that is not immediately detectable by the cocaine buyer. On the other hand, when cocaine is given in controlled laboratory conditions, the stimuli that may heighten or modify its effects are ordinarily absent. Knowledge of the acute effects of cocaine must come from a blend of individual descriptions, which may be biased or fanciful, and from the reports of laboratories, which may desiccate the drug experience beyond recognition.

Even in the laboratory the effects of the user's expectations cannot be eliminated entirely. The ethics of research on drugs with human subjects allow only experienced users of cocaine to be employed in the studies of its effects. Such people may skew experimental results because their expectations about cocaine have already been formed in settings far different from those of the laboratory. To minimize such biases it is important that neither the experimenter nor the subject know what dosage (if any) has been given; to control for expectations a placebo must be interspersed with active doses of cocaine.

To establish a framework within which to organize our subjects' responses to cocaine we required a measure of the cocaine actually present in the body. In 1975 Peter Jatlow and David Bailey of the Yale School of Medicine developed a sensitive and specific assay for determining the concentration of cocaine in blood plasma. Their method employs a gas chromatograph, an instrument in which the molecules of a sample gas are forced through a column packed with an adsorbing material. Various kinds of molecules in the gas are adsorbed and released at different rates, so that a substance can be identified by the characteristic time it takes to pass through the column. To increase the sensitivity of the device to cocaine, Jatlow and Bailey installed a detector particularly sensitive to compounds that contain nitrogen, as cocaine does. The method made it possible for the first time to measure concentrations of cocaine in the blood as low as five nanograms per milliliter. The effects of doses that are commonly taken in social settings and before surgical procedures can thereby be traced.

Until the work of Jatlow and Bailey the determination of cocaine concentrations in blood was hindered by the presence in blood of the enzyme pseudocholinesterase, which is responsible for the breakdown of the neurotransmitter acetylcholine and which also breaks down cocaine. By adding fluoride ions to fresh plasma our group found that the action of the enzyme could be inhibited. The technical advance has in turn made possible the determination of blood-plasma levels of cocaine among coca chewers in South America, in settings that are not directly accessible to laboratory measuring instruments.

In the form of the hydrochloride salt, cocaine is readily absorbed through mucous membranes and enters the bloodstream. For unknown reasons the most popular route of administration is through the mucous membranes of the nose, although our group has demonstrated that crystals of cocaine hydrochloride are efficiently dissolved and absorbed from the gastrointestinal tract as well. Cocaine can also be introduced intravenously, or it can be absorbed through the lungs by smoking the alkaloidal substance, which users call free base. In South America an intermediate product in the manufacture of cocaine hydrochloride, called cocaine paste or coca paste, is now smoked by urban youths. Cocaine paste is approximately 30 to 90 percent free-base cocaine. In the U.S. amateur laboratory kits are sold for converting cocaine hydrochloride into free-base cocaine, which is less susceptible to heat decomposition. The free base is vaporized by hot gases generated in a device called a base pipe, and the vapors are inhaled.

Cocaine has been given intravenously in some laboratory studies because the moment when the drug is completely absorbed can be defined precisely. The concentration of cocaine in the blood peaks immediately after the injection and thereafter falls off with a half-life of from 45 to 90 minutes. Experimental subjects report intense euphoria, sometimes followed by a "crash," or extreme dysphoria, and a craving for more cocaine.

The effects of intravenous cocaine are so short-lived that many of the rather time-consuming tests of its effects cannot be carried out. We chose instead to examine the physiological and psychological effects of cocaine introduced into the nose. We did not ask our subjects to snort the cocaine crystals through a straw or a rolled dollar bill; nor did we follow the common street ritual of administering relatively small amounts of cocaine (about 30 milligrams) at regular intervals. Instead we gave single but higher doses from a nasal spray so that we could dissect the time course of the action of the drug.

The physiological effects of cocaine introduced in this manner are not striking. Not surprisingly, we found that higher doses induced higher blood-plasma levels, although, in apparent contradiction to the reputation of cocaine as a short-lived drug, the peak plasma concentrations are reached about an hour after the drug is taken. Doses of from 25 to 100 milligrams increase the heart rate by between eight and 10 beats per minute and raise both systolic and diastolic blood pressure by about 10 millimeters of mercury. These effects peak about 15 to 30 minutes after the drug is administered. At the relatively high dose of two milligrams per kilogram of body weight (or 140 milligrams for a person of average weight) there is a slight temperature increase, but the pupils of the eyes do not necessarily dilate.

Although cocaine, like all other local anesthetics, causes convulsions at very high doses, we found no obvious effect on the electroencephalogram at a dose of two milligrams per kilogram of body weight. Professor Reese Jones at the University of California has, however, found EEG changes in man after administration of cocaine using evoked potential technique. Convulsions are seen in humans after single large doses. Chronic cocaine use can lead to the abrupt onset of behavior that appears to be psychotic. Some investigators have argued that this may be the result of a "kindling effect," whereby a series of small doses sets off a response normally expected only from a much larger dose. Repeated small doses of cocaine may eventually lead to convulsions.

One of the main reasons for our interest in cocaine is its ability to reliably produce positive feelings in many people. In order to measure the psychological effects of cocaine we adopted several tests commonly employed in the study of mood and pain. In one such test the subject is asked to mark a point on a line that is labeled to represent six levels of euphoric and dysphoric feelings. Another test presents the subject with a list of adjectives, such as "lively," "suspicious," "anxious," "attentive," "sleepy" and "discouraged" together with a scale on which he can indicate the degree to which each adjective applies to his current feelings.

In experiments done in other laboratories subjects could not distinguish a small, 10-milligram dose of cocaine from a placebo. This is about one third of the usual street dose. When 25 to 100 milligrams of cocaine was given intranasally, however, all the subjects reliably reported peak euphoria within 15 to 30 minutes. From 45 to 60 minutes after the 100-milligram dose two out of seven subjects experienced anxiety, depression, fatigue and a desire for more cocaine. There is often a crash or period of extreme discomfort after cocaine is smoked or injected, but it is less common after intranasal use. For the most part drugs are associated by the public with a single effect, but it is clear from both street and laboratory reports that the pleasurable effects of cocaine at relatively small doses are replaced by disturbing feelings at higher doses.

If the time course of the psychological effects of cocaine is compared with the time course of its concentration in the plasma of the blood, one finds that euphoria is most pronounced shortly before the plasma concentration has begun to fall. The euphoric effects disappear several hours before the plasma concentration returns to zero; a similar temporal relation between subjective feelings and plasma concentration can be seen in the effects of other drugs such as alcohol or the benzodiazepines. When cocaine is smoked or taken intravenously, discomfort can ensue when the plasma concentration is still half its peak level.

The lack of a match between the time course of plasma concen- n and that of euphoric feeling suggests that the psychological of cocaine may be related to the rate of change of the plasma centration rather than to its absolute level. Because plasma concentration changes much more abruptly when cocaine is smoked or injected than when it is snorted or taken by mouth, one would expect more potent psychological consequences from smoking or injecting if the rate of change is the controlling factor. Feelings reported by experimental subjects are in accord with this hypothesis. Alternatively, the rapid loss of euphoric feelings while the cocaine concentration in plasma remains high may result from decreased responsiveness of receptor sites once they have been occupied, so that there is the appearance of acute tolerance to the drug.

Another reason feelings of euphoria rise and fall so rapidly while the concentration of cocaine in the plasma remains high may be that cocaine is readily soluble in fatty tissue. Because of this solubility cocaine may be quickly taken up from the bloodstream into the brain; there is some evidence that the concentration of cocaine in the brain is much greater than the concentration in plasma. If the large initial concentration of cocaine in the plasma leads to a high concentration in the brain, subsequent equilibration would be achieved if the cocaine diffused out of the brain and into the plasma once again. The plasma concentration would thus remain high even after the cocaine began to flush out of the brain. Hence what is known about the relation between plasma concentration and euphoria is at least consistent with the hypothesis that the euphoria induced by cocaine is closely linked with its concentration in the brain.

The effects of a drug depend on the long-term behavior patterns of an individual with respect to the drug as well as on the discrete phenomena that can be observed after a single dose. Chronic use of a drug can have both social and pharmacological consequences. If a person becomes totally involved in the acquisition and consumption of a drug, his entire life structure may change. When cocaine is taken regularly, it can cause sleeplessness and loss of appetite; after high doses or chronic consumption the user may experience an anxious paranoid state. Whether or not cocaine causes true psychosis remains an undecided question, but there is increasing evidence that hallucinations and paranoia can result if the drug is taken frequently in large doses. Since 1980, because of the increased popularity of cocaine, psychosis and crashes are commonly observed in users.

Is cocaine addictive? The question appears to call for a simple answer, but a yes or no reply does not do justice to the tangle of medical definition, folk wisdom, legal classification and social recrimination that is summarized by the word "addictive." One longstanding medically accepted definition of the term is derived from the description of opiate effects. For a drug to be considered addictive a person must develop tolerance for it, in the sense that repeating the same dose causes a diminishing response. Moreover, the drug must lead to physical dependence, so that repeated doses are required to prevent the onset of a withdrawal syndrome.

According to this restrictive definition, cocaine may be addictive. While cocaine users can take the same dose every day and get the same effect, acute tolerance to cocaine effects has now been shown by researchers at the University of Chicago. There are withdrawal signs detectable on the electroencephalogram and in sleep patterns, but they are quite undramatic when compared with the withdrawal syndromes associated with opiates, barbiturates or alcohol.

On the other hand, cocaine certainly is addicting within the broader sense of the term that is accepted by most authorities. In this context the chronic consumption of cocaine through the nose is similar only in some respects to its regular injection and freebase smoking. Dependence on intranasal cocaine often manifests itself in a pattern of continued use while supplies are available and in abstention when supplies are lacking. Increased availability has made this less likely and some intranasal users become "addicts." Because it is often described as a "safe" drug, individuals are easily seduced into a belief that cocaine may be taken by some routes without discretion. We know from case histories that this is not true.

In contrast, the smoking or injection of cocaine almost always leads to continual consumption and drug seeking behavior, destructive to personal competence and productivity. Free-base smoking is probably also dangerous to the respiratory system because it constricts the blood vessels of the lungs. The high price of street cocaine, together with the relatively large amounts of the substance necessary for injections or free-base smoking, undoubtedly function to limit the damage people might otherwise inflict on themselves.

The public belief that cocaine is either "safe" or unequivocally pernicious is exaggerated. But efforts to control its importation are of vital importance. The U.S. Drug Enforcement Administration employed 1,950 agents worldwide with an operating budget of $227 million during the fiscal year ending in September, 1981. In that fiscal year agents devoted 31 percent of their investigative man-hours to cocaine-related work. Operatives of the agency are active in nine South American countries, and in all these countries except Colombia (where marijuana trafficking is also seen as a problem) the main concern is cocaine.

The State Department, moreover, has exerted a great deal of diplomatic leverage in persuading the governments of these countries to adopt policies desired by the U.S. toward the growing of coca and toward the enforcement of laws pertaining to the cocaine trade. The U.S. has now signed treaties that commit Peru and Colombia to the eradication of coca, although no such agreements have been made with Bolivia. United Nations agreements to limit the increase of coca production in Peru and Bolivia have been tied to financial incentives, and they are accompanied by plans to cultivate substitute crops.

It is not clear whether the potential for the abuse of cocaine justifies the intensity of such efforts. The social, political and economic effects certainly do. Deaths from cocaine use are rare—but becoming more common. In Andean Indian societies blood-plasma levels comparable to those encountered among intranasal cocaine users are found, yet there is little evidence of physical harm from coca chewing. In such cultures the use of coca cannot be termed drug abuse. The attack on the practice of coca leaf chewing is viewed by some as an attempt to suppress traditional Indian culture and by others as a reasonable attempt to suppress a dangerous and debilitating habit. The main threat to North American and European society from cocaine is the waste of human potential that results from widespread consumption. Use patterns, rather than specific pharmacological effects, are the issue for all abused substances. Regulations and laws most appropriately should relate to human behavior, not chemical entities. Our drug regulations in the past have been based neither on science nor on sense. We have legalized both alcohol and tobacco, which, although pleasurable to some people, are distinct hazards to both personal and public health.

One can learn from history that cocaine is a drug easily overused. One can learn from the present cocaine trade that if a demand is great enough, an industry will arise to meet it. In medical use by anesthesiologists cocaine is a relatively safe drug, but in the hands of naive people it can lead to self-destructive behavior. Many of the questions surrounding the issue of cocaine can be answered by scientific investigation, but the final decisions about cocaine will be political and economic, not scientific.

THE COCAINE SOCIETY[2]

The body was in a green plastic bag between two crumbling buildings not far from Wall Street. A policeman opened the bag and recognized Barry Stanford. The unfortunate youth had just finished his studies at Benington College, but he still owed the school $600. The policeman knew that Stanford, who came from a poor family, had paid for his education by providing cocaine to rich students.

One third of all Americans between eighteen and twenty-five, according to the National Drug Institute, sniff the "snow." Among well-to-do students (the powder costs more than seven times its weight in gold) the incidence of cocaine use is at least 60 per cent.

[2]Reprint of an article by Guy Sitbon, staff writer for Paris weekly *Le Nouvel Observateur*. Excerpted from Sitbon's article in *Le Nouvel Observateur*. *World Press Review*. p 43. F. '83.

To supply them, Stanford would go into poor neighborhoods where murder went unpunished but where, on the other hand, good cocaine could be obtained at reasonable prices.

That week Stanford's supplier had been arrested, and he wrongly believed that the student had turned him in. Stanford was killed while closing a deal for $1,000, enough to pay his college debt and have a lavish evening. The occasion would not have been capped with cocaine: Stanford never used the drug.

From Boston to Los Angeles a good meal frequently ends—and may also begin—with a good "line" of "Peruvian" if one has the means or wants to impress. Three grams—$500 worth—of cocaine added to a party menu insures the loyalty of quality guests.

In a stylish club in Manhattan a waiter holds a large tray from which customers select whiskey, champagne, or a foil-wrapped dose of cocaine. Drinks cost $2; powder costs $20. In a large New York bank Friday is cocaine day for up-and-coming executives. They meet in the boardroom at one minute past 5:00 and take out their paraphernalia. During the party they chat about the stock market, Reagan, the economic crisis.

Before it became the martini of the three-piece-suit set cocaine had been used for decades in Hollywood, where film moguls sniffed it quietly. In the past ten years use of the powder has filtered down to the lowliest of extras. While a film was being made recently in the mountains of Wyoming the production staff, to forestall problems with the crew, sent a messenger to Los Angeles twice a week for their cocaine ration. The stars ordered quantities commensurate with their rank.

Film producer Julia Phillips (*Close Encounters of the Third Kind*), having reached the point where her existence depended on cocaine, finally gave the drug up and admitted that she had been spending $100,000 a year on it. A New York business executive forfeited his career in order to sniff and sleep. To pay for his $70,000-a-year habit he has begun selling it—a common route. Professional football stars are also cocaine stars, as are some rock talents.

In the mid-1970s cocaine left its celebrity niche and descended to the middle classes. Today 15 million Americans, according to some estimates—and 30 million, according to others—use cocaine. It is as available as hamburgers.

It is sold at movie theater exists. Pushers peddle it door to door. One can arrange regular deliveries—like newspapers. Doctors and dentists sometimes collect it as fees.

Cocaine is the opposite of a narcotic; it does not dull the senses, but excites them. Still, whatever pleasure it may provide does not account for its popularity. An innocuous placebo can produce the same reaction.

In the current economic crisis cocaine remains a profitable industry. Sales reached some $35 billion in 1982, and annual profits exceed those of the ten largest American firms combined. These billions subsidize fleets of ships and planes that transport the merchandise to Florida, networks of banks that launder funds, private armies that keep the peace, and hundreds of thousands of other people in the distribution network. Economists say that if the flow of cocaine were cut off the economy of Florida would crumble.

Some experts believe that cocaine eventually will be legalized—like whiskey after the repeal of Prohibition. American enterprise has transformed a medicinal plant into a festering sore of society.

COCAINE SPREADS ITS DEADLY NET[3]

It can do you no harm and drive you insane, give you status in society and wreck your career, make you the life of the party and turn you into a loner, be the elixir for high living—and a potion for death.

Such are the paradoxical properties of cocaine—a drug that new findings show has been used by no fewer than 15 million Americans.

Dramatizing the grip cocaine has on the U.S., the National Institute on Drug Abuse reported on March 9 that almost one third of those between ages 18 and 25 have used the drug and that

[3]Reprint of article by John S. Lang, staff writer, from *U.S. News & World Report,* p. 27–29, Mr. 22, '82. Copyright © 1982 by *U. S. News & World Report, Inc.* Reprinted by permission.

cocaine-related admissions to drug clinics were up 300 percent in the last five years.

That same day, a Customs Service inspector in Miami poked a screwdriver into cardboard cartons from a Colombian plane and found nearly 4,000 pounds of cocaine with a street value of 925 million dollars—the largest drug interception in history.

The next day, Customs agents forced down a plane in the Bahamas carrying 130 million dollars worth of coke.

But it was the death of popular comedian John Belushi on March 5 that riveted attention to the cocaine threat. The Los Angeles coroner's office reported that Belushi—who swept to stardom on TV's "Saturday Night Live" and in the movie "Animal House"—died in a Hollywood hotel "of an overdose due to intravenous injections of heroin and cocaine."

Cocaine is now the nation's largest producer of illicit income. The Drug Enforcement Administration estimates that its sale in the U.S. generates a turnover in excess of 32 billion dollars annually. That's more than double the combined earnings last year of Exxon, Mobil, Socal, Gulf, Amoco, Arco and Shell.

The cost of cocaine makes it the ambrosia of the aristocrats—worth 7½ times its weight in gold. So subtle and so seductive is cocaine that few understand exactly what it does. For example, a recent study at Yale University found that its "recreational" use is neither addictive nor threatening to health. But the same research also determined that regular doses can "enslave" users.

The dangers that this fast-growing undergound industry poses are shown in reports from police, hospitals, research laboratories, morgues and schoolyards across the country—

- Emergency-room admissions related to the drug, according to best available data, topped 13,000 last year.
- In 1978, medical examiners in 26 major cities reported 103 deaths in which cocaine was a factor. By 1980, the number of cocaine-related deaths in those same cities had reached 250.
- A new survey of high-school students finds that 16.5 percent used cocaine in the past year.
- New York City has become a battleground for Colombian smugglers trying to control the lucrative cocaine trade. At least 25 Colombians have been executed gangland style in the city in the last two years.

• Narcotics wars in Miami, entry port for 70 percent of the cocaine arriving from South America, are reminiscent of mob strife in Chicago during Prohibition. Police estimate that more than one fourth of Miami's 614 homicides last year were drug related.

No longer merely a daring plaything of the affluent avant-garde, cocaine today is regarded as downright respectable by many young professionals. Typically, users are upper middle class, white, in their 20s or early 30s—doctors, accountants, lawyers, architects, entertainers, athletes and others with comfortable incomes.

In the words of psychopharmacologist Ronald K. Siegel of the School of Medicine at the University of California, Los Angeles: "It is a drug for the Protestant ethic and the spirit of capitalism, a drug for producers."

That is because people who snort cocaine in small doses believe it helps them focus on tasks, lets them be more comfortable and aware in social groups and increases sexuality—unlike alcohol, which has a dulling effect.

Bill, a San Francisco accountant, asserts: "I can grind out accounting studies all coked up. Do a little line at 9 p.m. and work far into the night, awake, alert and happy."

Dorothy, an Atlanta secretary, says that she sniffs cocaine on the job because, "No one notices, but I enjoy my typing and shorthand more."

Yet, laboratory tests at the University of Chicago on reaction time determined that those under the influence of cocaine frequently do worse in learning combinations of digits and patterns, while thinking they do better.

Cocaine use over long periods also is known to burn away mucous membranes in the nose, to actually eat holes in the septum separating the nose cavities, to cause temporary impotence and lead to paranoia.

New research does show, however, that recreational use is no more harmful than small doses of tobacco or alcohol. The pattern of use "is comparable to that experienced by many people with peanuts or potato chips," report Yale University's Robert Byck and Craig Van Dyke in the March issue of *Scientific American*.

But, at the same time, the doctors say, heavy intake "can make users so enslaved it can destroy lives."

Talking to snakes. Experts are especially worried about the effects of what is called free-basing. That is when cocaine is cooked down to its purest form and smoked—which psychopharmacologist Siegel says leads to "the most tenacious drug habit that we have in the world today." Free-basing can cause a severe form of psychosis that increasingly is blamed for some of the wildest and weirdest acts of violence in America today. One example of cocaine psychosis: A young man who saw snakes coming out of his hands.

"He proceeded to dissect his hand and filled up 10 little bottles full of these white snakes, which he presented to us as cocaine bugs. He said he was talking to the snakes and making friends with them," says UCLA's Siegel. "But our pathology department told us these were his dried skin tissue." While seeking treatment, the man became convinced that his wife and Siegel were secret agents, drew two guns and started firing. He was taken into custody.

Far more common is the economic ruin wrought by habitual use of a drug that sells for up to $2,500 an ounce and $150 a gram. In San Francisco, a young couple who inherited $18,000 early this year blew $5,000 on cocaine in the first week and $3,000 the second before deciding to remove the temptation by putting the balance into a safe-deposit box.

Michael Balfe Howard, grandson of an original partner in the Scripps-Howard publishing empire, blames a $6,000-a-week cocaine habit and his drug-induced behavior for his firing in 1980 as editor of the *Rocky Mountain News* in Denver. Since then, in an interview in *Rocky Mountain Magazine,* Howard said he has been arrested for a weapons offense, committed himself to mental hospitals, escaped from one of them, attempted suicide and spent time in drug-treament centers.

"Cocaine is more dangerous than heroin," asserts Howard, who has fought hard to overcome its temptations. "Cocaine is greedy. The more you take, the more you need. Cocaine is physically addictive; it's totally addictive. I had no intention of stopping using it when I got fired. In my perverse mind, I thought, 'Good, now I can take drugs all the time.'"

Jay, from an upper-middle-class Baltimore family, spent $1,200 a week on cocaine because it gave him "a sensation like bells ringing in my head. I loved it to the point I would have died for it." By age 24, Jay owned his own optical store, but lost the business after five months. "I started having a lot of problems with people, yelling at customers. . . . I was taking my profits, selling my merchandise, selling my equipment, selling everything to buy coke. I've literally blown a fortune."

The huge amounts of money that surround the cocaine trade often lead to corruption of public officials.

Early this year, Dade County, Fla., police arrested one of the department's commanders; officers said they found him sitting in his kitchen with a pound of cocaine.

The town marshall and a former councilwoman of Telluride, Colo., were arrested last year during the state's Organized Crime Strike Force probe of cocaine deals in ski-resort towns of the Rocky Mountains. The investigation was so unpopular in Telluride that business people raised bail and printed posters of arresting officers superimposed over drawings of pigs and rats.

It is the spreading social acceptability of cocaine that can make prosecution of users and dealers difficult. "In cases involving heroin," notes Capt. Larry Brohard of the Alexandria, Va., police force, "people cooperate with police. That's not the situation with cocaine."

Even though cocaine use is extensive in New York City, narcotics agents there devote less time to ferreting out its trade than they do to other drugs. Only 15 percent of 15,000 drug arrests in the city last year involved cocaine—while in previous years 25 to 30 percent involved cocaine. New York authorities say that since cocaine is a drug of middle and upper-class adults, community pressure is for police to devote more energy to stamping out the drugs that involve youths and the poor—marijuana and heroin.

"Before we will develop a major case in cocaine, we want to make sure it does not take up too much of our time and resources," says Deputy Chief Charles Kelly of New York's narcotics division.

In San Francisco, Deputy Police Chief George Eimil complains that courts do not take cocaine prosecutions very seriously and that a three-year suspended sentence for dealing, first offense, is the outcome all too often.

In Los Angeles, Police Lt. Ken Welty observes: "Serious penalties are not always applied. It's a felony to possess cocaine, but does a judge want to put this clean-cut kid with his three-piece suit in jail? He has come to court with his family behind him. He says he never did it before. How do you prove the guy uses it every day?"

Personality parade. The social cachet of cocaine appears rooted in its high price and snob appeal. Indeed, the names of those who have acknowldeged having problems with the drug read like a Who's Who of entertainment and sports: John Phillips, founder of the Mamas and the Papas rock group; his daughter Mackenzie Phillips, who starred on TV's "One Day at a Time"; Rolling Stones guitarist Keith Richards; basketball star John Lucas of the Washington Bullets, and former football players Carl Eller of the Minnesota Vikings and Thomas "Hollywood" Henderson of the Dallas Cowboys.

Such a mystique surrounds cocaine that some people get high just thinking they are taking it. In the Yale Medical School study, regular users of cocaine were consistently unable to tell the difference between a high-quality dose of the drug and a harmless substitute.

"If you pay $100 for a bottle of wine, you expect that it will be damned good," noted researchers Van Dyke and Byck. "It's the same with cocaine. If you pay $100 for a gram and take it in a social setting, you expect to get high and you get high."

In fact, narcotics agents have long observed that a $100 packet sold on the street often contains only a trace of cocaine, because dealers sometimes cut the drug with other substances to increase profits. Many people are filling their noses with ordinary novocaine, an Italian laxative called Mannite, baking soda—or even borax.

So concerned is the Reagan administration over drug smuggling and abuse that the 1982 budget of DEA, at first set for a 12 percent cut, was increased 6.5 percent to 230 million dollars after Atty. Gen. William French Smith personally appealed to the President.

Late last year, the Federal Bureau of Investigation—for the first time ever—was given a role in investigation of drug offenses. Steps are under way to put AWACS-type radar planes into the air around southern Florida to try to detect aircraft used to transport cocaine and marijuana smugglers.

Tracing cocaine's path, from the mountains of Colombia, Bolivia and Peru to coffee tables of the trendy, shows why it is so hard to stop its trade.

Coca leaves and marijuana are grown in terrain so wild and wide ranging, the DEA reports, that the Colombian Army uses its entire annual budget for gas and spare parts when it runs a drug sweep for two months. "We are not willing to pick up enough of the tab to have a serious impact," says one DEA official. "If you want to lay blame, lay it on the U.S. for not providing guidance, leadership and spending enough money."

Once cocaine has been produced, it is easy to smuggle. One method of getting it into the U.S. is for a smuggler to cut the tips off the fingers of surgical gloves, fill them with cocaine and tie them securely with dental floss. A person known as a "mule" will fast for several days, swallow up to 100 of the little "eggs," fly commercially to the U.S., take a laxative and pass the cocaine.

Authorities first became aware of this trick when one mule went into convulsions at the airport and died. An autopsy showed that one of the packets had split open, causing the uncut drug to spill into the stomach.

This nation's long coastline allows easy penetration for smugglers flying big loads of cocaine into the country. Last December, six duffel bags filled with cocaine were dumped from a turboprop jet near Tampa during a chase involving two Air Force jets and a U.S. Customs plane. Although an investigation continues, no formal charges have been filed, says an agent, "because all we had were two pilots in an empty airplane and we couldn't convict them on that."

Experst such as Dr. John Loomis of the University of Houston's drug-information center are skeptical of efforts to stop the flow. "The demand is here, and there is no sign that the supply is going to be seriously limited," he says.

"A lot of people had problems with the idea of sticking needles in their arms to use heroin, but they only have to breathe deeply to use cocaine. And we are seeing sports figures and other celebrities in effect endorsing drug abuse. So people say, 'It must be O.K.'

The only things keeping a lid on cocaine use are limited availability and high cost. If it were as cheap as marijuana or alcohol, we'd really have an epidemic."

INTERNATIONAL INITIATIVES TO CONTROL COCA PRODUCTION AND COCAINE TRAFFICKING[4]

Cocaine, which has been called the drug of the Eighties, is our most rapidly expanding drug problem. The objective of the Bureau of International Narcotics Matters (INM) is to reduce cocaine imports through control of coca production at its sources in Peru, Bolivia, and Colombia. We believe the policies we are applying in negotiations with these governments are necessary to improve prospects for gaining control. But obstacles are abundant in South America. We caution that control—to the point at which cocaine availability in the United States is substantially and permanently reduced—is a long-term effort.

In one or more of the three coca-producing countries, we have had to contend with: frequent changes in governments; local populations heavily dependent upon coca sales and cocaine trafficking for their principal income; populations indifferent to U.S. interests, especially where they have been insulated from drug abuse; traditional chewers of coca leaf whose needs must be met by continuing cultivation; a belief that cocaine abuse is a U.S. problem which creates the trafficking issue; demands that the United States virtually reconstruct the economies of large sections of such countries as an inducement to local cooperation on crop control and interdiction; and sometimes even alleged government involvement in the cocaine trade.

[4]Reprint of an article by Dominick L. Di Carlo, former Assistant Secretary for International Narcotics Matters. *Drug Enforcement*. p 6–9. Fall '82.

However, there are also incentives for these governments to act, including economic problems, domestic drug abuse problems, international pressure, and insurgencies that may be linked to narcotics trafficking. This interplay of incentives and disincentives defines our opportunities for action.

The three producer countries present different problems. Thus, our strategies vary, but our policy on cocaine control and its premises is uniform. Under the Single Convention on Narcotic Drugs, producer and transit nations like Peru, Bolivia, and Colombia have the primary responsibility for controlling coca and its derivatives within their borders. The international community should assist these nations, and the United States provides bilateral assistance, but we expect these governments to demonstrate their responsibilities through effective programs. Our policy is that the priority should be on coca eradication or other forms of crop control, while narcotics-related development assistance in traditional growing areas should be linked to agreements on crop reduction. We encourage other donor nations and development banks to adopt the same policies.

The problems in common to all three countries are the plant itself and its yields, in cocaine and in profits. Coca is a hardy, deep-rooted plant that is quite difficult to eradicate manually and is usually grown in isolated areas. Coca is an attractive crop for farmers because it has a life span of about 30 years; leaves can be harvested three to six times a year; and it can be grown on poor soils unsuitable for other agriculture. Because most holdings are small, and demand until recently was limited, coca production for the illicit market provided an attractive but not spectacular income. However, in response to increased demand, coca prices accelerated in 1980 to twenty times their previous level, and today illicit coca production is the principal and sometimes only income for thousands of farmers—an income that is many times the daily wages these farmers would earn from other crops.

The financial incentives favor coca cultivation, which is increasing in all three countries. A critical decision in negotiations on crop control, in which the political and economic consequences to the farmer are at issue with the government, is the mix of financial incentives or disincentives (or both) that will be needed to induce desired actions.

Peru

Our problems in Peru, whose coca provides about half of the cocaine consumed in the United States, begin with the fact that large numbers of Peruvians have grown and chewed coca for more than 2,000 years—and agreements must consider that the Government permits and licenses a substantial cultivation for traditional domestic as well as pharmaceutical purposes. The objective then is to curb production in excess of this level and control illegal diversions from the licit cultivation—a task compounded by present conditions: (1) Peru has a weak economy; (2) cocaine trafficking provides several hundred million dollars a year to that economy, making it one of Peru's four major foreign exchange earners; and (3) coca cultivation has expanded to an estimated 50,000 metric tons, versus an estimated 12,000–14,000 metric tons needed for licit domestic and international use.

The problem of competing interests is evident: Coca cultivation is the major source of income for more than 7,000 farmers in the Upper Huallaga Valley, where most of the production is sold on the illicit market, generating an estimated 60 percent of the region's economy as well as 25 percent of the cocaine consumed in the United States.

The government of President Fernando Belaunde Terry, elected in 1980 after 12 years of military rule, has doubled its resource commitment from $1.5 million to $3 million. The Government is concerned about reports from medical clinics pointing to a serious increase in the dangerous practice of smoking coca paste. In this semi-refined state, coca paste contains such harmful impurities as kerosene and cement. Inhaling into the lungs is especially harmful. Reports indicate widespread smoking of coca paste by high school–age youth. Sensitive to its international image, the Government is also concerned about the potential for official corruption that has occurred in other countries. Peru has increased the number of both people and organizations commited to controlling the coca trade.

Our support has shifted from a focus solely on enforcement to a more balanced program of enforcement, education, and income substitution. This shift reflects a change in strategy toward sustained efforts. For example, Operation Green Sea II in 1980 was a cooperative effort with the Peruvian Government which eradicated nearly 1,500 acres of coca and destroyed 12 million plants and 57 laboratories. While some of the coca fields remain abandoned, the long-term impact of this one-time effort was primarily psychological, putting the cocaine trade on notice to the risks faced, and emboldening the government to take more forceful action.

In contrast, a five-year coca eradication and enforcement project was initiated by INM in 1981, concurrent with the Agency for International Development's (AID) five-year rural development program in the Upper Huallaga Valley. the project is the first in which the long-advocated strategy of coordinating INM's support for enforcement with AID's development assistance is being implemented. This project targets 17,000 hectares (out of 40,000–60,000 under cultivation countrywide). The INM goal is to reduce coca cultivation through eradication and control, while the AID goal is to diversify agricultural production, thereby minimizing the social and economic effects of the control program. In addition to supporting the Guardia Civil's Mobile Rural Patrol Detachment (UMOPAR) in the Upper Huallaga, INM's efforts to enhance the operational and intelligence effectiveness of Peruvian narcotics enforcement agencies include support for other Guardia Civil and Peruvian Investigative Police activities.

While actual eradication has not yet begun in the Upper Huallaga, activities we are supporting were showing these results by mid-1982: About five percent of coca cultivation had been abandoned and other cultivations were not being fully harvested; UMOPAR had increased its arrest and seizures; many large-scale traffickers had departed, leaving small dealers smuggling a few kilograms of cocaine paste; and the profitability of coca cultivation had declined.

INM plans to support coca control programs in other regions by 1984. The Peruvian Government believes there should be an international emphasis on coca control, and the United Nations Fund for Drug Abuse Control (UNFDAC) is considering a Peruvian request for an Andean office.

Bolivia

In Bolivia, where coca cultivation and consumption have also had historic economic and cultural importance, licit demand requires an estimated 12,000 metric tons out of an estimated production of 50,500 metric tons. Not only has chewing of coca leaf been traditional for centuries but there are today an estimated 23,000 farm families engaged in growing coca, usually on holdings of one hectare or less, which complicates the eradication problem.

Moreover, the United States is faced with the necessity of starting from ground zero—again—in Bolivia.

Narcotics assistance programs began in Bolivia in 1972; a 1977 agreement provided assistance for narcotics control and a study of alternate crops. These activities were halted in 1980, after a coup by General Garcia Meza, who allegedly had the support of the "Santa Cruz Mafia," independent organizations in the Santa Cruz area who dominate the cocaine trade.

Narcotics control assistance and other U.S. aid were suspended after the coup to demonstrate our insistence that Bolivia curb coca production and trafficking as well as to satisfy other U.S. concerns.

After a change in government in August 1981 (Bolivia has averaged more than one government per year since the Republic was founded in 1825), discussions on a resumption of coca control assistance were begun with the new Torrelio government. INM is currently discussing an eradication program which, if successfully negotiated and implemented, could reduce Bolivia's enormous coca cultivation to levels needed for legitimate purposes. Under discussion is a program of both voluntary and involuntary crop eradication and controls, focusing first on illicit production in nonlicensed areas and then on controlling excess production in licensed areas (the key Chapare and Yungas regions).

In addition to factors of international image and responsibility, the incentives for action are Bolivia's need for resumption of U.S. economic assistance, and its need to control negative effects of drug trafficking on the Bolivian economy (for example, the disruption of the agricultural labor force, and the flow of inflationary, untaxed dollar into the legitimate economy), while, at the same time, overcoming the competing restraints of self-interest by offsetting the political and financial impacts control programs could have on the economies of the growing and trafficking areas.

Colombia

Colombia, the major exporter of marihuana to the United States and the major refining and transshipment center for Bolivian and Peruvian coca, now processes and distributes up to 70 percent of the cocaine entering the United States. Moreover, Colombian farmers are now cultivating about 7,200 acres of coca (4 tons of cocaine) and this cultivation could yield up to 13 tons of cocaine by 1985.

The value to the Colombian economy of cocaine and marihuana trafficking is estimated at $1 billion to $1.5 billion. Perhaps $500 million remains in country and there are indications that, as in other countries, this inflationary, untaxed drug money is undermining the legitimate economy. Traffickers launder narco-dollars through the over-invoicing of exports, through front companies, farm and cattle purchases and the conversion of dollars on the black market. Not only does this dollar flow frustrate fiscal and monetary planning, but it has become increasingly difficult to find farm labor for other crops, thus disrupting agricultural production.

Recently, there has been evidence that Colombian guerrilla groups are utilizing drug trafficking as a source of income to pay for arms shipments.

While the government of President Turbay, who has been sensitive to these negative effects on his government and country, has cooperated through narcotics control agreements with the United States, there is not a country consensus on drug control. Many Colombians consider drug trafficking a problem created by and pertaining solely to the United States. The National Association of Financial Institutions has even campaigned for legalizing the cultivation and export of marihuana to increase government tax revenues and to assist the growers.

However, both the government and private sectors have begun to realize the magnitude of the negative effects of the drug problem on Colombia. Corruption among government officials, the growth of an illegal economy the government does not regulate or tax, the influx of uncontrolled sums into the legitimate economy, and threats to political stability have increased Colombian awareness of drug traffic-related problems.

Building on U.S. support, which began in 1973, INM has since 1978 provided technical assistance and training, and financial resources to upgrade Colombian capabilities in drug interdiction and manual eradication, in judicial processing and intelligence collection, as well as in drug prevention to help the Colombians cope with their own drug abuse problems. A manual coca eradication program was begun in 1981. In 1981, Colombian authorities seized 349 kilograms of cocaine and destroyed 237,401 coca plants and 58 cocaine laboratories. With the exception of cocaine seizures, these figures compare favorably with 1980, when the totals were: 1,545 kilograms of cocaine seized, 106,665 coca plants destroyed, and 54 cocaine laboratories destroyed.

INM plans to discuss an intensified coca control program with the new Colombian government which took office in August 1981.

Conclusion

The world market for cocaine is presently estimated at less than 60 tons, with 40–48 tons imported into the United States. Current estimated production of coca is sufficient to produce as much as 156 tons of cocaine. This output and stockpiles in Peru and Bolivia are enough to supply the U.S. and world markets for years to come. To reduce cocaine availability substantially and permanently in the United States, we must achieve simultaneous control in Peru and Bolivia, while ensuring that Colombian production is contained and that new cultivation is prevented elsewhere.

While the reports on plant destruction, seizures and arrests show some progress, we have not yet achieved the levels of coca control desired in any of these countries.

The farmers' economic and political interests are issues of concern to these governments. But, there are also pressures on these governments to bring the coca problem under control: These governments are aware that the continued supply of cocaine to the United States, Canada, and Western Europe affects their international standing; the willingness of the United States to link development assistance to government actions to control coca production and trafficking has demonstrated to Peru and Bolivia the intensity of the U.S. concern; there are perceptions among government leaders of actual or potential links between narcotics trafficking and insurgent groups; the undermining of local economies and the impacts of their own emerging drug abuse problems add to these pressures. Buttressing these incentives to act is the U.S. policy that we will help provide the means not only to gain control of coca production and cocaine trafficking but—with other sources of economic assistance—will also consider financial alternatives to the farmers, conditioned upon commitments to crop control and reductions in production.

We are undertaking other initiatives in addition to direct U.S. efforts in the producing countries. We are encouraging European governments impacted by cocaine abuse to participate in coca control programs, and to apply their own international influence on the producer nations. We are cooperating with governments and private institutions to inform the peoples of Peru, Bolivia, and especially Colombia about the major efforts under way to reduce U.S. domestic drug abuse problems. We are supporting interdiction efforts in neighboring countries, like Ecuador and Brazil, as well as in the Caribbean, to interrupt trafficking and to deny processors access to precursor chemicals.

Throughout South America, we work in close cooperation with the Drug Enforcement Administration on these projects to halt the flow of cocaine to the United States. Our agencies have confidence in these policies and programs. But, as stated at the outset, cocaine control is a long-term effort in which we are dependent upon the actions of other governments to meet their agreed responsibilities.

COKE: THE RANDOM KILLER[5]

Toward the close of the '60s, that decade of rebellion and experimentation, a terse warning circulated through the drug subculture: speed kills. At the same time, word got around that cocaine, a drug all but forgotten in the U.S. after non-medical use was outlawed in 1914, created some of the same illusions of self-confidence, energy, and mental acuity that amphetamines did. Subtle and exotic, cocaine could make you euphoric, make you believe you were invulnerable and masterful. For a brief ecstatic moment it might even make you feel you would live forever.

For those enamored of the glitzy life, coke—snow, blow, nose candy, Bolivian Marching Powder—became *the* drug. Hollywood biggies, film stars, and rock and roll promoters served it up like jelly beans. On college campuses, hip students with plenty of money to spend on an evening's entertainment snorted it in darkened theaters and sniggered at the cult classic *Cocaine Fiends*. Everyone knew that the film's wild-eyed characters, driven to thievery and insanity by their cravings for more "headache powder," were exaggerated. Everyone knew that cocaine was safe and, unlike heroin and morphine, non-addictive. A few respectable pharmacologists even attested to its benignity. Among initiates—and by 1974 there were probably five million in the U.S. who tried it at least once—cocaine was known as the perfect recreational drug. If only it weren't so expensive . . .

Then the casualties began to mount among high-visibility users. There were Richard Pryor and John Belushi. There was the growing roster of professional athletes who admitted they were having difficulty controlling their cocaine intake and entered drug abuse programs to kick the habit. Still, some people rationalized, it was possible that it wasn't cocaine itself, but, as police speculate, Pryor's carelessness with the highly flammable ether used to "free-base" cocaine for smoking, that had sent him screaming into the streets. And Belushi had been injected with speedballs, a po-

[5]Reprint of an article by Gina Maranto, free-lance writer. *Discover*. p 16–21. Mr. '85. Copyright © Discover Magazine 3/85, Time Inc. Reprinted by permission.

tent mixture of cocaine and heroin. Maybe what was wrong with those professional athletes and entertainers was too much money and too much pressure and too many nights on the road. Because no one was really sure that cocaine was addictive, were they?

For a long time, the medical facts about the drug weren't clear. It has taken researchers more than a decade to run cocaine through the batteries of experiments designed to reveal its peculiar properties and the ways it interacts with and alters various cells, organs, and bodily systems in laboratory animals and in humans. It has also taken time for clinicians, gathering case histories in doctors' offices, emergency rooms, and morgues, to put together a picture of what moderate to heavy use of the drug does to someone over the course of months or years. On the basis of evidence from both avenues of research, several physicians and pharmacologists with no apparent moral or legal axes to grind have recently begun to try to bring the public image of cocaine into line with scientific reality.

Cocaine, they say, is one of the most dangerous drugs on the underground market. It's physically debilitating, whether you snort it, swallow it, inject it, or smoke it. A perpetually runny nose is the least of its drawbacks. Those who frequently snort substantial amounts of the drug can develop chronic sore throats, inflamed sinuses, hoarseness, and sometimes holes in the cartilage of the nose. Those who inject cocaine can contract hepatitis from dirty needles. Free-basers may destroy the ability of their lung cells to process gases, leaving them with a constant cough and often short of breath.

Those who use cocaine infrequently are rarely so plagued, but that doesn't necessarily mean they're escaping unscathed. "People reading stories about the bad things cocaine does to you say, 'None of those things ever happened to me,'" says Arnold Washton, director of drug abuse research and treatment at Regent Hospital, a private psychiatric institution in New York. "Well, this may be because there are serious things going on that we just can't see yet." Researchers at Duke University Medical Center, for instance, have discovered that the livers of mice injected with cocaine show cell death and produce lesser amounts of crucial enzymes. Gerald Rosen, the pharmacologist who performed the experiments, is naturally wary of extrapolating these results to people. However, even if cocaine alone doesn't poison the liver, speedballs do—so much so that the organ fails.

Doctors also have compelling clinical evidence that the drug can worsen pre-existing weaknesses of the heart, as well as trigger full-blown attacks. In a person with heart disease, the racing pulse and pounding that accompany the high can degenerate into a wild and fatal syncopation. Current research also points toward the possibility that cocaine causes permanent brain damage.

Over the long term, cocaine can severely disrupt the psyche. In fact, the crack-ups portrayed in the much derided *Cocaine Fiends* actually bear strong resemblance to reality. After a binge, heavy cocaine users may swing through four distinct psychological states, beginning with the euphoric high (which usually lasts ten to thirty minutes) and ending with depression, hallucination, and psychosis. After a long session, they are overwhelmed by lassitude and bleakness. "Not only is your physical energy gone," reports one user, "but your whole head changes too. [Good feelings] start dwindling and eventually dissipate into a very depressed state."

After weeks or months of regular bingeing the user is "coked out." Depression becomes chronic, he starts hallucinating, and signs of psychosis appear. Says Washton, "Well before psychosis, you see increased irritability, short temper, suspiciousness—especially of spouses, relatives, friends, and business partners." In a survey of 500 callers to the toll-free hotline, 800-COCAINE, researchers found that fully half reported symptoms of this nature. Eighty-three percent of the group, all of whom took cocaine almost daily, told interviewers they felt habitually depressed or anxious. At least half said they had difficulty concentrating or remembering things, were uninterested in sex, and sometimes had panic attacks.

Almost invariably, the more cocaine a person consumes, the more pronounced these symptoms become. Past a certain limit—which varies from person to person—anyone, no matter how mentally stable he might once have appeared to be, can slide into full-blown paranoid schizophrenia. It may last only a few weeks or months, or it may be permanent. All too permanent in the case of one 42-year-old engineer. After smoking three to five grams of cocaine a day for about four months, he began having elaborate delusions. He was convinced his wife and friends had tapped his phone. Were they in league with the police? His neighbors, he believed, were listening through the walls, spying on him. One day, after an argument with his wife, he set fire to their apartment—and some of her antiques. The police came, this time for real and took him to a psychiatric ward, where he stayed for 72 hours. A few months later he wrote on the wall with a crayon, "You see cocaine really can kill," climbed into a tub of warm water, slit his wrists, and died.

"He was an intelligent man," says Washton. "He would stop using cocaine for weeks at a time to see if he still had delusions. He did, so he wrongly concluded that they had nothing to do with the cocaine." Some scientists surmise that cocaine can skew brain chemistry enough to make an underlying disorder like schizophrenia flare up. Without this chemical prod, the mental illness might otherwise remain buried.

For the casual user, who considers himself immune to such physical and psychic depredations, the most frightening finding to emerge from the last decade of scrutiny is this: taken in any form, and at any dose from 60 milligrams—about two lines—on up, cocaine can be fatal. Sudden deaths from cocaine are still rare, considering that an estimated 22 million Americans have now tried the drug and some four million may use it at least once a month. But seemingly anyone is in jeopardy. The deaths to date have been totally random. Says Dr. Mark Gold, director of research at Fair Oaks Hospital in New Jersey, "We have no way of predicting who'll die from the drug and who won't. It could be a regular user or it could be a first-time user." Adds Todd Wilk Estroff, a psychiatrist at Fair Oaks, "Some people die after a small dose, some after massive doses. It depends on their tolerance."

Death can come in several ways. Often it is by respiratory failure, when the brain ceases to keep the vital functions of the nervous system going. Cerebral hemorrhages may also occur, as rising blood pressure bursts weak blood vessels in the brain. A very few people, lacking an enzyme that breaks down the drug, are likely to have fatal reactions to minute amounts of cocaine.

Others have died from allergic reactions to the drug or impurities mixed into it. Cocaine can induce epileptic seizures in a person with no previous signs of epilepsy, as well as heart fibrillations that lead to cardiac arrest. A typical case, involving a 15-year-old girl, was reported by Dr. Charles Wetli, a medical examiner in Florida's drug-flooded Dade County. "She went out one night to a disco party," Wetli says. "She drank, snorted some cocaine, and then told her friends she wanted to lie down. She lay down on a water bed, had a small seizure, got up, snorted some more cocaine, and then lay down again. She soon went into violent seizures which threw her off the bed." She died of respiratory collapse.

The direct cause of cocaine-induced sudden deaths can be hard to identify with certainty, since many users attempt to minimize the unpleasant feeling of coming off a cocaine high by drinking alcoholic beverages, popping barbiturates, or shooting heroin—all of which are also toxic. In fact, the bodies of some people killed by cocaine may not even contain the drug, since it's rapidly metabolized and continues breaking down after death. Not surprisingly, those who witness a fatal overdose are rarely eager to tell police the full story. Says Dr. Roger Mittleman, another Dade County medical examiner, "People on the scene don't want to say how much the victim took. In Florida, anyway, giving drugs to someone who then dies is considered homicide."

Nonetheless, even discounting masked deaths, overdoses seem to be on the rise. During the '70s, Mittleman and fellow coroners saw only about two deaths a year in the greater Miami area that could be pinned directly to the drug. Now they see two every month. In Washington, D.C., in 1984, cocaine was a contributing factor in 88 deaths, up from three in 1981 and 45 in 1983. In addition, there are an astonishing number of cocaine-related deaths in which the drug isn't the direct cause. Fatal motor vehicle accidents are common, and homicide is a very real possibility in the high-stakes game of dealing.

That it's possible to overdose on seemingly negligible amounts of cocaine worries physicians, especially since use of the drug has spread to all social classes. Approximately 14 tons of coke—80 to 90 per cent of it from Colombia—was seized by U.S. Customs in 1984, 30 times as much as in 1977. On the glutted New York and

Miami markets, the price has been chopped by a least a third over the past two years. At $60 to $100 a gram of coke—about 30 to 50 lines' worth—almost anyone can afford it.

At the same time, the age and income of the typical user have dropped. According to surveys conducted throught the national cocaine hotline, in 1983 the average user was male, 31, and made over $26,000 a year; last year he (or, increasingly, she) was 27 and earned $25,000. The average age and income will probably continue to fall. "Our statistics show that by the end of this year one out of five high school students will have tried cocaine before graduating, and ten per cent of suburban high school students will be regular users," says Gold. "I'm a child and adolescent psychiatrist," adds Estroff, "and I'm terrified. The evidence is everywhere and people have to relearn it: cocaine isn't the champagne of drugs. Cocaine kills."

That cocaine had such good press throughout the '70s seems the result of a kind of cultural and scientific amnesia. Doctors at the turn of the century knew that the drug was dangerous, and that some people died from the minute doses of pure cocaine used as an anaesthetic in surgery. In 1891 the *Medical and Surgical Reporter* carried this warning: "Toxic effects may [result from] a sequence of doses large or small, in patients young or old, the feeble or the strong." There was also cases of addiction among doctors. Freud, who spurred interest in the drug among the European medical community in 1884, was a lifelong cocaine addict, and was excoriated by the German chemist Emil Erlenmeyer for having released "the third scourge of humanity," after alcohol and opiates.

Freud, among others, described fairly fully many of the properties of cocaine, including a feeling of strength and energy that he attributed to excitation of the nervous system. Scientists didn't add much to that description for 90 years. In the mid-1970s the National Institute on Drug Abuse, concerned about the spread of the drug, began sponsoring studies to determine how cocaine produces its effects. Drawing on new knowledge of basic biochemistry and neurophysiology, researchers have explored at least two if its main actions.

Cocaine, an alkaloid derived from the waxy leaves of the tropical shrub *Erythroxylum coca,* can both incapacitate and excite neurons in the central and sympathetic nervous systems. Like lidocaine, novocaine, and other local anaesthetics, it numbs the parts of the body it touches first—for sniffers, usually the nose and throat. Like amphetamines and other stimulants, it sets the sympathetic nervous system humming—raising blood pressure, speeding heartbeat and respiration, and generally stepping up the body's metabolism.

Cocaine anaesthetizes by blocking the transmission of nerve signals. Usually when a nerve is stimulated, an electrical impulse speeds toward the next nerve or toward various other targets, including muscles, glands, and the brain. The impulse is actually a change in polarity that begins at the outer surface, or membrane, of the nerve, and travels like a wave down its long, tubular axon. Cocaine foils transmission by preventing the change of polarity from moving along the nerve.

When a person sniffs cocaine, it molecules are absorbed through the mucous membrane and carried in the blood stream to the heart, the lungs, and the rest of the body. After about three minutes the drug reaches the brain and the neurons of the sympathetic nervous system. (Injected, it arrives by the same route in about 15 seconds. Smoked, it takes a lightning seven seconds, producing a rush that "blows the top of your head off.") As a stimulant, cocaine excites these nerves, mimicking the body's natural fight-or-flight respose to fear or challenge. Biochemically, one way cocaine accomplishes this is by lodging in the molecular workings of excited neurons, preventing them from lapsing back into a neutral, resting state.

This stimulation is what makes cocaine so appealing to many. A not unusual example of a cocaine user is a high-powered international futures trader in his mid-30s who worked 20 hours a day. After 16 hours, he would take cocaine and be good for four more. Unfortunately, this routine didn't have a salutary effect on his financial judgment: he lost four million dollars in just a few months. Some people apparently believe the drug improves their physical powers. If it does so at all, that happens only at the very beginning. "A couple of athletes we've treated are now tearing up the league," says Estroff. "Their performance had deteriorated when they were on cocaine."

A few hours after snorting the drug or about 15 minutes after injecting it, a person slides into depression, which seems to be caused by a lack of norepinephrine and other neurotransmitters, chemical messengers used by the nervous system. These have been rapidly eaten up by the body in its hyper-excited state. A person's system usually bounces back after he has stopped ingesting cocaine and his nerves have had a chance to manufacture more neurotransmitters. But scientists suspect that over time the brains of some people may make a dangerous adjustment to these brief chemical changes by sprouting new neural branches. The more branches a nerve has, the greater its chance of picking up molecules of norepinephrine—or other neurotransmitters—that float by. This change in configuration may underlie the mysterious phenomenon known as kindling, in which a relatively small amount of cocaine can have tremendous impact. After taking the same amount of cocaine several times over the course of a few months or years, some people take that same amount, have seizures, and die. Researchers suspect that the altered structures of nerves may amplify the power of the drug.

Explaining the mechanism of cocaine's subjective effects—the biochemistry of euphoria—has proved far more complicated than tracking its physical effects. The euphoria continues to perplex and frustrate scientists. "Nobody really knows how cocaine produces it, or, physiologically speaking, what constitutes the feeling," says Roy Wise, a behavioral neurobiologist at Concordia University in Montreal. Researchers have tried to find out by studying the behavior, and the brains, of rats and other laboratory animals.

Since there is no way of knowing if an animal feels euphoric, scientists have proceeded obliquely. A well established principle of behavioral studies is that if you can get a rat to perform a task for a certain reward—a peanut, a pat on the head, a drug—then the reward is a "reinforcer." All classically addictive drugs, like the opiates, are reinforcers. In some disturbing lab tests in the '60s, cocaine proved the most potent reinforcer encountered. Monkeys were fitted with a syringe hooked by a tube to a container of cocaine. When they pressed a lever, they got a dose of the drug. In most cases, the monkeys pressed the lever for days, until they began to have convulsions and died.

Although scientists disagree about what bearing such experiments have on what occurs in people, most believe that monkeys engage in this obsessive, suicidal behavior when offered easy access to cocaine because the drug is compellingly pleasurable. Says Wise, "Somewhere a signal goes from being emotionally neutral to emotionally charged. Our best guess is that it occurs at dopamine [another neurotransmitter] synapses."

Those key synapses, or gaps between nerves, may lie in the part of the brain that scientists call the pleasure center, which may be located in the nucleus accumbens. Rats will perform tasks in order to receive shots of amphetamines in this spot. When it's destroyed, they stop performing the task. From this, researchers have concluded that the rats no longer get pleasure from the drugs. In a macabre version of this experiment, Bolivian doctors have severed nerves in the brains of cocaine addicts. But many such patients backslide into renewed addiction.

Case histories reveal that many people neglect jobs, family, and their personal welfare in order to procure and ingest cocaine. Take George, a 27-year-old sales manager who started out snorting and then began to shoot the drug: "All I could think about was cocaine. I wanted more of it more often. Everything else seemed unimportant. I was beginning to vomit after every hit, but I couldn't stop. Then one day I began to sweat all over; I felt so hot I thought I'd caught fire. I passed out. Next thing I knew I was in a hospital."

One thing that usually stops pharmacologists or psychiatrists from deeming cocaine addictive is the apparent absence of withdrawal symptoms. "We think of withdrawal in terms of an alcoholic with the DTs or a heroin addict lying in a gutter, retching," says Gold. "This doesn't happen with cocaine. But there are brain-related behavioral changes and a craving for the drug. An overwhelming majority of callers to our hotline say they feel addicted."

Many scientists are now revising their notions about cocaine addiction. People do seem to develop tolerance, which is part of the classical definition of addiction. They need larger quantities of the drug to get high, and many never again experience the ecstasy of their first episodes. Estroff believes that a person's brain chemistry makes him an addict: "The brain and cocaine may be like a lock and a key. some people say, 'That's what's been missing from my life to make me feel wonderful,' while others remain unaffected." Estroff adds that cocaine addiction—like alcoholism—isn't a sign of psychological weakness. "It's a result of the drug's interaction with a person's brain chemistry."

Scientists concede that there are those who can use small amounts of cocaine infrequently without showing any obvious physical damage or becoming obsessed with the drug. The latest hypothesis, hower, is that cocaine may wreck the brain by slow steps. Charles Schuster, a professor of pharmacology at the University of Chicago, has found that amphetamines lower the overall amounts of some neurotransmitters in the brains of rats, monkeys, and guinea pigs. The reduction persisted for as long as three years after the last time the animals were given the drugs, leading Schuster to believe that the neurons involved may be permanently incapacitated. More experiments are under way, but the prognosis doesn't look good. Says Schuster, "I suspect that cocaine will also damage the brains of these animals. When something happens across several species, you think more seriously about the pertinence to humans."

At present, doctors don't know how to predict who will develop a physiological need for cocaine and who won't. Gold and others argue that even by trying a toot or two, a person enters the risk group from which addicts emerge. Gold is right. There are bound to be more addicts, more deaths, and a greater outlay of money on health care for addicts in coming years, since use of the drug seems unlikely to diminish. "To offer marijuana at a party in the sixties showed you were cool, tuned in, on the cutting edge," says Washton. "The message is different now. We have yuppies instead of hippies. Cocaine is associated with their values—success, mastery, control. It's a self-marketing product."

III. MARIJUANA

EDITOR'S INTRODUCTION

Cocaine and heroin are not the only drugs of high visibility and concern. The use of man-made or synthetic drugs—such as PCP (known as "angel dust"), amphetamines, and barbiturates—has, according to a recent article, reached "epidemic proportions." Alcohol itself may be considered a drug, and alcohol abuse and alcoholism remain major problems in American society. Still another commonly used drug is marijuana. Like alcohol, marijuana is not in a strict sense addictive, but it may be abused, and there are many still-unanswered questions about how it acts on the human system. Research has indicated that marijuana has special appeal for those under twenty-five, but its consumption cuts across age and class lines, and estimates suggest that 20 million Americans now use it. Apart from its possible health hazards, its very prevalence creates a problem for drug enforcement officials. How, after all, can such a large segment of the population be treated as a criminal class? In an effort to deal with this baffling problem, Congress has partially decriminalized the use of marijuana, imposing slight fines rather than severe penalties. But policy toward marijuana use varies from state to state, and there is as yet no uniformity of attitude and regulation. A lobby for the legalization of marijuana (NORML) has argued that still further changes in the prohibited status of marijuana are necessary, but another vocal constituency absolutely opposes any encouragement of the use of the drug. Marijuana is unquestionably the most controversial of the "drugs of choice" in the United States today.

In this section, marijuana is viewed from many sides. John Lang, in his article "Marijuana: A U. S. Farm Crop That's Booming," from *U. S. News & World Report*, reports on the latest in marijuana production—away from importing it from Colombia and Mexico to large-scale cultivation of it in this country. In "Marijuana Overview," a chapter from *Correlates and Conse-*

quences of Marijuana Use, published by the U. S. Department of Health and Human Services and the National Institute on Drugs, Robert Peterson reviews various studies on marijuana use and discusses the continuing controversy over its potential dangers. In *Marijuana and Health: Report of a Study*, the Commission of the Institute of Medicine is equally wary about drawing final conclusions about marijuana use but warns that marijuana habituation "justifies serious concern." Finally, in a lengthy and detailed article, "Marijuana Policy and Drug Mythology," Louis Lasagna and Gardner Lindzey, members of the National Research Council of the National Academy of Science, discuss the problem of whether to prohibit marijuana, to curtail its use by preventing its supply, or to grant it legal status under governmental control.

MARIJUANA: A U. S. FARM CROP THAT'S BOOMING[1]

All across America, furtive farmers are racing early frost and police raids to bring in a record harvest of what is rapidly turning into a major cash crop—marijuana.

Amounts of the illegal weed already seized and destroyed in raids over recent weeks have convinced law-enforcement officials that pot farming is a multibillion-dollar national industry.

Authorities in California say marijuana is being grown commercially in 43 of the state's 58 counties. Unofficially, they estamate its worth at 1 billion dollars—a figure rivaling the grape crop and twice as valuable as the raisin harvest.

Lt. Louis Stiles of Kentucky's state police says marijuana may be a 200-million-dollar crop there. He adds: "When I started, I found it difficult to believe it could be Kentucky's biggest cash crop, but I don't find that too hard to believe any more."

[1]Reprint of an article by John S. Lang, staff writer. Reprinted from *U. S. News & World Report* p 63–64 issue of O. 12, '81. Copyright © 1981, U. S. News & World Report, Inc. Reprinted by permission.

Output climbs. Oklahoma officials predict growers there will produce 200 million dollars' worth of pot this year, ranking it second in value only to the 751-million-dollar wheat crop.

Between July 1 and mid-September, Virginia authorites made a record 71 seizures of marijuana, confiscating 21,000 pounds with an estimated street value of 9.7 million dollars. "There's nothing approaching this magnitude in my almost 20 years with the department," says Special Agent Dennis Robertson of the Virginia narcotics division.

The National Organization for the Reform of Marijuana Laws (NORML), the pro-pot lobby, claims that last year's domestic crop was worth 5 billion dollars and predicts that this year's output likely will be almost double.

Officials of the U.S. Drug Enforcement Administration argue that claims of a harvest worth billions are inflated—a self-serving estimate by growers who want to give the impression that everyone is growing marijuana and so it should be legalized. However, they admit they cannot disprove the figures and acknowledge attempts to increase their own budget from $60,000 to 1 million dollars to fight illicit farming.

Whoever is right, there is no question that high demand is boosting local marijuana farming as an underground business. According to the National Institute on Drug Abuse, some 22 million Americans smoke marijuana at least once each month. NORML contends that 1 million people grow small amounts for personal use and up to 100,000 do so for profit.

The boom in U.S. pot production dates from 1978, when it was reported that Mexican marijuana was being dusted with the herbicide paraquat, which could cause permanent lung damage.

NORML's political director, George Farnham, asserts: "The government thought that would be a deterrent, but instead it created a demand among American marijuana consumers for an uncontaminated product. So people turned to the U.S. as a source."

Law-enforcement officers believe another reason for the surge in homegrown marijuana is that there are less cost and risk in raising the weed here that in smuggling it in from the Caribbean and South America.

"The logistics are a lot easier," explains E. Wayne Dickey, an agent with the Florida Department of Law Enforcement. "It's easier than going to Colombia, making a deal and hoping you'll get out of there alive."

Smuggling drop-off. Thomas Dial of Mississippi's Bureau of Narcotics echoes that theory: "Within the next three to five years—if that long—domestic production of marijuana will rival output from Colombia, and that will eventually curtail the smuggler problem."

Some authorities worry that legitimate farmers will try to grow marijuana as they get bogged down in dwindling income and high interest rates. As Mississippi's Dial puts it: "Say the crops fail and the loans are past due and a person stands to lose everything. This may seem like a good way out. A drowning man will clutch at a straw."

Experts report that American marijuana farmers now are growing a strain of pot, cannabis indica, that is far stronger than Colombian or Mexican varieties. Some are specializing in trying to grow sinsemilla, seedless and unfertilized female buds that contain nearly 10 times as much THC—the intoxicating agent—as ordinary plants.

Officials content that pot growers often flourish with the connivance of respected local businessmen, who make money by selling the growers goods and services. Agents in California point to an $86,000 bank loan made on 40 acres of marijuana, due in full on November 15—after the harvest.

"We have an underground economy geared to marijuana production," reports Rick Pariser, head of a four-county effort to stop drug traffic around Carbondale, home of Southern Illinois University. "You see a lot of people under 30 driving expensive, flashy cars and young people with no apparent source of income spending 50 to 75 bucks a night in the college bars. We call them the Southern Illinois Dope Growers Association."

"Marijuana is the difference between a profit and a loss for many local business people," says Ted Eriksen, agriculture commissioner of Mendocino County, Calif. "Take a 3-to-4-acre field of 4,000 plants, notes Harold W. Brown, chief DEA agent in Louisville. "You're talking about 2,000 pounds of marijuana, with sales ranging from $300 to $1,600 per pound. Even at the low end, that's big money."

The lure of easy money, police busts and competition have made marijuana farming a sometimes deadly business.

Officers descending by helicopter on hidden fields often must face explosive booby traps, tripwires rigged to shotgun shells, sharpened punji sticks like those used by guerrillas to cripple soldiers in Vietnam—even live rattlesnakes tied to marijuana stalks.

"Serious game." The struggle over pot has been particularly vicious in eastern Oklahoma, a region whose history includes the likes of Belle Starr, Pretty Boy Floyd, Ma Barker and Bonnie and Clyde. Oklahoma's chief narcotics agent, Fred Means, says: "These are not good old boys distilling moonshine. This is a serious game, with serious consequences and serious money."

Police report that marijuana growers took three young Oklahomans to a mountainside last spring and shot them to death one at a time because the youths had stolen 3 pounds of weed. Two other recent homicides in the area are suspected of being drug related.

Narcotics agents note that most violence is aimed at rivals in the drug trade rather than at the law. Yet increasingly lawmen are being killed or injured in searches for marijuana farms. An officer in Riverside, Calif., was wounded last year while on aerial surveillance. A pilot for the Oklahoma Narcotics Bureau was killed in a crash in August during a search.

While fulfilling a campaign pledge to curb the spread of drugs in Braxton County, W.Va., newly elected Sheriff Vincent Zummo was killed on September 11 when his helicopter crashed during a search for marijuana fields.

On August 7, Kentucky detective Darrell Phelps was killed in a gun battle with armed guards stationed at a hidden pot farm. State Police Commissioner Marion Campbell reports: "It's dangerous, not just for police but for hunters who might walk in there by mistake and be shot or killed."

Many growers take elaborate measures to avoid detection. In California, some decorate marijuana plants with red Christmas-tree balls so that they look from a distance like tomato plants.

Midwestern pot farmers camouflage their fields with rows of corn. The fields still can be spotted from the air, so some scatter the plants in tiny plots.

In the hollows of West Virginia and bottom lands of Kentucky and Oklahoma, marijuana farms are not laid out in orderly fashion. Plants fill narrow strips along creek beds. Often, underbrush in a forest will be cleared for the plants, with just enough branches left on tall trees to afford cover and filter sunlight.

For many pot tenders, public lands and Indian reservations are popular sites because they are remote and growers cannot be traced through deeds.

Water-bed methods. With more money at stake, marijuana cultivation becomes steadily more sophisticated. Narcotics agents have discovered marijuana in greenhouses, in caves under special lights and in plots with automatic sprinklers and electronic soil stimulators. California officers found one plantation where an ingenious grower used four water beds on a hillside to provide drip irrigation for his plants.

Indiana police report "marijuana factories" with drying kilns, production lines and trash compactors to bale goods.

While the guile and equipment of large-scale pot farmers grow, the audacity of some small-time operators astonishes police. In the resort area of Virginia Beach, Va., officers made 61 arrests this summer after seizing marijuana growing in 26 apartments. Reports Sgt. Earnest Marrow; "The ironic point about it was all we did was walk through the apartment complexes. The plants were in plain view where you could see them—in hanging baskets, regular pots and makeshift pots."

While some pot users assume that relaxed narcotics laws and tolerant social attitudes mean no one notices or cares, police everywhere are gearing up for tougher enforcement.

As one Oklahoman put it: "If it runs away with us, we face an explosion of official and political corruption—murder for hire, larceny, corruption of the criminal-justice system. We'll be a harbinger of things to come in the U.S."

MARIJUANA OVERVIEW[2]

Marijuana research has been controversial since the inception of the modern era of cannabis investigation in the mid-1960s. This is hardly surprising. Given the concern about the millions of children and youths using marijuana, it was almost inevitable that such research would be the source of widespread misunderstanding. Although the controversy has been most heated among the general public, scientists, too, have become embroiled. Even those who should have known better have sometimes taken an uncritical view of seriously flawed research consistent with their personal prejudices and have ignored creditable studies that conflicted with their preconceptions. The desire to achieve premature certainty about this controversial substance has also led many to ignore much that we know about drug effects more generally and about the importance of dose, frequency, and circumstances of use in determining the use implications of a drug. No drug, taken in small enough quantities, is inevitably toxic, and few drugs are completely nontoxic at high doses.

Part of the difficulty in interpreting findings is that many years of use by millions are often required for use implications to become clear. Animal data and limited human laboratory experimentation can provide some evidence of long-range consequences, but these are often inconclusive. Cigarette smoking is an apt example. Smoking cigarettes on a mass scale began about the time of World War I, with the advent of high-speed machinery to produce them and the growing awareness that cigarettes were more convenient than cigars and pipes. And, unlike traditional modes of tobacco use, which were viewed as "unladylike," cigarette smoking by women soon became acceptable. However, it was not until 50 years after the initial upsurge in cigarette use that sufficient evidence of serious health effects was amassed for the Surgeon-General to issue the first smoking and health report (U.S.

[2]Reprint of a chapter "Marijuana Overview" by Robert C. Petersen from *Correlates and Consequences of Marijuana Use,* edited by Meyer D. Glantz. Published by the U. S. Department of Health and Human Services and the National Institute on Drugs.

Public Health Service 1964). The bulk of the evidence linking cigarette smoking with many kinds of disease is epidemiological—that is, based on a statistical association between smoking and disease in many thousands of persons in the general population. While this in no sense indicts epidemiological research, it underscores the difficulty of anticipating the health impact of a substance before use has become well established, when it may be extremely difficult to discourage use.

As was true of early tobacco use, many thoughtful clinicians are convinced that marijuana has serious health implications, although many of its possible chronic effects are still unproven. Clinical evidence of a causal association between a substance and a set of symptoms is usually initially based on a small number of patients who have sought medical attention and in whom the symptoms are found to be associated with some aspect of their lifestyle or their exposure to the presumptive disease agent. With cigarettes, pulmonary surgeons suspected a carcinogenic role as early as the 1930s based on their observation that almost all their lung cancer patients smoked (Muller 1939). But since not all smokers develop lung cancer, it required the study of much larger numbers of smokers and nonsmokers to verify that smokers' overall rate of lung cancer is many times that of the nonsmoker.

Widespread use of cannabis, particularly on a habitual basis, is little more than a decade and a half old. Initially, use was largely limited to young adults occasionally using marijuana that had a lower potency than that currently being used. Early attempts to determine its possible adverse effects compared these occasional users collectively with nonusers. Such a comparison was as unlikely to detect marijuana-related health effects as would be a comparison of occasional cigarette smokers with nonsmokers. When intensity of use was taken into account, it was—and still is—usually defined by drug use frequency with little distinction made in the actual quantities consumed.

For convenience, marijuana has often been studied in isolation from other drugs. Frequently, its principal psychoactive ingredient, delta-9-tetrahydrocannabinol (THC), is isolated and administered orally to humans or animals. Although there are good arguments for studying marijuana in this way, it is not the way in which cannabis is usually consumed. Marijuana is generally smoked and is quite commonly used concurrently with alcohol, tobacco, and frequently other illicit drugs as well. This is especially true for the heavy user. THC is only one of several hundred ingredients in marijuana smoke, and to smoke contains several dozen additional chemical compounds that are unique to marijuana. Much less is known about the action of these other chemicals, although they are thought to modify THC's psychological and toxic effects as well as to have effects of their own (Turner 1980).

The "drug scene" is a rapidly changing one. There is good reason to believe that today's marijuana is significantly more potent, that is, higher in THC content, than the cannabis available as recently as 5 years ago. Street samples exceeding 1 percent THC were fairly uncommon at that time; samples with a THC content of 5 percent or more are now common (C. E. Turner, personal communication 1981). Systematic experimental study of marijuana in humans has generally used weaker material than is now available. Research based on older users smoking less potent varieties of marijuana may have little relevance to the use of stronger cannabis by young children and adolescents today.

Since cannabis use has been traditional in some cultures for hundreds of years, there have also been attempts to study its effects in those societies using modern research methods. The appeal of studying traditionally using groups is obvious; the limitations of such research may not be. Groups studied typically consist of men in middle life, since almost all traditional users are male. This is in marked contrast to the large numbers of children, adolescents, and females using marijuana in contemporary America. Moreover, there is reason to believe that traditional users' concurrent use of tobacco—the two substances are frequently smoked simultaneously as a mixture—leads them to inhale less deeply and to retain the smoke in their lungs for shorter periods than does the American user (Petersen 1979). A roughly analogous case is pipe versus cigarette smoking, in which the health effects are importantly different. If the analogy holds for traditional versus nontraditional cannabis use, it would not be surprising if traditional use were less hazardous to health. Even where cannabis-related health problems or dysfunction have been reported in traditional settings, it is uncertain what role cannabis plays compared to that of poor nutrition. Frequently, among the poorest segments of the society, the cost of users' cannabis supply may reduce the amount of money available to support an already poor dietary standard. Traditional users are also frequently employed in intellectually undemanding roles in agrarian societies in which any effect on thinking may be less important than it would be in a highly industrialized urban culture.

The many limitations characteristic of cannabis research that we have briefly outlined here often make the interpretation of the world's medical and scientific literature concerning the drug difficult. Although there are more than 8,000 articles dealing with some aspect of cannabis, many of these are of only marginal relevance to contemporary use patterns by American users. Many would not meet present-day scientific standards for research adequacy. Some represent little more than undocumented assertions about the putative effects of cannabis use without regard to other possible causal factors that may have played a role in the symptom pictures described. A much smaller number of studies are based on modern research methods that adequately specify the material used and take into account other contributing factors relevant to the clinical picture observed.

Even the best contemporary research leaves many important questions unanswered, particularly with regard to the longer term consequences of use. As a result, there is a considerable danger that the absence of adequate evidence for a possible effect may be interpreted as an indication that such an effect is unlikely. As evidence from other widely used toxic substances, such as alcohol and tobacco, so amply demonstrates, clinical impressions are sometimes more accurate as a distant early warning of potential health hazards than is the much more modest amount of research data available when a substance initially becomes popular.

Epidemiology of Marijuana Use

Although there have been many local, State, and national surveys done over the past two decades to determine the nature and extent of American marijuana use, only two of these provide trend data that are likely to be of more enduring national significance. (Others, of course, provide important and useful information about correlates and predisposing factors related to use.) The first of these, the National Household Survey, is based upon interviews with a random sample of persons 12 years old or older living in households in the coterminous United States. It was conducted in 1971, 1972, 1974, 1976, 1977, 1979, and, most recently, in 1982 (National Institute on Drug Abuse, in press, a). The data were collected in a generally uniform fashion and thus provide good trend information for a decade of heightened American drug use. A second important survey source is an annual study of a random sample of high school seniors that was begun in 1975 and has been done annually each year since (the latest, *Student Drug Use in America, 1982,* National Institute on Drug Abuse, in press, b). Questionnaires are administered to high school seniors and to a portion of the original respondents in subsequent years. This provides not only a cross-sectional picture of American youths at a point of transition but also an opportunity to learn about changes in their drug use over time. Although both these national surveys are well designed and executed, they do have limitations that should be kept in mind in interpreting their results. Since the national household survey is confined to those living in household units and the high school senior survey to those still enrolled in high school in their senior year, some important groups are omitted. These include persons without regular addresses or those living in institutional settings such as dormitories and military bases, or transients. School dropouts and chronic absentees are likely to be omitted in the high school senior survey. Some of those missed may have atypical rates of marijuana (or other) drug use. We know, for example, that school absentees and dropouts are likely to have significantly higher rates of marijuana use than their peers who are still attending regularly (Kandel 1975).

Although a detailed discussion of the findings of these and other surveys can be readily obtained elsewhere, some of their highlights are worth summarizing:

• Both marijuana experimentation and current use (within the month preceding the survey) have increased markedly since the 1960s. Between 1971 and 1982, the latest year for which data analysis is complete, the percentage of youths (ages 12 to 17) who had ever used nearly doubled—from 14 percent to 27.3 percent. Among those ages 18 to 25, an increase of over 50 percent occurred in the same period—from 39.3 to 64.3 percent. The percentage of those currently using (i.e., those reporting use in the 30 days prior to the survey) is roughly half that of those who have ever used. This has been a consistent pattern over time for young adults and adolescents.

• Among high school seniors, nearly half (47.3 percent) of the class of 1975 had experimented with marijuana, compared with about 60 percent of the classes of 1978 to 1982. As with other adolescent and young adult groups, the percentage of current users is approximately half that of those who have ever tried the drug.

• Daily use has not been surveyed in the National Household Survey, but among high school seniors, it rose from 6 to nearly 11 percent between 1975 and 1978 and has since fallen to 6.3 percent in the class of 1982.

• Use among those older than age 25 is much lower than among those younger. Only 6.7 percent of those 26 and over reported current (past month) use of marijuana in 1982, compared to 1.3 percent in 1971.

Other significant aspects of use have been found in these and other studies. For example:

• The lower the age of initial use of alcohol and cigarettes, the more likely the individual is to use marijuana (Rittenhouse 1980).

• Age of first use of marijuana has steadily decreased. A little over a third (37 percent) of the high school senior class of 1975 had used marijuana prior to the tenth grade, but just over half (51 percent) of the class of 1981 began use that early (National Institute on Drug Abuse, in press, b).

• "Daily" use (20+ days per month) is positively correlated with absenteeism and poor school achievement among high school seniors and negatively correlated with religious involvement and plans for college attendance (Johnston 1980).

• Seniors who spend little time at home are more likely to be daily users than are those less socially active—of those who are out six nights per week on dates, a third use marijuana daily (Johnston 1980).

• Daily-using seniors are much more likely to use other drugs than are less frequent users—nearly half (47 percent) currently use amphetamines; nearly a third (31 percent) currently use cocaine (Johnston 1980).

Psychosocial Correlates of Marijuana Use

The concern that marijuana use might play a role in social deviance or in other forms of impaired psychosocial functioning has led a number of researchers to study the correlates of use. By "correlates" is meant those behaviors, attitudes, and interpersonal patterns together with social demographics that are associated with marijuana use. A number of longitudinal and cross-sectional studies have now found that use, is associated with such characteristics as poor academic performance and low academic motivation, various kinds of delinquent behavior, problems with authority, and a lack of self-esteem (Jessor and Jessor 1977; Kandel 1978a; Kellam et al. in press). The most striking aspect of these findings is that they have typically been found to precede drug use rather than to be the result of such use. This is in contrast to individual case studies, which frequently have observed that use itself, particularly at higher levels, results in diminished motivation and performance. The explanation may lie in the differences between studies of those who have sought treatment or been referred because of their drug-related problems as opposed to studies of more general population samples. This is not unique to marijuana. Even with drugs that are known to have causal significance in deviant behavior and diminished performance, such as alcohol, many heavy users do not show these effects even though they may be evident in users seeking or referred to treatment for drug-use-related problems. The fact that not every heavy user shows obvious use-related problems does not, of course, prove that a drug does not have serious adverse effects on more susceptible individuals.

Among the predictors of future marijuana and other drug use that have been found in longitudinal studies are such characteristics as rebelliousness (often reflected in rejection of parental and school authority), a dislike for school, a sense of alienation, normlessness, trauncy, and the like. Prospective users place a higher value on independence than they do on achievement and tend to be more peer-oriented than parent-oriented in their value systems. They tend to have more positive attitudes toward the use of legal drugs such as alcohol and tobacco and are likely to be earlier users of such drugs than their peers. They are also likely to have lower self-esteem, a lower sense of phychological well-being, and greater degrees of personal dissatisfaction and depression (Kandel et al. 1978; Smith and Fogg 1978; Kandel 1973).

Studies that have focused specifically on delinquency, deviance, and drug use have found that such behavior as theft and vandalism, lying, and interpersonal aggression are more characteristic of future drug users than of nonusers. By contrast, youngsters who are more conventional in their values, who are more religious, and who espouse more traditional academic and vocational achievement goals are less likely to become drug involved at an early age or on an intensive basis.

One of the most consistent findings is that an individual's drug use is highly correlated with that of his or her peers. Users are much more likely than are nonusers to have friends who are users. In fact, they are more likely to resemble their friends in their drug use than in almost any other dimension except for age and sex (Kandel 1978b). The more extensive the individual's involvement in the peer culture, the greater the likelihood of marijuana use on a regular basis. Thus, adolescents who date extensively, who spend most of their free time with their peers, and who feel remote from their parents are more likely to be regular users than are those less peer oriented (Johnston et al. 1980).

Another question of enduring interest has been the extent to which marijuana use plays a role in the subsequent or concurrent use of other illicit drugs. Statistically, there is little question that use, particularly heavier use, is associated with a greater likelihood of experimentation with other drugs. This is also true of use of alcohol and cigarettes. Those who use alcohol and tobacco are far more likely to begin using marijuana early and to use it more extensively than those who do not. The role of these nominally legal drugs as "gateway" substances to later illicit drugs has led to a reappraisal of prevention strategies primarily emphasizing the prevention of illicit drug use and to a recognition that the use and abuse of both types of substances cannot readily be separated.

As national surveys have clearly indicated, over the past 20 years there has been a marked increase in the acceptability of occasional marijuana use among adolescents and young adults, although there has been some degree of increasing disapproval since 1980. Nevertheless, there is good evidence that heavier use is not approved by the majority. In fact, the percentages of high school seniors who view regular marijuana use as posing "great risk" have significantly increased over the past several years. While 35 percent of the class of 1978 viewed regular use as posing great risk, 58 percent of the class of 1981 perceived it as such (Johnston et al. 1981).

Although the studies briefly reviewed here have enhanced our understanding of the correlates of marijuana use, it should be emphasized that the periods of time over which users and prospective users have been studied have been relatively brief—rarely exceeding 5 years. While some research done on older users (post-college age) suggests that use drops with the assumption of adult roles such as marriage, parenthood, and full-time employment, much remains to be learned about drug-use careers and just how the various factors interact in affecting drug use (O'Donnell et al. 1976). Another important consideration is the rapidly changing nature of the "drug scene" itself. Marijuana use has shifted from a clearly minority behavior closely associated with social deviance to a majority behavior (at least on an "experimental" basis) and may now in 1983 be again becoming less acceptable, judging by the attitude shifts that have been reported. Since the nature of the drug itself has also changed, it is also possible that future studies may find greater evidence that heavier marijuana use is not only a part of a larger pattern of social deviance but that it contributes to such deviance to a greater extent than earlier longitudinal studies indicate.

Acute Psychological Effects of Marijuana Intoxication

Uncertainty over the implications of chronic marijuana use should not obscure the basic agreement concerning the drug's immediate intoxicant effects. While marijuana intoxicated ("high"), the user shows many indications of impaired psychological functioning, including effects on memory, thinking, speaking, various kinds of problem solving, and concept formation. Early clinical descriptions of these effects are strikingly similar to more recent experimental observations of the past decade. Most of these effects seem to share in common an impairment of short-term memory, which leads to fragmented speech, disjointed thinking, and a tendency to lose one's train of thought (Institute of Medicine 1982).

Many specific types of performance are impaired. Examples include digit/symbol substitution, in which the subject is required to replace a series of random digits with symbols representing each digit; the number of orally presented digits that can be recalled (digit span); serial subtraction in which the subject subtracts a number repeatedly from an initially large number; and reading comprehension. Time perception is also affected and is reflected in an overestimation of elapsed time intervals. Most users are aware of this tendency to distort time (Ferraro 1980).

As with other drugs, marijuana's effects are dose related. The higher the dose, the more likely that performance disruption will occur. At least with simpler tasks, experienced users become tolerant of the drug's psychological effects and when strongly motivated may be able to attenuate the drug's effects (Cappell and Pliner 1974). Most laboratory research has been done with experienced users who are highly motivated to perform well so as to demonstrate that use is not disruptive. Under more usual conditions, performance might be expected to be poorer than in the laboratory.

Research has been done primarily with young adult males. Systematic research has not been carried out on the effects of marijuana use on much younger users or on how it affects classroom functioning directly. If anything, however, effects on younger users might be expected to be still more disruptive than effects on older users, and the similarity of classroom tasks to those experimentally investigated leaves little doubt that marijuana is likely to interfere with classroom learning. The more complex, unfamiliar, and demanding the task to be performed, the greater the likelihood that being high will cause impairment.

Marijuana use also produces acute effects on perception, affect, and social interaction. Perceptually, users typically report a heightened awareness of visual, auditory, and tactual sensations (Goode 1970). This subjective enhancement of sensation is usually seen as desirable, and coupled with the time distortions alluded to earlier, it may be responsible for the reported enhancement of sexuality. The latter may also be a response to a generally disinhibiting effect of marijuana similar to that of alcohol. Like alcohol, however, higher doses may be sedative and may reduce responses.

Unlike the alterations in time perception that can be measured in the laboratory, the enhancement of other types of sensation has not been detected experimentally. There is no evidence that improved auditory or visual acuity, for example, results from marijuana intoxication. Despite marijuana's street reputation as a social facilitator, laboratory research indicates that even at moderate doses communication is impaired by the intrusion of irrelevant ideas and words and that there is even greater disruption at higher doses (Dornbush et al. 1971; Miller and Cornett 1978; Paul and Carson 1973).

Acute Physiological Effects

The most obvious—and well verified—effect of marijuana on humans is a dose-related temporary increase in heart rate, which may become as high as 160 beats per minute (Beaconsfield et al. 1972; Perez-Reyes et al. 1973) In animals, by contrast, heart rate in response to marijuana is often slowed (Cavero et al. 1972). Blood pressure levels while the subject is standing tend to drop but typically remain unchanged or even increase slightly while the subject is sitting or reclining (Beaconsfield et al. 1972). In the past, the acute increase in heart rate accompanying use has been viewed as benign. More recently there has been concern that it may have more serious implications for those who are older or who already have impaired heart functioning. In patients with angina pectoris—chest pain as a result of poor cardiac circulation—there is evidence to indicate that they experience such pain more rapidly and following less exertion after smoking marijuana cigarettes than after smoking conventional cigarettes (Prakash and Aronow 1976). Most recently (1982), health scientists at the National Academy of Sciences' Institute of Medicine who comprehensively reviewed marijuana's health effects suggested that marijuana use may become a threat (as the user population ages) to those with hypertension, cerebrovascular disease, and coronary atherosclerosis (Institute of Medicine 1982).

Conjuctival congestion, a reddening of the eyes, is also a common physiological reaction to acute marijuana use. That this effect is not simply a result of the irritating effects of the smoke is indicated by its occurrence even when the drug is orally ingested.

Effects on Psychomotor Performance

When we turn to research on various aspects of psychomotor coordination and performance, there is generally good agreement about the acute effects of marijuana. As early as 1944, work done for the New York Mayor's Committee on Marihuana found that hand steadiness, measured by the ability to hold a stylus within a small hole without touching the hole's sides, was reduced. "Body sway" while standing erect was also increased (Mayor's Committee on Marihuana 1944). More recent variations on these original experiments using better specified doses of marijuana have been generally consistent with the earlier experiments (Clark et al. 1970; Evans et al. 1973; Kiplinger et al. 1971). Reaction time experiments have had varying results depending on the complexity of the task demands. When the experiment has demanded an uncomplicated response to a simple stimulus, say pressing a key in response to a light or sound, marijuana has been found to have little effect (Borg et al. 1975). But when the research task has required complex discrimination or complex responding or when the task required continuous attention, performance was impeded in a generally dose-related fashion (Clark et al. 1970; Moskowitz and McGlothlin 1974; Peeke et al. 1976). What appears to be involved in these experiments is not reaction time as such, but the task's demands for continuous attention or more complex information processing.

Tracking, the ability to follow a moving stimulus, which requires continous rather than intermittent attention, is a good example of an experimental task impaired by marijuana intoxication. It is an important function since it is involved in driving, flying, and many other types of man/machine interactions. In critical tracking, in which task difficulty is increased until the subject is unable to track, deficits in performance have been found for as long as 10 hours after initially becoming high, long past the period of subjective intoxication (Moskowitz et al. 1981). In experiments in which subjects detect and respond to peripheral light cues in their visual field, performance is adversely affected by marijuana (Casswell and Marks 1973; Moskowtiz et al. 1972). Such defects in signal detection may have practical significance in driving and similar man/machine interactions requiring alertness to peripheral visual cues

Driving Studies

Because of its practical importance, driving behavior as related to marijuana use has been studied in a variety of ways. These include experiments that more closely resemble the complex demands of actual driving than do reaction time and other simpler performances; driving-simulator performances as well as driving on test courses and under actual traffic conditions have been investigated.

Virtually all simulator research has found clear deficits in performance related to marijuana intoxication. In general, the more closely the driving-simulator demands have resembled those of actual driving, the greater the disruption resulting from performing while high. The greatest effect has been on response to the perceptual demands of driving rather than on car control variables. However, there is good experimental evidence that the resistance of such control variables as braking time and tracking may be an artifact of the rather simple demands of most simulators. In an interactive, computer-controlled simulator in which performance more closely resembled actual driving, more serious marijuana-induced deficiencies were found (Smiley et al. 1981). In this more realistic experimental model, marijuana use produced significant variability in the control of car velocity and poorer car positioning when responding to simulated wind gusts and negotiating curves. The ability ot maintain following distance was also affected, as was the ability to maintain lane position. "Drivers" were also likely to make errors in responding to route signs while high. Their responses to simulated emergencies were impaired to an extent that would have produced accidents in actual driving. Overall, the simulator studies clearly indicate that marijuana impairs driving performance in ways that have serious practical consequences for traffic safety.

A study of pilot behavior while marijuana-intoxicated using a flight simulator found serious disruption of psychomotor and cognitive functioning involved in piloting an aircraft under instrument flying conditons (without visual flight cues outside the aircraft). Following social doses of marijuana, pilots had difficulty in maintaining their flight pattern and often forgot just where they were in the flight sequence. Performance of those pilots who were tested for several hours after initial marijuana intake did not return to normal until 4 hours after smoking. The authors of this study point out that the simulator flight test was simpler than many flying situations, and still greater impairment might be expected in actual flight (Janowsky 1976; Janowsky et al. 1976).

There have been several attempts to determine marijuana's effects on driving under test course or traffic conditions. With the exception of one poorly reported study in which marijuana doses and other details of the experimental procedures are described too inadequately to evaluate the work, the remainder of the studies have all reported impaired performance. In a Canadian close-course experiment, 12 male and 4 female subjects traversed a course of 1.1 miles, which was defined by poles and traffic cones, at a speed of 25 to 30 mph (40 to 48 km/hr). Marijuana, alcohol, and placebo were administered on a double-blind basis. The higher dose of marijuana and the alcohol dose (sufficient to produce a 0.07 percent blood alcohol level) produced performance impairment to about the same extent (Hansteen et al. 1976).

A second Canadian study using 43 male and 21 female subjects studied driving under closed-course and actual traffic conditions. In traffic, performances were rated on behavioral rating scales. At the higher of the two marijuana levels used, judgment and concentration were clearly impaired. Dose-related impairment was also found in five of eight tests used on the closed course (Klonoff 1974).

A third closed-course experiment was done at speeds approaching those of highway driving (up to 50 mph or 80km/hr). Although the number of subjects was small (eight), the author reports that multivariate analysis showed that marijuana, alcohol, and a combination of the two all adversely affected performance (Attwood et al. 1981).

Since these experiments were done without the usual distractions of additional passengers in the car or a car radio or stereo, and with strong motivation to perform well, a greater impairment of performance might be expected under more ordinary conditions.

Attempts have been made to determine the role of marijuana in motor vehicle fatalities or highway accidents. A serious problem is encountered, however, in the measurement of blood cannabinoid levels in a way analogous to the measurement of blood alcohol levels. Blood cannabinoid levels drop within minutes of smoking and by the end of two hours may have decreased to a level below that at which they can readily be detected. Moreover, unlike blood alcohol levels, blood cannabinoid levels are not clearly correlated with reduced performance. Finally, quantitative analysis requires blood samples, which accident-involved drivers are often unwilling to supply. Blood alcohol determinations can be based on urine or breath analysis, and although urinalysis can determine whether marijuana has been used within several days of an accident, at present there is no way of determining a direct connection between the use of marijuana and the accident.

Despite these limitations, there have been several studies indicating that marijuana, like alcohol, plays a causal role in the production of motor vehicle fatalities and accidents. Perhaps the most ingenious of these utilized an "index of culpability" to measure the role of several drugs in motor vehicle accidents. The frequency with which each drug was found in the blood of drivers judged responsible for an accident was compared with that for drivers in the same sample who were not found responsible. The index ranged from 1, meaning a drug is not related to accidents, to 1.8, indicating a much greater use frequency in those found culpable. Using this method, marijuana was found to have a culpability index similar to that for alcohol (Warren et al. 1981). A very recent (1982) study of teenage driving after using marijuana or alcohol found that teenagers who drove 6 or more times per month after smoking marijuana were 2.4 times more likely than those who did not to have been involved in traffic accidents. Still heavier users (driving 15 or more times per month after marijuana use) were 2.9 times more likely to have had an accident. These figures are based on a random telephone survey of nearly 6,000 16 to 19-year-olds in which appropriate controls were used for the number of miles driven, age, sex, education, and whether those queried were married, students, or living with parents (Hingson et al. 1982b).

While these studies suggest that marijuana is a significant factor in accidents, much more needs to be done to better specify its role in causing accidents. The few studies done to date probably underestimate the frequency with which marijuana is involved because of the drug-use detection problem and the likelihood that self-reports underestimate the role of marijuana use in impaired driving.

Chronic Effects

The brevity of the American experience with large-scale marijuana use and the extended period often required for chronic effects of drug use to become apparent makes this an area in which our present knowledge is almost clearly deficient and inconclusive. As already noted, heavier users of marijuana are likely to make extensive use of other licit and illicit drugs, making the chronic implications of their marijuana use difficult to isolate.

Respiratory Effects

Because marijuana smoke is deeply inhaled, retained in the lungs, and contains many ingredients similar to those in tobacco smoke, adverse respiratory effects are to be expected. Such effects have been clinically reported among traditional users in the older clinical literature (Indian Hemp Drug Commission 1969), and there is a range of more recent experimental and clinical research suggesting that marijuana has many effects similar to those of cigarette smoking. Unlike research on cigarettes, however, the body of data currently available is much smaller and less conclusive. No large-scale epidemiological studies have been done, and the still-small minority of heavy users who have used for periods of many years make confirming these effects epidemiologically difficult.

Studies based on much shorter periods of exposure) to marijuana have found lung effects ranging from the statistically but not practically significant (probably because of the brevity of exposure) to more serious respiratory problems reported by self-referred users of hashish. A study of normal volunteers after periods of up to 2 months of smoking an average of about five standard marijuana cigarettes found detectable decreases in specific airway conductance, forced expiratory flow, and diffusion capacity (Tashkin et al. 1976). Another study of moderately heavy street users who were compared with nonusers found evidence that such users showed greater effects from marijuana use than from comparable cigarette use (Tashkin et al. 1980). Given the facts that virtually the entire "joint" (marijuana cigarette) is consumed by deeply inhaling it and that the smoke is usually unfiltered, the greater effect is not surprising.

A study of 31 hashish-using American soliders in Europe, self-referred for physical reasons, found bronchitis, rhinophryngitis, asthma, and sinusitis all related to heavy use (100 grams per month for up to 15 months) (Tennant et al. 1971). A similar larger study of 200 self-referred soldiers found similar symptoms related to use. In a small subsample of this group, tissue biopsy found bronchial changes similar to those found in much older heavy cigarette smokers (Auerbach et al. 1961). For 20 of the heavier hashish users, vital capacity was reduced to 60 to 85 percent of normal (Henderson et al. 1972).

Chronic studies of animals exposed to quantities of marijuana smoke that produced blood levels similar to those in human users found degenerative changes in the lungs (Rosenkrantz and Fleischman 1979). Other studies of human lung tissue in tissue culture have found malignant cellular changes after shorter periods of exposure to marijuana smoke than to tobacco smoke (Leuchtenberger et al. 1976).

The possibility that marijuana can ultimately produce lung cancer in humans is suggested by several types of additional research evidence. Chemical analysis of marijuana smoke indicates that it contains several chemical compounds similar to those found in tobacco smoke that are known to be carcinogenic (Novotny et al. 1976). Marijuana smoke residuals, like those of tobacco, cause skin tumors when applied to the shaved skin of experimental animals (Hoffmann et al. 1975). The fact that marijuana smokers are also frequently cigarette smokers may well pose an additional risk beyond that of either marijuana or tobacco smoked alone. The shorter life span in traditionally using countries and the lack of systematic studies of causes of mortality in those countries may have obscured the possible role of marijuana in lung carcinoma. Since lung cancer and other chronic lung diseases are usually diseases of later life, many person-years of exposure to marijuana may be needed before clear epidemiological evidence of a connection is demonstrated.

Reproductive Effects

Because marijuana users are largely either in or about to enter their reproductive years, a possible effect on reproduction has long been of concern. Some studies have found evidence of a reduction in testosterone levels in males. Where reductions have been found, they have generally been within normal limits (Kolodny et al. 1974; Cohen 1976). Even a modest reduction might, however, have significance for those whose endocrine functioning is marginal or possibly in younger users at the point of transition from childhood to adolescence. Clinical evidence of these theoretical possibilities has generally been lacking.

Diminished sperm counts found in some heavily using males may also have greater significance for those who are already marginally fertile. In a study of Greek users, evidence of abnormal sperm structure was found in some users, although its clinical significance is not clear (Issidorides 1979).

Work with animals has suggested that marijuana may have adverse reproductive effects in females, including the suppression of ovulation and altered progesterone levels. One study of female monkeys given dosages of THC that would be consistent with heavier human use found a greater incidence of reproductive failure than that found in drug-free animals (Sassenrath et al. 1979).

Research on human females has been quite limited. One study of 26 young women using unspecified street marijuana three or more times per week for 6 months or more compared these users with nonusers of similar age. While the authors reported a higher frequency of anovulatory menstrual cycles and a shortened luteal phase, which may be related to reduced fertility, the results must be regarded as suggestive at best. Users differed from nonusers in their level of alcohol use and of sexual activity, which may have affected the results (Bauman et al. 1979).

A recent study of fetal growth and development in 1,690 mother/child pairs in Boston found an association between marijuana use, lowered birth weight, and fetal abnormalities resembling the fetal alcohol syndrome. Although the exact causal role of marijuana, especially in conjunction with alcohol or tobacco use, is not clear, the authors conclude that "women who used marijuana during pregnancy were five times more likely to deliver infants with features considered compatible with the fetal alcohol syndrome." Because of uncertainity of causation, the authors "caution against the firm conclusion that marijuana use causes fetal growth retardation" (Hingson et al. 1982a). Despite the limitations of the research thus far completed, there is a consensus that marijuana use by women during pregnancy is particularly unwise.

A possible role of marijuana in mutagenicity has been suggested (Stenchever et al. 1974). Although the bulk of the better controlled research suggests that marijuana does not have mutagenic or cytogenic effects, research in this area must be regarded as incomplete, and the issue as still unresolved.

Effects on the Immune System

A variety of animal studies have suggested that marijuana may have an effect on the body's immune system, its principal defense against disease (Petersen and Lemberger 1976; Lefkowitz and Klager 1978; Pruess and Lefkowitz 1978). In humans, the data are clearly inconclusive. Some studies have found evidence of a diminished immune response in some users, but others have not (Gupta et al. 1974; Silverstein and Lessin 1974; Nahas et al. 1974; Petersen et al. 1976). There is no epidemiological evidence that marijuana users at any level of use are more frequently susceptible to disease that might result from an impaired immune response. But since such large-scale studies have not yet been done and most users are relatively young and have high degrees of immunity, such effects may not yet have been detected.

Chronic Effects on Brain and Behavior

A wide range of marijuana's effects make it apparent that the drug has acute effects on brain function. The question of whether continuing use leads to persistent changes in brain function or morphology is more difficult to answer at this time.

In 1971, a British study suggested that brain atrophy related to marijuana use had occurred in 10 multiple-drug users who had various neurological symptoms (Campbell et al. 1971). The facts that other drugs had been used and that there were other serious methodological deficiencies made the connection between marijuana use and the brain damage tenuous at best. Two better controlled subsequent studies of healthy chronic marijuana users using a noninvasive technique for measuring the brain found no evidence of brain atrophy in any of the subjects studied (Co et al. 1977; Kuehnle et al. 1977).

A study of a very limited sample of monkeys treated with either marijuana smoke or intravenous THC has reported evidence of drug-related brain changes detectable by electron microscopy (Heath et al. 1979). The limited number of animals studied, the lack of replication, and some question of the significance of some of the changes reported all make the interpretation of these findings difficult. Even in the absence of structural changes in the brain, the possibility that marijuana produces persistent functional changes can not be dismissed. With other known neurotoxic drugs, such as alcohol, not all users are equally affected. There can be clear evidence of disturbed functioning, such as memory defects, despite lack of clear evidence of structural change.

Attempts have been made to study the effects of marijuana on the electrophysiology of the brain as measured by electroencephalography (EEG). While acute effects have been identified, these have neither been unique to marijuana nor chronically persistent in the absence of marijuana intoxication (Rodin et al. 1970; Fink 1976). Studies have also been done in traditional chronic user groups (Rubin and Comitas 1976; Karacan et al. 1976). These too have found no evidence of persistent EEG changes related to use, but since the samples chosen for study were screened on several health variables the possibility exists that the screening process itself eliminated those who might have shown such changes.

Clinical reports of isolated cases of abnormal EEG findings presumably related to marijuana use are difficult to interpret since any EEG findings may have preceded use or may have resulted from the use of other drugs or from other causes.

Behavioral Effects

A variety of adverse behavioral-psychological effects of marijuana have been described as resulting from acute and chronic cannabis use. Users frequently report reactions that are negative although not severe enought to seek medical or other outside assistance. These range from mild anxiety to acute panic reactions. Transient mild paranoid feelings are common (Tart 1970). Such reactions seem to be more frequent in inexperienced users who lose the perspective that what they are experiencing is a drug reaction rather than a basic change in their mentation. An acute brain syndrome marked by disorientation, confusion, and memory impairment has been reported (Spencer 1970; Talbott and Teague 1969). These acute reactions may occur when the individual ingests an unexpectedly potent variety of marijuana or uses the drug in larger quantities than usual. Since it is more difficult to self-titrate dosage when the drug is taken orally, overdoses from such use are probably more common.

In countries such as India, a cannabis psychosis has been described that resembles schizophrenia, althought it is not clear whether this results from the drug use itself or is the product of an underlying schizophrenia exacerbated by the use of the drug (Chopra and Smith 1974). A cannabis psychosis has not been commonly reported in the United States, although there have been clinical reports that marijuana use in psychotic patients who were in remissison has precipitated a recurrence of their schizophrenia (Treffert 1978; Smith and Mehl 1970). Mostly recently, a Swedish report (Palsson et al. 1982) has found an apparent causal link between heavy hashish use and a schizophrenic-like illness characterized by confusion, aggressiveness, and affective lability in individuals with little evidence of preexisting psychosis. The disorder appeared to be rare and disappeared in a period of weeks or months following cessation of cannabis use.

The question of whether long-term cannabis use produces a loss of conventional motivation and an inability to persist in achieving long-term goals—a so-called "amotivational syndrome"—has been raised both in countries of traditional use and with respect to contemporary American use. At one extreme, it appears likely that chronic marijuana intoxication interferes with functioning in this way. But the question of whether regular, heavy use at levels less than chronic intoxication causes this is more difficult to answer. For some, a lack of strong motivation to pursue long-term goals precedes drug use. But there are a number of clinical observers who are convinced that these motivational effects are directly related to use and that following cessation of marijuana use normal motivation may return (Kolansky and Moore 1971; National Institute on Drug Abuse 1982). It is also noteworthy that among high school seniors who discontinued use, over half did so because of their concern about use-related "loss of energy or ambition." Almost two out of five daily users in the class of 1981 thought their cannabis use caused a loss of interest in other activities and interfered with their ability to think. There has been little systematic study of the effect of chronic use on work performance in American populations, although there have been attempts to look at work functioning and social functioning in several populations of traditional users. The overseas groups studied showed little evidence of amotivation, but this may reflect a different mode of use or the lower demands involved, or it may be an artifact of the methods of subject selection.

Of paramount concern has been the possible effect of frequent marijuana use on the psychological, emotional, and social development of children and adolescents. In this area, firm research evidence is seriously lacking, and we are dependent on clinical impressions and individual case studies. Among clinicians who see children and adolescents who are frequent users, there is growing consensus that such use seriously interferes with functioning and development. While it may be argued that clinicians are more likely to see those who are experiencing drug-related difficulties even though they may not be representative of users more generally, such evidence must be taken seriously. As with other drugs, it is likely that not all users are equally susceptible to drug-induced disruption of functioning. But it is those groups that are most likely to be adversely affected, children and early adolescents, who have not been systematically studied. Further, there are many individual case reports by older users indicating that their marijuana use, frequently coupled with other drug use, has been seriously disruptive of their lives. The question of whether it is marijuana use itself that is responsible or some combination of drugs and other lifestyle factors may be of only modest significance since we have good reason to believe that heavier users of marijuana are likely to be multiple-drug users whose lives increasingly revolve around their use. Undoubtedly as previously noted, there are some heavy users who continue to function reasonably well despite their marijuana use, as is true of other types of drug use.

Future Directions

As this and other reviews so amply demonstrate, much remains to be learned about marijuana. Despite the street belief that different types of marijuana have different psychological and possibly different physical effects, the major defining property that has been studied in relation to human behavior has been dose as measured in terms of THC content. While other chemical constituents have been identified and studied to a limited extent, much less is known about the ways in which they may affect the user. In virtually all retrospective surveys, frequency of use has been the primary gauge of use intensity, with little regard to the actual quantities consumed, their varied potency, or the circumstances of use. Although marijuana is often used with other licit or illicit drugs, very little work has been done on possible interactive effects. The possibility that contaminants such as herbicides, bacteria, and fungi may play a role in marijuana's effects has been raised by recent reports, although again there has been little or no systematic investigation in these areas.

Studies of marijuana use have been largely limited to populations of adult males. Little attention has been paid to the possible effect of acute or chronic use on both younger and older users or, more specifically, on adolescent and adult females. Virtually no epidemiological research has been done to determine any statistical association between use and disease. Early studies of traditional cannabis users in other countries have not been followed up to determine just how much of the cannabis consumed actually plays a physiological role. Recently developed blood cannabinoid assays could readily assess the comparability of traditional use patterns and contemporary American use.

The deficiencies in the research literature to date suggest a number of approaches that would be useful in the future:

• Epidemiological research on patterns of marijuana use should be expanded to include better definitions of level of use based on measures in addition to frequency.

• Longitudinal studies of heavy users should begin at younger ages, and already existing longitudinal health studies should include marijuana and other drug use. Incidence of disease that might be related to a diminished immune response resulting from heavy use should be examined.

• In addition to heavy users, other populations that may be at high risk should be studied in connection with marijuana use. These would include the marginally fertile, offspring of women who used marijuana during pregnancy, prepubertal users, and persons who have medical or psychological conditions that may be affected by use (e.g., cardiac irregularities, hypertension, respiratory problems, or histories of serious psychological problems).

- Since much of the research on the acute effects of marijuana has been based on the use of low potency marijuana, replication of some of these studies using more potent materials may be needed.
- Studies of marijuana should include an examination of its effects on development and academic performance in younger users. Earlier studies based on moderate use by college populations may have little relevance to current use patterns by younger users.
- Animal studies suggesting that alterations in brain structure result from marijuana use should be replicated and extended to include the study of behavioral effects in both younger and older animals.
- Possible long-term cognitive deficits should be examined in populations of heavy users. The availability of standardized test results from testing done by school systems before the indivdual began drug use may provide a useful baseline against which to assess change. Since not all users are likely to be equally affected, populations of users reporting impaired functioning should also be carefully studied.
- Systematic study of drug use over extended periods of time may be useful in better determining the impact of use on functioning and in identifying factors that affect drug use transitions, including cessation of use.

References

Attwood, D.; Williams, R.; McBurney, L.; and Frecker, R. Cannabis, alcohol and driving: Effects on selected closed-course tasks. In: Goldberg, L., ed. *Alcohol, Drugs and Traffic Safety, III.* Stockholm, Sweden: Almqvist and Wiksell, 1981. Pp. 938–953.

Auerbach, O.; Stout, A.P.; Hammond, E.C.; and Garfinkel, L. Changes in bronchial epithelium related to cigarette smoking and in relation to lung cancer. *New England Journal of Medicine,* 265:253–267, 1961.

Bauman, J.E.; Kolodny, R.C.; Dornbush, R.L.; and Webster, S.K. Efectos endocrinos del uso cronico de la mariguana en mujeres. In: *Simposio Internacional Sobre Actualizacion en mariguana.* Vol. 10. Tlalpan, Mexico, July 1979. Pp. 85–97.

Beaconsfield, P.; Ginsburg, J.; Rainsbury, R. Marijuana smoking. Cardiovascular effects in man and possible mechanisms. *New England Journal of Medicine,* 287:209–212, 1972.

Borg, J.; Gershon, S.; and Alpert, M. Dose effects of smoked marijuana on human cognitive and motor functions. *Psychopharmacologia,* 42:211–218, 1975.

Campbell, A.M.G.; Evans, M.; Thompson, J.L.G.; and Williams, M.R. Cerebral atrophy in young cannabis smokers. *Lancet,* 2:1219–1225, 1971.

Cappell, H.D., and Pliner, P.C. Cannabis intoxication: The role of pharmacological and psychological variables. In: Miller, L.L.; ed. *Marijuana: Effects on Human Behavior.* New York: Academic Press, 1974. Pp. 233–264.

Casswell, S., and Marks, D. Cannabis induced impairment of performance of a divided attention task. *Nature,* 241:60–61, 1973.

Cavero, I.; Buckley, J.P.; and Jandhyala, B.S. Parasympatholytic activity of (-)-delta-9-transtetrahydrocannabinol in mongrel dogs. *European Journal of Pharmacology,* 19:301–304, 1972.

Chopra, G.S., and Smith, J.W. Psychotic reactions following cannabis use in East Indians. *Archives of General Psychiatry,* 30:24–27, 1974.

Clarke, L.D.; Hughes, R.; and Nakashima, E.F. Behavioral effects on marijuana: Experimental studies. *Archives of General Psychiatry,* 23:193–198, 1970.

Co, B.T.; Goodwin, D.W.; Gado, M.; Mikhael, M.; and Hill, S.Y. Absence of cerebral atrophy in chronic cannabis users. *Journal of the American Medical Association,* 237 (12):1229–1230, 1977.

Cohen, S. The 94-day cannabis study. *Annals of the New York Academy of Sciences,* 282:211–220, 1976.

Dornbush, R.L.; Fink, N.; and Freedman, A.M. Marijuana, memory and perception. *American Journal of Psychiatry,* 128:194–197, 1971.

Evans, M.A.; Martz, R.; and Brown, D.J. Impairment of performance with low doses of marijuana. *Clinical Pharmacology and Therapeutics,* 14:936–940, 1973.

Ferraro, D.P. Acute effects of marijuana on human memory and cognition. In: Petersen, R.C., ed. *Marijuana Research Findings: 1980,* National Institute on Drug Abuse. Research Monograph 31. Washington, D.C.: Supt. of Docs., U.S. Govt. Print. Off., 1980.

Fink, M. Effects of acute and chronic inhalation of hashish, marijuana, and delta-9-tetrahydrocannabinol on brain electrical activity in man:

Evidence for tissue tolerance. *Annals of the New York Academy of Sciences,* 282:387–398, 1976.

Goode, E. *The Marijuana Smokers.* New York: Basic Books, 1970.

Gupta, S.; Grieco, M.; and Cushman, P. Impairman of rosette-forming T-lymphocytes in chronic marihuana smokers. *New England Journal of Medicine,* 291:874–877, 1974.

Hansteen, R.W.; Miller, R.D.; Lonero, L.; Reid, L.D.; and Jones, B. Effects of cannabis and alcohol on automobile driving and psychomotor tracking. *Annals of the New York Academy of Sciences,* 282:240–256, 1976.

Heath, R.G.; Fitzjarrell, A.T.; Garey, R.E.; and Myers, W.A. Chronic marijuana smoking; Its effect on function and structure of the primate brain. In: Nahas, G.G., and Paton, W.J.D., eds. *Marijuana: Biological Effects.* Oxford: Pergamon Press, 1979. P. 713.

Henderson, R.L.; Tennant, F.S.; and Guerry, R. Respiratory manifestations of hashish smoking. *Archives of Otolaryngology,* 95:248–251, 1972.

Hingson, R.; Alpert, J.J.; Day, N.; Dooling, E.; Kayne, H.; Morelock, S.; Oppenheimer, E.; and Zuckerman, B. Effects of maternal drinking and marijuana use on fetal growth and development. *Pediatrics,* 70 (4):539–546, 1982a.

Hingson, R.; Heeren, T.; Mangione, T.; Morelock, S.; and Mucatel, M. Teenage driving after using marijuana or drinking and traffic accident involvement. *Journal of Safety Research,* 13(1):33–38, 1982b.

Hoffmann, D.; Brunnemann, K.D.; Gori, G.B.; and Wynder, E.L. On the carcinogenicity of marihuana smoke. *Research Advances in Phytochemistry,* 9:63–81, 1975.

Indian Hemp Drugs Commission. *Report of the Indian Hemp Drugs Commission 1893–94.* Facsimle reprinted as *Marijuana Report of the Indian Hemp Drugs Commission 1893–94.* Silver Spring, Md.: Thomas Jefferson Publishing, 1969.

Institute of Medicine, National Academy of Sciences. Behavioral and psychosocial effects of marijuana use. In: *Marijuana and Health—Report of a Study by a Committee of the Institute of Medicine Division of Health Sciences Policy.* Washington, D.C.: National Academy Press, 1982.

Issidorides, M.R. Observations in chronic hashish users: Nuclear aberrations in blood and sperm and abnormal acrosomes in spermatozoa. In: Nahas, G.G., and Paton, W.D.M., eds. *Marihuana: Biological Effects. Analysis, Metabolism, Cellular Responses, Reproduction and Brain.* Oxford: Pergamon Press, 1979. Pp. 377–388.

Janowsky, D.S. Marijuana effects on simulated flying ability. *American Journal of Psychiatry,* 133(4):384–388, 1976.

Janowsky, D.S.; Meacham, M.P.; Blaine, J.D.; Schoor, M.; and Bozzetti, L.P. Simulated flying performance after marihuana intoxication. *Aviation, Space, and Environmental Medicine,* 47(2):124–128, 1976.

Jessor, R., and Jessor, S.L. *Problem Behavior and Psychosocial Development: A Longitudinal Study of Youth.* New York: Academic Press, 1977.

Johnston, L.D. "The Daily Marijuana User." Paper presented at the Meeting of the National Alcohol and Drug Coalition, Washington, D.C., September 18, 1980.

Johnston, L.D.; Bachman, J.G.; and O'Malley, P.M. *Highlights From Student Drug Use in America, 1975–1980,* National Institute on Drug Abuse. DHHS Pub. No. (ADM)81-1066. Washington, D.C.: Supt. of Docs., U.S. Govt. Print. Off., 1980.

Johnston, L.D.; Bachman, J.G.; and O'Malley, P.M. *Highlights From Student Drug Use in America, 1975–1981,* National Institute on Drug Abuse. DHHS Pub. No (ADM)82-1208. Washington, D.C.: Supt. of Docs., U.S. Govt. Print. Off., 1981.

Kandel, D. Adolescent marihuana use: Role of parents and peers. *Science,* 181:1067–1070, 1973.

Kandel, D. Reaching the hard-to-reach: Illicit drug use among high school absentees. *Addictive Diseases,* 1:465–480, 1975.

Kandel, D.B., ed. *Longitudinal Research on Drug Use: Empirical Findings and Methodological Issues.* Washington, D.C.: Hemisphere, 1978a.

Kandel, D.B. Similarity in real-life adolescent friendship pairs. *Journal of Personality and Social Psychology,* 36:306–312, 1978b.

Kandel, D.B.; Kessler, R.; and Margulies, R. Antecedents of adolescent initiation into stages of drug use: A developmental analysis. In: Kandel, D.B., ed. *Longitudinal Research on Drug Use: Empirical Findings and Methodological Issues.* Washington, D.C.: Hemisphere, 1978. Pp. 73–99.

Karacan, I.; Fernandez-Salas, A.; Coggins, W.J.; Carter, W.E.; Williams, R.L.; Thornby, T.I.; Salis, T.J.; Okawa, M.; and Villaume, J.P. Sleep electroencephalographic-electrooculographic characteristics of chronic marijuana users: Part I. *Annals of the New York Academy of Sciences,* 282:348–374, 1976.

Kellam, S.; Simon, M.; and Ensminger, M.E. Antecedents in first grade of teenage drug use and psychological well-being: A ten year community-wide prospective study. In: Ricks D., and Dohrenwend, B., eds. *Origins of Psychopathology: Research and Public Policy*. Cambridge: Cambridge University Press, in press.

Kiplinger, G.F.; Manno, J.E.; and Rodda, B.G. Dose response analysis of the effects of tetrahydrocannabinol in man. *Clinical Pharmacology and Therapeutics*, 12:650–657, 1971.

Klonoff, H. Marijuana and driving in real-life situations. *Science*, 186:317–324, 1974.

Kolansky, H., and Moore, W.T. Effects of marihuana on adolescents and young adults. *Journal of the American Medical Association*, 216:486–492, 1971.

Kolodny, R.C.; Masters, W.H.; Kolodner, R.M.; and Toro, G. Depression of plasma testosterone levels aftrer chronic intensive marijuana use. *New England Journal of Medicine*, 290:872–874, 1974.

Kuehnle, J.; Mendelson, J.H.; Davis, D.R.; and New, P.F.J. Computed tomographic examination of heavy marihuana smokers. *Journal of the American Medical Association*, 237(12):1231–1232, 1977.

Lefkowitz, S.S., and Klager, K. Effect of delta-9-tetrahydrocannabinol on *in vitro* sensitization of mouse splenic lymphocytes. *Immunological Communications*, 7:557–566, 1978.

Leuchtenberger, C.; Leuchtenberger, R.; Zbinden, J.; and Schleh, E. Cytological and cytochemical effects of whole smoke and of the gas vapor phase from marijuana cigarettes on growth and DNA metabolism of cultured mammalian cells. In: Nahas, G.G., ed. *Marihuana: Chemistry, Biochemistry, and Cellular Effects*. New York: Springer-Verlag, 1976. Pp. 243–256.

Mayor's Committee on Marihuana. *The Marihuana Problem in the City of New York. Sociological, Medical, Psychological and Pharmacological Studies*. Lancaster, Pa.: Jaques Cattell, 1944.

Miller, L.L., and Cornett, T.L. Marijuana: Dose effects on pulse rate, subjective estimates of intoxication, free recall and recognition memory. *Pharmacology, Biochemistry and Behavior*, 9:573–577, 1978.

Moskowitz, H., and McGlothlin, W. Effects of marijuana on auditory signal detection. *Psychopharmacologia*, 40:137–145. 1974.

Moskowitz, H.; Sharma, S.; and Schapero, M. A comparison of the effects of marijuana and alcohol on visual functions. In: Lewis, M.I., ed. *Current Research on Marijuana*. New York: Academic Press, 1972. Pp. 129–150.

Moskowitz, H.; Sharma, S.; and Zieman, K. Duration of skills performace impairment. In: *Proceedings of the 25th Conference of the American Association of Automotive Medicine.* San Francisco, Calif.: the Association, 1981. Pp. 87–96.

Muller, F.H. Tabakmissbrauch und lungencarcinom. *Zeitschrift Krebforsch,* 49:57–84, 1939.

Nahas, G.G.; Suciu-Foca, N.; Armand, J.P.; and Morishima, A. Inhibition of cellular mediated immunity in marijuana smokers. *Science,* 183:419–420, 1974.

National Institute on Drug Abuse. *Marijuana and Youth—Clinical Observations on Motivation and Learning.* Washington, D.C.: Supt. of Docs., U.S. Govt. Print. Off., 1982.

National Institute on Drug Abuse. *National Survey on Drug Abuse, 1982.* Washington, D.C.: Supt. of Docs., U.S. Govt. Print. Off., in press, a.

National Institute on Drug Abuse. *Student Drug Use in America, 1982.* Washington, D.C.: Supt. of Docs., U.S. Govt. Print.Off., in press, b.

Novotny, M.; Lee, M.C.; and Bartle, K.D. A possible chemical basis for the higher mutagenicity of marihuana smoke as compared to tobacco smoke. *Experientia,* 32(3):280–282, 1976.

O'Donnell, J.A.; Voss, H.L.; Clayton, R.R.; Slatin, G.T.; and Room, R. G.W. *Young Men and Drugs—A Nationwide Survey,* National Institute on Drug Abuse. Research Monograph 5. DHEW Pub. No. (ADM)76-311. Washington, D.C.: Supt. of Docs., U.S. Govt. Print. Off., 1976.

Palsson, A.; Thulin, S.O.; and Tunving, K. Canabis psychoses in south Sweden. *Acta Psychiatrica Scandinavica,* 66:311–321, 1982.

Paul, M.I., and Carson, I.M. Marihuana and communication. *Lancet,* 2:270–271, 1973.

Peeke, S.C.; Jones, R.T.; and Stone, G.C. Effects of practice on marijuana-induced changes in reaction time. *Psychopharmacology,* 48:159–163, 1976.

Perez-Reyes, M.; Lipton, M.A.; Timmons, M.C.; Wall, M.E.; Brine, D.R.; and Davis, K.H. Pharmacology of orally administered delta-9-tetrahydrocannabinol. *Clinical Pharmacology and Therapeutics,* 14:48–55, 1973.

Petersen, B.H., Graham, J.; and Lemberger, L. Marihuana, tetrahydrocannabinol and T-cell function. *Life Sciences,* 19:395–400, 1976.

Petersen, B.H., and Lemberger, L. Effect of delta-9-tetrahydrocannabinol administration of antibody production in mice. *Federal Proceedings,* 35:333, 1976.

Petersen, R.C. Importance of inhalation patterns in determining effects of marijuana use. *Lancet,* 1:727–728, 1979.

Prakash, R., and Aronow, W.S. Effects of marihuana in coronary disease. Reply. *Clinical Pharmacology and Therapeutics,* 19(1):94–95, 1976.

Pruess, M.M., and Lefkowitz, S.S. Influence of maturity on immunosuppression by delta-9-tetrahydrocannabinol. *Proceedings of the Society for Experimental Biology and Medicine,* 158:350–353, 1978.

Rittenhouse, J.D. "Learning Drug Use. From 'Legal' Substance to Marijuana and Beyond." Paper presented at the American Psychological Association Annual Convention, Montreal, Canada, September 1980.

Rodin, E.A.; Domino, E.F.; and Porzak, J.P. The marihuana-induced "social high." Neurological and electroencephalographic concomitants. *Journal of the American Medical Association,* 213:1300–1302, 1970.

Rosenkrantz, H., and Fleischman, R.W. Effects of cannabis on lungs. In: Nahas, G.G., and Paton, W.D.M., eds. *Marihuana: Biological Effects. Analysis, Metabolism, Cellular Responses, Reproduction and Brain.* Oxford: Pergamon Press, 1979.

Rubin, V., and Comitas, L. *Ganja in Jamaica: The Effects of Marihuana.* New Hork: Anchor/Doubleday, 1976.

Sassenrath, E.N.; Banovitz, C.A.; and Chapman, L.F. Tolerance and reproductive deficit in primates chronically drugged with delta-9-THC. *Pharmacologist,* 21:210, 1979.

Silverstein, M.D., and Lessin, P.J. Normal skin test response in chronic marijuana users. *Science,* 186:740–742, 1974.

Smiley, A.M.; Moskowitz, H.; and Ziedman, K. Driving simulator studies of marijuana alone and in combination with alcohol. In: *Proceedings of the 25th Conference of the American Association for Automotive Medicine.* San Francisco, Calif.: the Association, 1981. Pp. 107–116.

Smith, D.E., and Mehl, C. An analysis of marijuana toxicity. *Clinical Toxicology,* 3:101–115, 1970.

Smith, G.M. and Fogg, C.P. Psychological predictors of early use, late use, and nonuse of marihuana among teenage students. In: Kandel, D.B., ed. *Longitudinal Research on Drug Use: Empirical Findings and Methodological Issues.* Washington, D.C.: Hemisphere, 1978. Pp. 101–113.

Spencer, D.J. Cannabis-induced psychosis. *British Journal of Addiction,* 65:369–372, 1970.

Stenchever, M.A.; Kunysz, T.J.; and Allen, M.A. Chromosome breakage in users of marihuana. *American Journal of Obstetrics and Gynecology,* 118:106–113, 1974.

Talbott, J.A., and Teague, J.W. Marihuana psychosis: Acute toxic psychosis associated with the use of cannabis derivatives. *Journal of the American Medical Association,* 210:299–302, 1969.

Tart, C.T. Marijuana intoxication: Common experiences. *Nature,* 226:701–704, 1970.

Tashkin, D.P.; Calvarese, B.M.; Simmons, M.S.; and Shapiro, B.J. Respiratory status of seventy-four habitual marijuana smokers. *Chest,* 78:699–706, 1980.

Tashkin, D.P.; Shapiro, B.J.; Lee, E.Y.; and Harper, C.E. Subacute effects of heavy marijuana smoking pulmonary function in healthy young males. *New England Journal of Medicine,* 294:125–129, 1976.

Tennant, F.S.: Preble, M.; Prendergast, T.J.; and Ventry, P. Medical manifestations associated with hashish. *Journal of the American Medical Association.* 216:1965–1969, 1971.

Treffert, D.A. Marijuana use in schizophrenia: A clear hazard. *American Journal of Psychiatry,* 135:1213–1215, 1978.

Turner, C.E. Chemistry and metabolism. In: Petersen, R.C., ed. *Marijuana Research Findings: 1980,* National Institute on Drug Abuse. Research Monograph 31. DHHS Pub. No. (ADM)80-1001. Washington, D.C.: Supt. of Docs., U.S. Govt. Print. Off., 1980. Pp. 81–97.

U.S. Public Health Service. *Smoking and Health. Report of the Advisory Committee to the Surgeon General of the Public Health Service.* Washington, D.C.: Supt. of Docs., U.S. Govt. Print. Off., 1964.

Warren, R.; Simpsom, H.; Hilchie, J.; Cimbura, G.; Lucas, D.; and Bennett, R. Drugs detected in fatally injured drivers in the Province of Ontario. In: Goldberg, L., ed. *Alcohol, Drugs and Traffic Safety.* Stockholm, Sweden: Almqvist and Wiksell, 1981. Pp. 203–217.

MARIJUANA AND HEALTH: REPORT OF A STUDY[3]

The Institute of Medicine (IOM) of the National Academy of Sciences has conducted a 15-month study of the health-related effects of marijuana, at the request of the Secretary of Health and Human Services and the Director of the National Institutes of Health. The IOM appointed a 22-member committee to:

- analyze existing scientific evidences bearing on the possible hazards to the health and safety of users of marijuana;
- analyze data concerning the possible therapeutic value and health benefits of marijuana;
- assess federal research programs in marijuana;
- identify promising new research directions, and make suggestions to improve the quality and usefulness of future research; and
- draw conclusions from this review that would accurately assess the limits of present knowledge and thereby provide a factual, scientific basis for the development of future government policy.

This assessment of knowledge of the health-related effects of marijuana is important and timely because marijuana is now the most widely used of all the illicit drugs available in the United States. In 1979, more than 50 million persons had tried it at least once. There has been a steep rise in its use during the past decade, particularly among adolescents and young adults, although there has been a leveling-off in its overall use among high school seniors in the past 2 or 3 years and a small decline in the percentage of seniors who use it frequently. Although substantially more high school students have used alcohol than have ever used marijuana, more high school seniors use marijuana on a daily or near-daily basis (9 percent) than alcohol (6 percent). Much of the heavy use of marijuana, unlike alcohol, takes place in school, where effects on behavior, cognition, and psychomotor performance can be particularly disturbing. Unlike alcohol, which is rapidly metabolized and eliminated from the body, the psychoactive components of

[3]Reprint of "Summary," prefatory statement of *Marijuana and Health: Report of a Study*, by the Commission of the Institute of Medicine. p 1-5. National Academy Press '82. Reprinted by permission of the National Academy Press, Washington, D.C.

marijuana persist in the body for a long time. Similar to alcohol, continued use of marijuana may cause tolerance and dependence. For all these reasons, it is imperative that we have reliable and detailed information about the effects of marijuana use on health, both in the long and short term.

What, then, did we learn from our review of the published scientific literature? Numerous acute effects have been described in animals, in isolated cells and tissues, and in studies of human volunteers; clinical and epidemiological observations also have been reported. This information is briefly summarized in the following paragraphs.

Effects on the Nervous System and on Behavior

We can say with confidence that marijuana produces acute effects on the brain, including chemical and electrophysiological changes. Its most clearly established acute effects are on mental functions and behavior. With a severity directly related to dose, marijuana impairs motor coordination and effects tracking ability and sensory and perceptual functions important for safe driving and the operation of other machines; it also impairs short-term memory and slows learning. Other acute effects include feelings of euphoria and other mood changes, but there also are disturbing mental phenomena, such as brief periods of anxiety, confusion, or psychosis.

There is not yet any conclusive evidence as to whether prolonged use of marijuana causes permanent changes in the nervous system or sustained impairment of brain function and behavior in human beings. In a few unconfirmed studies in experimental animals, impairment of learning and changes in electrical brain-wave recordings have been observed several months after the cessation of chronic administration of marijuana. In the judgment of the committee, widely cited studies purporting to demonstrate that marijuana effects the gross and microscopic structure of the human or monkey brain are not convincing; much more work is needed to settle this important point.

Chronic relatively heavy use of marijuana is associated with behavioral dysfunction and mental disorders in human beings, but available evidence does not establish if marijuana use under these circumstances is a cause or a result of the mental condition. There are similar problems in interpreting the evidence linking the use of marijuana to subsequent use of other illicit drugs, such as heroin or cocaine. Association does not prove a causal relation, and the use of marijuana may merely be symptomatic of an underlying disposition to use psychoactive drugs rather than a "stepping stone" to involvement with more dangerous substances. It is also difficult to sort out the relationship between use of marijuana and the complex symptoms known as the amotivational syndrome. Self-selection and effects of the drug are probably both contributing to the motivational problems seen in some chronic users of marijuana.

Thus, the long-term effects of marijuana on the human brain and on human behavior remain to be defined. Although we have no convincing evidence thus far of any effects persisting in human beings after cessation of drug use, there may well be subtle but important physical and psychological consequences that have not been recognized.

Effects on the Cardiovascular and Respiratory Systems

There is good evidence that the smoking of marijuana usually causes acute changes in the heart and circulation that are characteristic of stress, but there is no evidence to indicate that a permanently deleterious effect on the normal cardiovascular system occurs. There is good evidence to show that marijuana increases the work of the heart, usually by raising heart rate and, in some persons, by raising blood pressure. This rise in workload poses a threat to patients with hypertension, cerebrovascular disease, and coronary atherosclerosis.

Acute exposure to marijuana smoke generally elicits bronchodilation; chronic heavy smoking of marijuana causes inflammation and pre-neoplastic changes in the airways, similar to those produced by smoking of tobacco. Marijuana smoke is a complex mixture that not only has many chemical components (including carbon monoxide and "tar") and biological effects similar to those of tobacco smoke, but also some unique ingredients. This suggests the strong possibility that prolonged heavy smoking of marijuana, like tobacco, will lead to cancer of the respiratory tract and to serious impairment of lung function. Although there is evidence of impaired lung function in chronic smokers, no direct confirmation of the likelihood of cancer has yet been provided, possibly because marijuana has been widely smoked in this country for only about 20 years, and data have not been collected systematically in other countries with a much longer history of heavy marijuana use.

Effects on the Reproductive System and on Chromosomes

Although studies in animals have shown that Δ-9-THC (the major psychoactive constituent of marijuana) lowers the concentration in blood serum of pituitary hormones (gonadotropins) that control reproductive functions, it is not known if there is a direct effect on reproductive tissues. Delta-9-THC appears to have a modest reversible suppressive effect on sperm production in men, but there is no proof that it has a deleterious effect on male fertility. Effects on human female hormonal function have been reported, but the evidence is not convincing. However, there is convincing evidence that marijuana interferes with ovulation in female monkeys. No satisfactory studies of the relation between use of marijuana and female fertility and child-bearing have been carried out. Although Δ-9-THC is known to cross the placenta readily and to cause birth defects when administered in large doses to experimental animals, no adequate clinical studies have been carried out to determine if marijuana use can harm the human fetus. There is no conclusive evidence of teratogenicity in human offspring, but a slowly developing or low-level effect might be undetected by the studies done so far. The effects of marijuana on reproductive function and on the fetus are unclear; they may prove to be negligible, but further research to establish or rule out such effects would be of great importance.

Extracts from marijuana smoke particulates ("tar") have been found to produce dose-related mutations in bacteria; however, Δ-9-THC, by itself, is not mutagenic. Marijuana and Δ-9-THC do not appear to break chromosomes, but marijuana may affect chromosome segregation during cell division, resulting in an abnormal number of chromosomes in daughter cells. Although these results are of concern, their clinical significance is unknown.

The Immune System

Similar limitations exist in our understanding of the effects of marijuana on other body systems. For example, some studies of the immune system demonstrate a mild, immunosuppressant effect on human beings, but other studies show no effect.

Therapeutic Potential

The committee also has examined the evidence on the therapeutic effects of marijuana in a variety of medical disorders. Preliminary studies suggest that marijuana and its derivatives or analogues might be useful in the treatment of the raised intraocular pressure of glaucoma, in the control of the severe nausea and vomiting caused by cancer chemotherapy, and in the treatment of asthma. There also is some preliminary evidence that a marijuana constituent (cannabidiol) might be helpful in the treatment of certain types of epileptic seizures, as well as for spastic disorders and other nervous system diseases. But, in these and all other conditions, much more work is needed. Because marijuana and Δ-9-THC often produce troublesome psychotropic or cardiovascular side-effects that limit their therapeutic usefulness, particularly in older patients, the greatest therapeutic potential probably lies in the use of synthetic analogues of marijuana derivatives with higher ratios of therapeutic to undersirable effects.

The Need for More Research on Marijuana

The explanation for all of these unanswered questions is insufficient research. We need to know much more about the metabolism of the various marijuana chemical compounds and their biologic effects. This will require many more studies in animals, with particular emphasis on subhuman primates. Basic pharmacologic information obtained in animal experiments will ultimately have to be tested in clinical studies on human beings.

Until 10 or 15 years ago, there was virtually no systematic, rigorously controlled research on the human health-related effects of marijuana and its major constituents. Even now, when standardized marijuana and pure synthetic cannabinoids are available for experimental studies, and good qualitative methods exist for the measurement of Δ-9-THC and its metabolites in body fluids, well-designed studies on human beings are relatively few. There are difficulties in studying the clinical effects of marijuana in human beings, particularly the effects of long-term use. And yet, without such studies the debate about the safety or hazard of marijuana will remain unresolved. Prospective cohort studies, as well as retrospective case-control studies, would be useful in identifying long-term behavioral and biological consequences of marijuana use.

The federal investment in research on the health-related effects of marijuana has been small, both in relation to the expenditure on other illicit drugs and in absolute terms. The committee considers the research particularly inadequate when viewed in light of the extent of marijuana use in this country, especially by young people. We believe there should be a greater investment in research on marijuana, and that investigator-initiated research grants should be the primary vehicle of support.

The committee considers all of the areas of research on marijuana that are supported by the National Institute on Drug Abuse to be important, but we did not judge the appropriateness of the allocation of resources among those areas, other than to conclude that there should be increased emphasis on studies in human beings and other primates.

Conclusions

The scientific evidence published to date indicates that marijuana has a broad range of psychological and biological effects, some of which, at least under certain conditions, are harmful to human health. Unfortunately, the available information does not tell us how serious this risk may be.

Our major conclusion is that what little we know for certain about the effects of marijuana on human health—and all that we have reason to suspect—justifies serious national concern. Of no less concern is the extent of our ignorance about many of the most basic and important questions about the drug. Our major recommendation is that there be a greatly intensified and more comprehensive program of research into the effects of marijuana on the health of the American people.

MARIJUANA POLICY AND DRUG MYTHOLOGY[4]

Since the early 1960's the use of marijuana as an intoxicant by a growing proportion of the American population has been an issue of major national concern. Despite repeated warnings of possible adverse health consequences and persistent efforts by law enforcement agencies to restrict the supply and use of marijuana, available data indicate that experimentation with or regular use of the drug is no longer restricted to a small minority of Americans. In 1979, for example, 68 percent of young adults between the ages of 18 and 25 reported having tried marijuana; 35.4 percent reported having used marijuana in the last month. Among adults over age 26, the proportion having ever used marijuana has more than doubled since 1971, from 9.2 percent to 19.6 percent.

[4]Reprint of an article by Louis Lasagna and Gardner Lindzey, members of the Committee on Substance Abuse and Habitual Behavior, National Research Council, National Academy of Sciences. *Society*. p 67–80. Ja.–F. '83. Published by permission of Transaction, Inc. from *Society*, Vol. 20, No. 2, copyright © 1983 by Transaction, Inc.

Although "the marijuana problem" may be viewed as of recent origin, marijuana is not a new drug. The cannabis plant has been cultivated and used both for its intoxicating properties and for its fiber (hemp) throughout the world for more than ten thousand years. At various times and places attempts have been made to restrict its use as an intoxicant; at other times and places its virtues have been extolled for medical purposes, and it has played a significant role in religious ritual. Because cannabis is easily grown—indeed, it is one of the hardiest of all plant species—its resin has been used for centuries along with tobacco, fermented distillates of grains and fruits (alcohol), and opium derivatives as one means of relieving stresses associated with daily life.

Despite its long history, the use of cannabis as an intoxicant was relatively unknown in the United States until the latter part of the nineteenth century, and even then its use as a drug was restricted to a tiny fraction of the population, primarily immigrants from Mexico. The first efforts to restrict its use in this country did not occur until 1911, when Congress, which at that time was considering proposals for federal antinarcotics legislation, listened to arguments that cannabis should be included in the list of illegal drugs. That effort failed, but during the next two decades a number of state legislatures moved to prohibit the possession of marijuana unless prescribed by a physician. It was not until 1937, when the Marijuana Tax Law was enacted, that the federal government became involved in the attempt to control its use. Even this law recognized the industrial uses of hemp and also exempted the seeds of the plant, which were then being sold as bird feed. In 1956, Congress included marijuana in the Narcotics Act of that year and, in 1961, the United Nations adopted the Single Convention on Narcotic Drugs, the terms of which state that each participating country could "adopt such measures as may be necessary to prevent misuse of, and illicit traffic in, the leaves of the cannabis plant." Congress approved participation in the convention in 1967 and three years later passed the Comprehensive Drug Abuse Prevention and Control Act, which provides the basis for current federal prohibitions regarding marijuana use.

Despite this history it was not until the 1960s that most Americans became aware of marijuana. The political and cultural protests of that period focused public attention on young people, their life-styles, and their use of drugs, including marijuana. That period created the context in which public policies regarding marijuana use have been debated since the early 1970s. For the first time marijuana use was not restricted to minority groups and fringe elements of society: many of the new users were native-born, middle-class, white college students. Without doubt, the political and cultural context in which marijuana emerged as an issue of national concern has strongly influenced the subsequent policy debate about its use.

The policy debate about marijuana use has also brought into sharp focus two conflicting but deeply held beliefs of large and overlapping segments of the American population. To many, the use of drugs of any kind solely for the purpose of producing states of intoxication is abhorrent, entirely apart from any presumed health effects. At the same time, many people strongly defend the right of individuals privately to indulge their desires, so long as others are not adversely affected. Adding to the complexity of the issues are continuing uncertainties about the health and developmental consequences of marijuana use, concern over the growing number of adolescent users, the social consequences of prosecuting otherwise law-abiding citizens for possession and use of marijuana, the relationship between the distribution of marijuana and that of other illegal drugs, the costs of enforcement of current laws, and the economic implications of the persistence of very large illegal markets.

Marijuana is not a harmless drug. Although available evidence suggests that marijuana may be less likely than opiates, barbiturates, or alcohol to induce psychological and physical dependence in its users, it has the capacity to reduce the effective functioning of individuals under its influence, and prolonged or excessive use may cause serious harmful biological and social effects in many users.

The recent report, *Marijuana and Health*, of the Institute of Medicine, concludes: "The scientific evidence published to date indicates that marijuana has a broad range of psychological and biological effects some of which, at least under certain conditions, are harmful to human health. Unfortunately, the available information does not tell us how serious this risk may be." Overall, the report concludes: "[W]hat little we know for certain about the effects of marijuana on human health—and all that we have reason to suspect—justifies serious national concern."

Dangers of Marijuana

Over the past forty years, marijuana has been accused of causing an array of antisocial effects, including: in the 1930's provoking crime and violence; in the early 1950's, leading to heroin addiction; and in the late 1960's, making people passive, lowering motivation and productivity, and destroying the American work ethic in young people. Although beliefs in these effects persist among many people, they have not been substantiated by scientific evidence.

Concerns about how marijuana affects citizenship, motivation, and job performance have become less salient in recent years as marijuana has moved into the mainstream of society and has become less exclusively associated with radicals, hippies, or disadvantaged minorities. Though there is still widespread belief that haevy marijuana use may be incompatible with a responsible, productive life, evidence that marijuana has not adversely affected either the productivity or the sense of social responsibility of some groups of users has tempered earlier fears of a widespread "amotivational syndrome." Research that correlates marijuana use with undesirable behavior, such as alienation or inattention to school studies, has not established the direction of causality or ruled out spurious associations. This issue, however, continues to be the subject of lively controversy and the Institute of Medicine report concludes that "it appears likely that both self-selection and authentic drug effects contribute to the 'motivational' problems seen in somes chronic marijuana users."

Recently, a body of literature has accumulated that reports on links between marijuana use and such health impairments as lung disease, chromosome damage, reduced reproductive function, and brain dysfunction. In some areas—for example, effects on the nervous system and behavior and on the cardiovascular and respiratory systems—there is clear evidence that marijuana produces acute short-term effects. According to *Marijuana and Health*:

With a severity directly related to dose, marijuana impairs motor coordination and affects tracking ability and sensory and perceptual functions important for safe driving and the operation of other machines . . . [It also] increases the work of the heart, usually by raising the heart rate and, in some persons, by raising blood pressure.

There is as yet no such clear evidence on the possible long-term effects in these areas, or of other potential health consequences of marijuana use; further research is needed. In addition, most studies on human populations have been laboratory studies of young, healthy, adult males. Differential effects of marijuana use on the elderly, on pregnant women, on groups that are psychiatrically vulnerable or at risk for disease or dysfunction, and particularly on adolescents have not been studied systematically.

In our view, the most troublesome aspects of marijuana use are its potential effects on the development of adolescents. Parents as well as a number of clinicians and researchers are concerned that the social and intellectual development of teenagers may be harmed by chronic marijuana use. There is good evidence that intoxication may seriously impair such important skills as comprehension and retention of newly presented educational materials. Rapidly growing tissues have been shown to be particularly vulnerable to some, although by no means all, toxic agents, and there is at least a possibility that toxic effects may be subtle and not clearly manifest until adulthood. Scientifically, these are difficult relationships to identify, and the research to date is still insufficient to strongly support any relationship.

Perhaps more significant than any lasting biological effect is the effect of the drug in different patterns of use on emotional development, on the formation of habits, and on the acquisition of coping skills for stress situations. Indeed, although the many issues raised by the use of intoxicants to escape stressful challenge have not been systematically studied, the evident attractiveness of marijuana to many adolescents, and its possible dose-related interference with the study and hard work needed for intellectual development in the crucial high-school years, make this a special matter for concern. This is particularly so in light of the fact that, unlike alcohol, marijuana is used by many adolescents during school hours. Finally, reports of the effects of marijuana use on automobile driving skills are worrisome.

This Committee has reviewed the scientific literature surveys of marijuana effects on health and behavior, including the major recent study conducted by the Institute of Medicine and those by the National Institute on Drug Abuse, Tashkin et al., Nahas, and Fried. We agree with the conclusions of the Institute of Medicine report that it is likely that long-term heavy marijuana use will be shown to result in measurable damage to health, just as long-term chronic tobacco and alcohol use have proven to cause such damage. It is evident that the full impact of marijuana use on human health will not be clear without careful epidemiological studies involving substantial populations of users—a matter of some decades—even though it is predictable that this drug—like all others—will cause harm in some of its users, particularly in its heaviest users, and among these, in its heaviest adolescent users. At this time,, however, our judgement as to behavioral and health-related hazards is that the research has not established a danger both large and grave enough to override all other factors affecting a policy decision.

Current Marijuana Policies

Current federal and state marijuana laws are in part governed by international treaty. The major federal law relevant to marijuana is the Comprehensive Drug Abuse Prevention and Control Act of 1970, which repealed all prior federal legislation and reduced federal penalties for possession and sale. Although marijuana possession and sale are still prohibited, possession has been reduced from a felony to a misdemeanor offense; the maximum penalty for a first offense is $5,000 and one year's imprisonment. The Act also provides for conditional discharge by which first offenders found guilty of simple possession or casual transfer (which is treated as simple possession) may be placed on probation for up to one year.

The Uniform Controlled Substance Act of 1970, drafted by the National Conference of Commissioners on Uniform State Laws, was designed to make state laws more compatible with the new federal law. Like the federal act, the Uniform Act reclassified marijuana as a hallucinogen rather than a narcotic and reduced the penalty for possession from the felony to the misdemeanor level; a majority of the states have adopted the Uniform Act. Eleven states have withdrawn the criminal sanction from possession for personal use. In these states, arrest has been replaced with a traffic-ticket type of citation, and a small fine is the sole allowable penalty. About thirty states include some provision for conditional discharge of first offenders, and about a dozen of them provide for all records of the offense to be expunged. The Alaska Supreme Court ruled in 1975 that possession for personal use by adults at home was protected by the constitutional right to privacy and hence was not subject to any penalty.

State penalties for second-offense possession and for selling marijuana are extremely variable. Sale is almost always a felony, with maximum sentences ranging from two years to life, although casual transfer, or "accommodation," is sometimes exempt from felony treatment. All but fifteen jurisdictions punish cultivation as heavily as they do sale; the Uniform Act includes the two in the same classification (manufacture), with the same penalty provisions.

Federal prohibition of small-scale possession is virtually unenforced. At the March 1977 House of Representatives hearings on decriminalization, the chief of the criminal division of the Department of Justice testified that the federal government no longer effectively prosecuted the use of marijuana, "nor do we, under any conceivable way, in the Federal Government have the resources to do so." In terms of its effects from a law enforcement point of view, the present official federal policy of complete prohibition does not differ in fact from a policy of prohibition of supply only. Complete prohibition is the federal law, but partial prohibition is the practice. However, the law, even though partly unenforced, has probably had a restraining influence on the willingness of states to adopt policies of less than complete prohibition. The states traditionally have followed the federal lead in drug abuse legislation, although they are not legally required to do so. In summary, in most states and according to federal law, U.S. marijuana policy is one of *complete prohibition*—that is, prohibition of both supply and use.

Major alternatives to complete prohibition include *prohibition of supply only*—called partial prohibition—and *regulation*. Prohibition of supply only means having no penalty (or only civil penalties) for use, possession, or, sometimes, "casual transfer" of small quantities of marijuana, while having criminal penalties for manufacture, importation, or commercial sale of marijuana. Regulation means not only eliminating penalties for use but also allowing controlled production and distribution. In this discussion, the terms "complete prohibition" and "prohibition of supply and use" are used interchangeably. The terms "partial prohibition," "prohibition of supply only," and "decriminalization" are also used as equivalent. The terms "partial prohibition" or "prohibition of supply only" are preferable since many people seem to regard decriminalization as the equivalent of legalization or regulation—which it most certainly is not. (The policy of partial prohibition has also been called the vice model.) Finally, "regulation" and "legalization" are used as equivalent terms.

Within each of the three broad policy options—complete prohibition, prohibition of supply only, and regulation—numerous subsidiary policy choices exist. For example, a policy of complete prohibition necessitates decisions about the resources to be devoted to enforcement, the appropriate penalties to be imposed for violations, and whether marijuana should be made available for any medical uses. Under a policy of prohibition of supply only, decisions must still be made about penalties and permitted medical uses. In addition, one must also determine how to distinguish between users and suppliers; whether cultivation should be permitted; how strong preparations of the cannabis plant, such as hashish, should be treated; whether to criminalize small-scale casual transfers, made with or without payment; and what should be done about certain specific behaviors, such as the public use of marijuana and the operation of motor vehicles under the influence of the drug. Under a policy of regulation, some of the issues to be decided are the type of control system (e.g., state monopoly or licensed sale), the rules as to potency and quality, and appropriate penalties for violation of the system's rule.

The variety of choices within each of the broad policy options suggests that none can be characterized in a monolithic way. Some regulatory systems could be so stringent as to have results similar to prohibitory laws: e.g., a regulatory system that raised the price drastically above what the illegal market charges. Similarly, lack of enforcement could strongly reduce the impact of a prohibitory option. As already noted, this latter effect has already occurred in some jurisdictions in which the law provides for complete prohibition but users are not in fact prosecuted.

An attempt to describe a full array of policy options together with associated benefits and detriments of each of them was made by the National Commission on Marijuana and Drug Abuse in its 1972 report, *Marijuana: A Signal of Misunderstanding*. With respect to the major policy choices, the Commission did a thorough job. The members and staff recognized the limited knowledge base for their deliberations and subsequently recommended that a second commision be appointed to review the situation four years later. Such a follow-up commission was never appointed. It seems appropriate, then, that this Committee reappraise the Commission's work in light of subsequent research findings, especially those relating to recent changes in marijuana policies.

The Commission examined the spectrum of social policies available to control marijuana use and the benefits and detriments of implementing each policy. The legal alternatives presented included those identified above: complete prohibition, prohibition of supply only, and regulatory approaches. The Commission emphasized that choosing among the three approaches requires consideration of the social milieu, cultural values, and practicalities of implementation. The Commission considered such social conditions particularly important in examining marijuana controls because both use of the drug and the laws prohibiting supply and use had symbolic importance, representing a clash of values between a dominant culture that opposed marijuana use and a large minority that either used marijuana or condoned its use. The probable effects of the various policies considered by the Commission include changes in use patterns, enforcement costs, and influence on related social concerns such as the marketing of other illicit drugs and general respect for law.

The Commission commented on all three broad policy options. It suggested first that total prohibition has resulted in costly enforcement, alienation of the young, discrimination through selective enforcement, some deterrence of supply (especially to middle-aged and middle-class potential users), but minimal deterrence of use by those with access to the drug. Second, the Commission stated its belief that prohibition of supply only would support the official policy of discouraging use, but at the same time would recognize the practical difficulties of attempting to eliminate use. The report listed a number of choices that might be made under a system of partial prohibition and described some of the practical problems they might entail (e.g., the need to distinguish between casual and commercial distributors). Finally, the Commission described regulation as a policy that only mildly disapproved of occasional use and that concentrated on controlling excessive use, but was mostly designed to lower the costs of prohibiting the drug. The Commission argued that marijuana consumption would increase considerably if complete prohibition were replaced by regulation. In additon, the Commission considered a major drawback of any regulatory system to be that its elimination of the main symbol of society's disapproval—criminal sanctions—would cause resentment among the nonuser majority of the population. Marijuana was described as being symbolic of countercultural life-styles: "the drug's symbolism creates a risk of strong political reaction to any liberalization of the present laws by older members of the society."

On balance, the Commission concluded that, since the threat of punishment had not apparently deterred the millions of people who had already used marijuana, the replacement of complete by partial prohibition would not produce a significant increase in marijuana use. Consequently, the Commission recommended that individual marijuana users should not be subject to criminal prosecution for their private use or possession of small amounts of the drug, and that, on balance, the best policy was one of prohibition of supply only. In accordance with this view, the Commission recommended that federal and state laws should be amended to achieve partial prohibition. In the decade since the Commission report, a number of states have changed their laws in varying ways. These legal changes can be viewed as natural experiments, and the data from them can be used to reassess the Commission's conclusions regarding these policies.

Complete and Partial Prohibition

To compare the two types of marijuana control policies presently used in the United States—prohibition of supply and use and prohibition of supply only—we need to consider only the one particular in which they differ: the application of criminal sanctions against marijuana users. To compare the effects of the two policies, we can examine the effects of the prohibition of use and determine whether prohibition results in more costs than benefits or vice versa.

In recent years the prohibition of marijuana use has come under increasing criticism. Many students of the U.S. marijuana situation, including the National Commission on Marijuana and Drug Abuse, members of Congress, political analysts, and legal experts, have suggested that existing laws prohibiting marijuana use be repealed. These suggestions have been prompted by the failure of current policies to deter large numbers of users, the consequent criminalization of large numbers of young Americans, and the high social costs of such law enforcement. A number of professional associations and agencies have also gone on record in support of the removal of all criminal penalties for the private possession and use of marijuana as a means of reducing the economic costs of law enforcement and the social costs of arrest or imprisonment (criminalization) of young people who are otherwise not criminally involved or labeled. The organizations and agencies that have expressed this view include the American Medical Association, the American Bar Association, the American Public Health Association, the Canadian Commission of Inquiry into the Non-Medical Use of Drugs, the National Council of Churches, the National Advisory Commission on Criminal Justice Standards and Goals, the National Commission on Marijuana and Drug Abuse, among others. Eleven states, with one-third of the nation's population, have adopted some version of partial prohibition or "decriminalization." (In Oregon, Alaska, Maine, Colorado, California, Ohio, Minnesota, Mississippi, New York, North Carolina, and Nebraska, citations and small fines have replaced arrests and incarceration for use-only marijuana-related offenses.)

At first glance, criminalizing the selling of marijuana might appear inconsistent with failing to punish its purchase. But in the drafting of laws, a line is often drawn between legal and illegal conduct so that the maximum reduction in the proscribed behavior can be gained at minimim social cost. Frequently it turns out that laws aimed solely at suppressing sales are more cost-effective in reducing both the possession and use of a substance than are laws that attempt to suppress possession directly. There are several reasons for this. First, there are fewer sellers than buyers; this permits a concentration of law enforcement efforts where they do the most good. Second juries are likely to be more sympathetic to a "mere" user, who may be ill-advised, than to a dealer making a profit from the weakness of others. Offenses treated under the vice model (partial prohibition) range from gambling—the person who takes illegal bets is guilty of a crime while the person who places them is not—to the offense of selling new automobiles not equipped with seat belts—the seller, not the buyer, is guilty of an offense. Even Prohibition in 1919 never criminalized the possession or use of alcohol, only its manufacture and sale.

Probably the most important fact about a policy of prohibition of supply only is that where it has been adopted it has apparently not led to appreciably higher levels of marijuana use than would have existed if use were also prohibiited. The National Commission on Marijuana and Drug Abuse's speculations about the lack of change in use pattern resulting from repeal of prohibitions on use have been confirmed by data since 1972. Reports from California, Oregon, and Maine indicate no appreciable increase in use following decriminalization of use, at least in the short term.

Oregon, the first state to repeal prohibition of use (in October 1973), has been studied in a series of Drug Abuse Council surveys. Surveys in 1974 and 1975 showed no major increase following decriminalization. While the percentage of adults who were current users had increased by January 1977 (from 20 to 24 percent), use had increased similarly nationwide in the same period, suggesting that the causes for the adult increase in Oregon were the same as those for increases in the rest of the country rather than the result of changes in the law. Indeed, the percentage of adult ever-users in Oregon in 1976 (24 percent) was lower than the average percentage of adult ever-users in the western United States (28 percent) in 1975–1976, although higher than the national average (21.3 percent). (It should be noted that the aggregate use rates in the western United States are heavily weighted by use rates in California, the largest western state, which had relatively high rates even prior to the state repeal of prohibition of use.) That the increase in use in Oregon from 1973 to 1976 was probably not due to the new law is suggested by other survey data. Only a small proportion of nonusers said fear of legal prosecution was a reason for nonuse in 1974, 1975, and 1976. On the question of the fear of health dangers, Drug Abuse Council survey data show that such fear decreased significantly over those years but has increased since 1976.

The state of Maine, which repealed criminal penalties for marijuana use in May 1976, surveyed the effects of legislation in July and August 1978. Its study concluded that the change from criminal to civil penalties has not caused a large increase in marijuana use: less than 1 percent of all adults and 3.1 percent of all high-school students reported any increase in their use as a result of the new law, 3.5 percent of adult regular users and 7 percent of high-school regular users reported any increase in their use directly attributable to the change in the law. There is also preliminary evidence, based on a nationwide study of high-school students between 1975 and 1979 and given in testimony in 1980 before the Senate Subcommittee on Criminal Justice, that "any increase in marijuana use in the decriminalized states, taken as a group, was equal to or less than the increases being observed in the rest of the country where decriminalization was not taking place." It could be argued that because de facto repeal of prohibition of use has been taking place throughout the country, one should not expect to see larger increases in use in states that legally decriminalize than in others. Even if this is true, however, the important point is that the legal change to decriminalization does not, in itself, appear to lead to increases in use.

This lack of change is not particularly surprising. The statistical chance that any person would be apprehended for his or her use is, in fact, extremely low throughout the United States (though the large number of users is sufficient to generate a substantial volume of arrests in states that do prohibit use). As a result, it is hard to imagine that the deterrent effect of prohibition laws on any given user would be very great.

It has been suggested that repeal of government prohibitions might change attitudes related to health or morals, perhaps symbolizing that health officials certify marijuana use to be safe. The absence of large increases in marijuana use in repeal states, however, indicates that either the change in policy has not had such a symbolic effect, or that, if it has, its causal significance is not appreciable—though it must be acknowledged that changes of this type might take generations to occur.

The costs of policies directed at the user are not negligible, although actual savings in law enforcement costs attributable to repeal of prohibition of use per se are difficult to estimate. The difficulty arises in part because marijuana arrests have decreased nationally in recent years, reflecting the overall tendency to relax enforcement of marijuana laws, and that change could lead to inaccurate estimates of the impact of repeal. Nevertheless, reduced law enforcement activities seem to have led to substantial savings in states that have repealed laws that prohibit use.

California made a careful study of the economic impact of its law repealing prohibition of use, which went into effect in January 1976. The law reduced the penalty for personal possession of one ounce or less of marijuana from a possible felony to a citable misdemeanor, punishable as an infraction with a maximum fine of $100 without regard to prior possession offenses. Criminal custody, booking, and pretrial incarceration procedures were eliminated. Possession of more than one ounce was also made a misdemeanor, with a maximum fine of $500, six months in jail, or both. According to the study, these changes resulted in a 74 percent reduction in what the state had been spending yearly to enforce its marijuana laws. (Estimates of what the state had been spending ranged from $35 million to more than $100 million yearly.)

In addition to its economic benefits, repealing prohibition of use saves the social costs of criminalizing the marijuana user. In recent years, close to four hundred thousand people have been arrested each year for marijuana-related offenses despite the general nonenforcement of criminal sanctions for use. Only a small fraction of the arrests are made under federal law, largely for importation of marijuana. About 85 percent of all marijuana-related arrests are for possession, usually of one ounce or less.

A study by the National Commission on Marijuana and Drug Abuse of a sample consisting of some three thousand of the people arrested for marijuana-related offenses in 1970 indicated that the marijuana arrest was usually the arrestee's first experience with the criminal justice system, particularly among juveniles. Yet, according to the 1977 testimony of Jay Miller of the American Civil Liberties Union to the Select Committee on Narcotics Abuse and Control, "it is standard practice for law enforcement agencies to report such offenses to prospective employers, licensing agencies, and other authorities as 'narcotic drug arrests.'" Thus young users, who are often otherwise law-abiding people, are subject to an arrest record, or even a prison term, with implications extending into many aspects of their lives.

Alienation from the rule of law in democratic society may be the most serious cost of current marijuana laws. The National Commission on Marijuana and Drug Abuse was concerned that young people who see no rational basis for the legal distinction between alcohol and marijuana may become cynical about America's political institutions and democratic process. The American Bar Association report concurs in the view that marijuana laws that criminalize the millions of Americans who have used marijuana engender disrespect for the law.

Although the National Commission on Marijuana and Drug Abuse concluded that prohibition of supply only would be a better policy than prohibition of supply and use, it felt that a serious disadvantage of such a course would be the upset and moral outrage such a policy would engender. Hindsight now shows that the Commission was mistaken in predicting a strong uniform public reaction to the adoption of partial prohibition policies. Experience since 1973 has shown that repeal of criminal penalties for use of marijuana has not been accompanied by massive public protest in the states in which it occurred and, in fact, has had the approval of the majority of citizens in those states.

Nationally, attitude trends are consistent with the experience of the repeal states. R. Roffman, in a 1978 issue of *Contemporary Drug Problems*, reports that public opinion surveys indicate a slowly increasing preference for a reduction in penalties for marijuana offenses; a 1975 national survey by the National Institute on Drug Abuse found that 52 percent of American adults favored only a fine or probation for small marijuana offenses; and a 1977 Gallup poll showed that 28 percent of the public favored legalization, compared with 12 percent in 1969.

Prohibited and Regulated Markets

Policy implementation does not occur in an ideal world. Prohibition of supply has not, in practice, meant that no one has had access to marijuana—though this may have been the intent of those who framed that law. Similarly, regulation of supply does not mean that everyone who uses marijuana will use it moderately, minimizing its harm. Prohibition of supply does make marijuana less accessbile than it might otherwise be to a large number of Americans, and thus it almost certainly reduces the total amount of the drug used and the number of users. Such reduction is the purpose of a partial prohibition policy and to some extent it is accomplished. Arguments for a regulated, legal supply of marijuana are largely based on the social cost and incomplete effectiveness of prohibition of supply and on the belief that regulating rather than prohibiting the supply would not lead to an unacceptable large increase in use.

Under a regulatory policy, the cultivation, importation, manufacture, distribution, retailing, and, of course, use of marijuana would no longer be illegal per se. Within this broad category, specific policy options range from a virtual withdrawl of the government from marijuana control (allowing the drug to be freely produced, advertised, and sold, very much as coffee is today—but protecting the consumer against harmful adulterants), to a carefully controlled system of licensing, to a government monopoly on retail sales, wholesale distribution, or manufacture of marijuana. Thus, controls might be placed on such factors as quality, potency, amount purchased, time and place of sales, age of buyers, etc. If marijuana were regulated as is alcohol, restrictions would derive from federal, state, or local statutes, with the majority of them not at the federal level. Regulations might also include legally fixed prices—as in state-controlled alcohol beverage retailing or as a consequence of the levying of excise taxes.

The specific form and content of any proposed regulatory system are very important for those faced with the decision as to whether and under what conditions to remove penalties for the distribution of marijuana, but such details are beyond the scope of this report.

The advantages of a policy of regulation include the disappearance of most illegal market activity, the savings in economic and social costs of law enforcement directed against illegal supply systems, better controls over the quality and safety of the product, and, possibly, increased credibility for warnings about risks. The major disadvantages are a consequence of increased marijuana use—increases in harm to physical health and to individual development and behavior.

The number of arrests for violations related to supply is much lower than for those related to use. But enforcement of prohibition of supply is far more costly per arrest. Long undercover investigations, the purchase of expensive hardware, and the major consumption of trial and correctional resources are largely attributable to the prohibition of supply.

The National Institute on Drug Abuse estimated that in 1974 costs for enforcement of marijuana laws totaled $600 million for state and local agencies. If we extrapolate from the 1977 date of the California State Office of Narcotics and Drug Abuse, about three-fourths of the total is spent enforcing the law against marijuana supply. The total federal drug abuse law enforcement budget was more than $400 million in 1979, about half of which was the budget for the Drug Enforcement Administration. At the federal level, authorities do not break down their expenditures on enforcement between marijuana and other drugs; virtually all of the federal resources that are allocated to marijuana are spent in attempting to enforce the laws against supply.

The task of attempting to make the prohibition of supply effective is, of course, formidable. In 1969 Operation Intercept demonstrated the practical difficulty of sealing off the Mexican border. In the weeks the operation lasted, hundreds of thousands of vehicles and passengers were searched every day; ensuing traffic jams caused expenditures by U.S. tourists and commuters to Mexico to drop 50–70 percent below normal. The situation was intolerable and the program was halted. However, the federal government has continued efforts to improve border surveillance and to penetrate trafficking networks. The White House Strategy Council on Drug Abuse notes that more than 5.6 million pounds of marijuana was seized at the Mexican border over a 12-month period in 1977–1978; a large increase over the 1.5 million pounds seized during the previous 12 months, "but a fraction of marijuana entering the country." Recently, the Council has suggested strengthening border surveillance by cooperative efforts of the Drug Enforcement Administration, the Customs Service, the Coast Guard, and the Department of State and by the use of the detection capabilities of the armed forces as well.

In our view, the prospects for major success in these ventures are not great. Nor is there much likelihood that some recently suggested measures against marijuana production outside the U.S. would make future prohibition of supply more effective. For example, the White House Strategy Council on Drug Abuse has supported crop eradication programs, provided that the proposed method of eradication is evaluated for possible health and environmental consequences and that a readily distinguishable marker is added to any chemical herbicides that are used, but the political obstacles to this course would be signficant. Entirely apart from the views of producer nations, which are likely to be quite negative, the public is unlikely to support the use of chemicals of unknown toxicity on an import product, legal or not, that may be used by large numbers of Americans. And irrespective of the degree of success of controlling imports, the problem of domestic production under a policy of partial prohibition remains. Although the illegal domestic industry is thought to account for only about 15 percent of American marijuana consumption, marijuana grows easily in many parts of the United States. The National Commission on Marijuana and Drug Abuse cited a Department of Agriculture estimate that in 1972 there were 5 million acres containing wild marijuana in the United States and an undetermined but obviously growing number of acres under cultivation.

Law enforcement costs are by no means the only costs of prohibition of supply. There are large amounts of money being made in marijuana—which, like any illegal business, carries with it the likelihood of corruption of public officials and the loss of tax dollars. Violence is also a cost of attempting to prohibit marijuana supply; this problem is not confined to illegal marijuana production abroad. There has been violence in marijuana-growing regions in the United States. The extent of such violence is not known with any precision, but there have been popular press reports of kidnappings, assaults, burglaries, and homicides known to be connected with the marijuana business in northern California and elsewhere.

Another major cost of attempts to prohibit the suply of marijuana is related to the fact that many illegal sellers of marijuana also sell other illegal drugs, e.g., PCP, amphetamines, and barbiturates. It is likely, therefore, that prohibition of the supply of marijuana increases access to and use of other illegal drugs through the creation of an illegal marketing system for all drugs. Little is known about the structures and activities of illicit drug markets. It is clear, however, that there are many small-scale marijuana dealers that many sellers service only their friends and acquaintances, and that those who sell marijuana are thereby more likely to come into contact with users and sellers of more dangerous drugs, to use such drugs, and to make them available to their clientele. Moreover, there is reason to believe that marijuana sellers may become socialized into other illegal activites.

The wide availability and use of marijuana are not only major factors in the cost of attempts to prohibit the supply of the drug, they also have implications for the likely magnitude of increases in use that could be expected under a regulatory policy. Greater use of marijuana under a regulatory policy is regarded as the most significant cost of such a policy. In an analysis of this potential cost, however,it is important to note that under the present policy of prohibition, prevalence and frequency of marijuana use are substantial and have increased in recent years. (The data indicating rates of use are based on self-reports; as such, their reliability and validity may be questioned. Nevertheless, studies of questions on drug use have consistently demonstrated reliable responses within the same instrument and over time. Furthermore, there are indications that most drug surveys do not have serious validity problems.)

A National Institute on Drug Abuse general household survey shows that 35.4 percent of the 18–25-year-olds in the United States report having used marijuana in the month preceding the survey. Yearly surveys show a steady increase from 1971 to 1979 in the percentage of people who report having ever used marijuana as well as in the percentage of people who report being current users. These survey results also indicate that between 1976 and 1977, the percentage of current users among 12–17-year-olds increased from 12.3 to 16.6 percent; this trend had leveled off by 1979 and has since shown a decline. *Student Drug Use in America 1975–1981*, an annual survey of national samples of some 17,000 high-school seniors published by the National Institute on Drug Abuse, indicates that 7.0 percent of the class of 1981 reported daily marijuana use, compared with 6.0 percent in 1975 and 10.7 percent in 1978, the peak year. There has been a similar trend in initial use at younger ages.

Although the present policy of prohibition of supply is not preventing the current levels of marijuana use, including use among the very young, it is probable that most strategies under a regulatory policy would result in an overall increase in use. Even more important than overall use rates, however, are likely changes in consumption patterns; such patterns are the most difficult changes to predict. The smallest increases in numbers of users can be expected to occur among those to whom marijuana is now most readily available—the young. *Student Drug Use in America* found that close to 90 percent of the high-school seniors in its national sample survey report that marijuana is "fairly easy" or "very easy" for them to get. This percentage remained relatively stable over the seven years, 1975–1981. At the same time the reported availability of most other illegal drugs (except cocaine) declined considerably. For example, while 46.2 percent of the 1975 high-school seniors said that LSD would be "fairly easy" or "very easy" to get, only 32.2 percent of the class of 1978 gave those responses. It would appear, therefore, that the reports of easy availability are not due to a tendency of adolescents to report any illegal drug as easy to get, but reflect their actual access to the drug. It might also be noted that only 13.9 percent of the class of 1978 reported having no friends who smoke marijuana; thus it is reasonable to expect that at least 86 percent have a factual basis for estimating the availability of the drug.

Other survey data corroborate these findings. A 1975 national survey by the Drug Abuse Council found that at least 70 percent of the high-school students in their sample reported marijuana "easy to get"; *Young Men and Drugs*, a 1976 monograph of the National Institute on Drug Abuse, reports similar results. There are no contrary reports for recent years. In sum, one can be reasonably confident that, at least with respect to older adolescents, the prohibition against supply does not succeed in suppressing access to marijuana.

Regulation could be expected to provide the greatest increase in availability to those to whom the drug is now least available, i.e., older adults who are not in contact with marijuana sellers or a drug-using subculture and who are most likely to avoid illegal "connections."

It has been argued that a serious cost of the adoption of a regulatory policy for marijuana is the likelihood that such a change might delude many people into believing that the drug is safe. As noted above, there is no indication that the elimination of penalties for marijuana use has caused the drug to be regarded as any less dangerous. Moreover, alcohol and tobacco are almost universally regarded as involving risks to health, and these drugs are already made available under regulatory systems.

To the extent that marijuana use causes harm, one is necessarily concerned about policy changes that will lead to increases in use. As previously noted, however, it is a fact that marijuana is already widely available despite the legal prohibition of supply and that, despite the best efforts of government under any foreseeable set of conditions, it will continue to be. Though a regulatory policy would increase the availability of the drug, estimates of the size of these increases, and associated increases in harm, must be weighed against estimates of the costs and weakness of continuing prohibitions of supply. In pragmatic terms, the issue is whether more harm would be done, overall, by retaining the partly effective, costly prohibition of supply or by moving to a system of legalized regulated sales—wherein presumably more people would use more marijuana, but some of the the costs imposed by prohibition of supply would be removed.

To this point, a policy of regulation has been discussed rather abstractly in contrast with the more concrete discussion of prohibition policies. Experimentation with varying systems of regulation followed by adjustment and readjustment based on experience would be necessary before those most appropriate for particular circumstances could be developed. This can be a complex matter. For instance, U.S. alcohol policy, developed with the repeal of Prohibition, consists of an umbrella of national policy and a wide variety of supporting state and local regulation. The national policy umbrella includes controls on importation, taxation, potency, packaging, labeling, advertising, use in fedearl jurisdictions (e.g., parks, military installations), and use in systems regulated by the federal government (e.g., air transportation); it also provides funds and guidelines for the treatment of casualties of excessive use. Under the umbrella policy, states and local jurisdictions regulate taxes, retail sales, hours of availability, age limits, and the like, where supply is legal, or prohibit sales entirely. Some states have monopoly systems for package sales, others use licensed private stores. Historically, under this system, the strictness of controls has reflected local sentiment about the consumption of alcohol. Although few "dry" jurisdictions exist today, various degrees of local "dryness" were quite widespread until very recently.

A regulated system of marijuana sale might attempt to moderate use by inhibiting the frequency of use and the amounts used, as well as by prescribing conditions of purchase and use. However, it is likely that under a regulatory system consumption would in great part be controlled by informal social norms—as it is today.

Manipulating the price of the drug is an obvious means of inhibiting use. It has been argued that most adults would be willing to pay a higher price for legal marijuana than they currently pay for illegal supplies in return for not having to seek out "connections" and being relieved of the feeling that they may be supporting organized crime. A high price would be comparatively more restrictive for young people—precisely those whom one would most want to discourage from use—since, though they seem affluent compared with young people in previous times, their budgets are in fact more constrained than those of adults. The possibility of illegal markets selling to young people remains, but today's kind of illegal market for marijuana would probably shrink greatly under a regulatory system in the same way that illegal alcohol distribution systems have become so scarce. Young users would be much more likely to gain access to marijuana by diversion from the legal market—as they do today for alcohol—or from homegrown plants than from a wholly illegal chain of distributors. Such a development would make marijuana selling a less profitable and status-producing occupation among the young.

It has been said that if legal limits were imposed on the potency of legally available marijuana, a substantial illegal market for high-potency forms of the drug, including hashish, would still exist. Since it is likely that there would continue to be some users who prefer high-potency forms of cannabis, this is a reasonable concern. But there is no compelling a priori reason to believe that a legal structure for retail marijuana sales, which includes limits on potency, would result in any increase in the availability and use of high-potency products.

Cultivation of marijuana by users is another issue that would have to be confronted in devising a regulatory system. Growing marijuana without payment of a tax might be treated as a revenue offense. Without criminal penalties or vigorous enforcement, however, deterrent effects would be minimal since marijuana can be grown indoors anywhere in the United States using artificial light—and at comparatively little expense. A recent British study of options for marijuana control, *Cannabis: Options for Control*, suggests that, from a law enforcement perspective, it is not feasible to attempt to control home cultivation. Whether users would take the trouble to grow their own marijuana would depend in part on the legal price. The relatively high prices that might be charged in order to discourage use and to increase revenues would also tend to encourage home cultivation. Whatever its disadvantages, however, the use of homegrown marijuana at least would not bring users into contact with those who illegally sell the drug. With respect to young people, moreover, marijuana under cultivation is much harder for children to hide from parents than is the purchased prepared drug, and cultivation by juveniles could remain illegal if age limits on use were imposed. Nonetheless, the treatment of home cultivation represents a major issue for the design of a regulatory system.

Excessive use may be discouraged by policies aimed at public education and at the use of the media, including a ban on commercial advertising. Although information on how to use drugs, on drug hazards, and on the attributes of drugs is passed along most effectively through informal channels, media nd education programs can make such information far more readily available.

Research on the communication of messages to the public has identified source credibility as a major factor contributing to the persuasive power of a message. It appears that the public is now extremely wary of some government information programs that attempt to influence health behaviors. The credibility of the federal government may be especially suspect when it issues health warnings about an illegal substance that it is clearly trying to prohibit. M. Rosenthal, in a 1979 article in the *Houston Law Review*, asserts that distrust of the government and the medical establishment has grown because of past exaggerations and distortions of the effects of some mind-altering drugs.

In an assessment of possibilities for governmental controls under a regulatory system, the operation of informal norms for controlling substance use practices must be taken into account. National experience with alcohol use, for example, provides evidence that there are informal rituals and sanctions that generally encourage moderation in the use of recreational drugs. Moreover, moderation is encouraged when a drug is introduced gradually, that is, to a growing population of users, like marijuana in the 1960s and early 1970s. One might expect that when a new drug is introduced into a society, governmental control would be particularly important since no informal controls for teaching people appropriate rules for use would have developed. If a potent drug is made widely available precipitously and very cheaply to a novice population, severe societal disruptions may occur: for example, the gin epidemics of early eighteenth-century England. Because in the past two decades informal norms for controlling marijuana use have spread in the United States under conditions of greatly increased availability of marijuana, there is reason to believe that widespread uncontrolled use would not occur under regulation. Indeed, regulation might facilitate patterns of controlled use by diminishing the "forbidden fruit" aspect of the drug and perhaps increasing the likelihood that an adolescent would be introduced to the drug through families and friends who practice moderate use, rather than through their heaviest-using, most drug-involved peers.

As has historically been the case with respect to alcohol, state governments differ in their approaches to marijuana. So long as present federal law continues to prohibit cultivation and distribution of marijuana, states cannot adopt a regulatory system, although they are legally free to reduce or eliminate their own penalties for sale and are not compelled to enforce federal laws. If federal law were changed, however, the institution of a regulatory system in one state would have reverberations in other states. Residents of states that continued to prohibit marijuana could be expected to cross state lines to purchase the drug in a state with a regulated system, thus further compromising the ability of states to enforce prohibition of supply among its residents. Furthermore, states that attempt to curtail consumption by raising prices might find their populations turning to lower-cost marijuana from neighboring states with lower prices. This is a familiar situation. Large numbers of both cigarettes and guns are smuggled illegally into New York from other states. Moreover, New Yorkers may travel to New Jersey to gamble in a casino, or Virginians to the District of Columbia to buy cheaper liquor. It is difficult to see how state prohibitions could remain effective if the number of states with regulatory systems grew very large unless the changes occurred in only one region of the country. However, there may be advantages in permitting a state-by-state approach. Conditions governing the costs and benefits both of partial prohibition and of regulation vary among the states. In this area of uncertainty, we may learn from experiment. If one regulatory system proved successful, other states would be more likely to adopt similar systems; similarly, if it worked poorly in one state, other states would be less inclined to adopt a regulatory policy.

The 1961 Single Convention on Narcotic Drugs, which now obligates the U.S. government to prevent the importation of marijuana and to prohibit the adoption of a licensing system by any state, is a serious (although not an insurmountable) obstacle to the adoption of a federal regulatory policy and the development of state licensing. The treaty allows a signatory to terminate its adherence to the agreement at any time after two years from the date of the convention. Of course the general impact of any move to withdraw from the convention includes a broad foreign policy context, which is beyond the expertise of this Committee to judge.

For the last decade, concern with health hazards attributable to marijuana has been rising. The hearts, lungs, reproductive functions, and mental abilities of children have been threatened by marijuana, and such threats are not to be taken lightly. Heavy use by anyone or any use by growing children should be discouraged. Although conclusive evidence is lacking of major, long-term public health problems caused by marijuana, they are worrisome possibilities, and both the reports and the a priori likelihood of developmental damage to some young users make marijuana use a cause for extreme concern.

Unanswered Questions

At the same time, the effectiveness of the present federal policy of complete prohibition falls far short of its goal—preventing use. An estimated fifty-five million Americans have tried marijuana, federal enforcement of prohibition of use is virtually nonexistent, and eleven states have repealed criminal penalties for private possession of small amounts and for private use. It can no longer be argued that use would be much more widespread and the problematic effects greater today if the policy of complete prohibition did not exist: The existing evidence on policies of partial prohibition indicates that partial prohibition has been as effective in controlling consumption as complete prohibition and has entailed considerably smaller social, legal, and economic costs. On balance, therefore, we believe that a policy of partial prohibition is clearly preferable to a policy of complete prohibition of supply and use.

We believe, further, that current policies directed at controlling the supply of marijuana should be seriously reconsidered. The demonstrated ineffectiveness of control of use through prohibition of supply and the high costs of implementing such a policy make it very unlikely that any kind of partial prohibition policy will be effective in reducing marijuana use significantly below present levels. Moreover, it seems likely to us that removal of criminal sanctions will be given serious consideration by the federal government and by the states in the foreseeable future. Hence, a variety of alternative policies should be considered.

At this time, the form of specific alternatives to current policies and their probable effect on patterns of use cannot be determined with confidence. It is possible that, after careful study, all alternatives will turn out to have so many disadvantages that none could command public consensus. To maximize the likelihood of sound policy for the long run, however, further research should be conducted on the biological, behavioral, developmental, and social consequences of marijuana use, on the structure and operation of drug markets, and on the relations of various conditions of availability to patterns of use.

The persistent concern about the health-related effects of marijuana requires both an immediate and continuing response. First, as the report of the Institute of Medicine recommends, there should be "a greatly intensified and more comprehensive program of research into the effects of marijuana on the health of the American people." An important goal of this research program should be the identification of subgroups at high risk for physiological and psychological damage in relation to patterns of use and doses of marijuana. The report presents a detailed agenda of needed research. Second, to the extent that potential health hazards are identified, policy research should address possible safeguards and precautions to protect the user.

If marijuana use can be scientifically shown to entail grave risks—to the brain, the cardiovascular and respiratory systems, or to reproductive functions, for example—that are currently not known, it can be argued that, as was the case with cigarette smoking, knowledge of those effects will be more effective than criminal enforcement as a deterrent to use.

Research on the price elasticity of demand in legal and illegal markets is a clear priority. The result of such research will be important in determining the likelihood of controlling heavy use through price mechanisms and in computing the amount of money—if any—that could be realized in taxation of marijuana.

Present knowledge of the structure and activities of drug markets and networks is insufficient to allow prediction of the effects of policy changes on them. Research in this area is difficult but the questions are important. If many dealers who sell cocaine, PCP, amphetamines, and barbiturates as well as marijuana would be put out of business if marijuana were available through legal channels, it might result in a curtailed market for a variety of other drugs. On the other hand, it is also possible that the market structure is so loosely organized, and dealers so transiently involved, that removing marijuana from the illegal markets would have little effect. To be sure, much research on some of these questions could not be conducted unless a regulatory system were in place in some state. Nonetheless, some research, particularly ethnographic and economic studies, should be undertaken now to discover the importance of marijuana profits to drug-dealing networks; the transiency, size, and nature of such networks; etc. It is essential for research in this area to be supported by appropriate government agencies.

Although many questions remain to be answered before the most informed choices can be made between prohibiting and regulating supply, there are many things that cannot be known unless some jurisdiction tries a regulatory policy. Although adoption of a regulatory policy is likely to result in increased use, little is known about changes in patterns of use that are likely to result. If federal laws prohibiting supply are changed to allow states to license marijuana sales, epidemiological research programs must be ready to monitor any changes in use and their consequences. To do so, research should be organized and operating well in advance of any such policy changes in order to determine rates of use before the change. Although the shift in the law from complete to partial prohibition in eleven states has apparently had little effect on consumption patterns there, we do not know the degree to which legally available marijuana would attract a larger market. The impact on use of educational campaigns, health warnings, and informal social controls under a regulatory system should be investigated.

In the absence of the opportunity for states to adopt regulatory policies, there can only be educated guesses about which age groups are likely to increase use or whether individuals who now use marijuana will use more, etc. Meanwhile, every bit of analysis to predict the answers to these questions, by surveying public attitudes, assessing past experiences with the spread of drug use in society (e.g., alcohol use following the repeal of Prohibition), and critically reviewing the experience of other societies in which marijuana is more readily available, will be valuable.

Marijuana regulation would permit systematic provision of comprehensive, clearly communicated health warnings on package inserts or covers, in public health education, by medical practitioners, and by public health interest groups as well as by the government. The extent to which such warnings would have more credibility for users than current health warnings, generated in an atmosphere of prohibition, is an important subject for research. Despite widespread pessimism about the failures of drug education campaigns, there are encouraging results in educational approaches based on the Stanford Heart Disease Prevention Program experience. With appropriate, research-based models and techniques, public health education may be an attractive means for limiting excessive use.

IV. DRUGS AND CELEBRITIES

EDITOR'S INTRODUCTION

Public consciousness of drugs has been heightened by the many stories in newspapers and magazines of celebrities who use them or have come to grief because of them. Show business personalities have frequently been the subject of such articles, giving an impression that drug use is pervasive in the entertainment industry. But public figures in all sectors of American life—in politics and business as well as show business—have come to the attention of the public through their involvement with drugs. Inevitably, drug involvement among the prominent reflects upon the rest of society. If drug use is part of the life-style of the most advantageously placed, what should be expected of the middle class and the less well-off? Indeed, such widespread use of drugs by the rich and famous may suggest that narcotic use is one of the rewards of success in America.

Section IV begins with an article, "Reconstructing Richard Pryor," by Micki Siegel, which appeared in *Health* magazine. It recounts the work of the two surgeon brothers who saved the life of the comedian after he accidentally set himself on fire while "freebasing" cocaine. A following piece by John Lahr from *The New Republic* is a review of Bob Woodward's biography of John Belushi, who died of an overdose of "speedball," a mixture of cocaine and heroin. In an acerbic style, Lahr discusses the fast, short life of Belushi, who had long been a cocaine addict. "Again, Death in the Family," by Pete Axthelm in *Newsweek*, describes the brief, unhappy life and drug death of David Kennedy in May 1984. "From Cars to Cocaine," also from *Newsweek*, covers the career of John DeLorean at the time of his indictment for cocaine trafficking—one of the most sensational trials of the 1980s. The issue of entrapment was a major theme in the trial which, though it resulted in DeLorean's acquittal in August 1984, left his career in ruins.

RECONSTRUCTING RICHARD PRYOR[1]

It happened on June 9, 1980: Two policemen patrolling the northwest area of the San Fernando Valley in California heard what they thought was someone screaming. Then they saw an incredible sight: a man running, his body a mass of flames from face to waist. The policeman jumped out of their car, wrestled the burning man to the ground and rolled him in the grass to put out the fire.

Later, they realized the burnt man was actor/comedian Richard Pryor. Later still, they heard varying accounts of how he had set himself ablaze—from preparing a potentially explosive mixture of cocaine and ether to fueling cigarette lighters on a rug damp with spilled rum. But at that moment one thing was clear—in his panic, instead of rolling on the floor to smother the flames, Pryor had run out of his house and into the street. And now, unless he got help *fast*, Pryor would certainly die.

The officers made an instant decision. Sirens wailing, they rushed Pryor to the Sherman Oaks Burn Center—the largest private burn center in the country—and into the care of two extraordinarily dedicated doctors: Richard Grossman, MD, a plastic surgeon, founder and director of the center, and his younger brother, Jack Grossman, MD, also a plastic surgeon.

Dr. Richard Grossman founded the center in 1969 because there was no adequate place to treat burn patients in the entire San Fernando Valley. As he explains, "If plastic surgery is my vocation, burn surgery is my avocation." His brother joined him later. Together, the two have worked out a series of imaginative innovations and new techniques proving so successful that last year, out of 400 patients, only six percent died. Pryor says flatly, "I owe my life to God and the Grossmans." The Grossmans tell the story of how they saved Pryor's life a little reluctantly because they don't want to intrude on their patient's privacy. But they *do* want people to know that there is hope for burn victims—even those as badly burned as Pryor was.

[1]Reprint of an article by Micki Siegel, free-lance writer. Reprinted by permission from *Health*, p 54+. S. '82.

At 8 o'clock on the night of Pryor's accident, Dr. Jack Grossman had just finished a long and difficult operation. He was tired and ready to go home when the call from the emergency room came: A patient had just been brought in with burns on his face, ears, chest, back, abdomen and arms—50 percent of his body. Much of the damage was life threatening, and they didn't know if the man was going to make it. A team of four nurses and technicians was already working on him—would Grossman come and help? Forgetting his weariness, Grossman started for the emergency room.

When Grossman arrived, Pryor was in excruciating pain and terror. Rapidly and quietly, Grossman and his team went to work. Their first task was to calm the frightened man and treat him for shock. Because burn victims lose an enormous amount of body fluids, their kidneys can shut down. Other vital organs may also stop functioning. When enough of the essential machinery is turned off, death comes swiftly. The essential task of the rescuers, then, was to prevent this. Grossman literally flooded Pryor's body with massive doses of intravenous fluids. Then, moving rapidly, he administered drugs to ease the pain and oxygen to help Pryor breathe through lungs damaged by smoke inhalation.

But the battle had barely begun. Severely burned people are at risk of death from not one or two but a dozen sources. Grossman's next step was warding off another potential killer: blood poisoning. Normally, bacteria called *pseudomonas* live on our skin and do us no harm. But when the skin is burned, pseudomonas invade the bloodstream, and in that vastly different environment they become lethal enemies, causing blood poisoning. Gently, the burn team began to apply dressings soaked in topical antibiotics to Pryor's wounds in an effort to prevent pseudomonas from entering his blood.

Throughout this period of swift, purposeful activity, one member of the burn-center team handled a camera, quietly snapping photos—part of the Grossman brothers' standard medical protocol. "We keep photographic records of all our patients," Dr. Richard Grossman explains. As the medical team works, a fluorescent dye, administered through an IV, moves through the patient's bloodstream. Using a camera fitted with special filters to record the solution's progress, the doctors can determine whether they are dealing with second-degree burns, third-degree burns, or a combination of both. Second-degree burns, which destroy only the top layers of skin, are far easier to treat. But third-degree burns destroy all layers of skin, threatening life and demanding eventual skin grafts. The camera showed that Pryor's injuries included many third-degree burns.

By 9 PM, Pryor was out of the emergency room and carefully installed in a remarkable bed representing some of the latest technology in burn therapy. Instead of conventional cotton sheets, the bed was covered with a disposable plastic sheet containing rows of tiny bubbles to help keep the supersensitive burned body from feeling the pressure of its own weight. Over the bed hung a Plexiglass heat shield made of the same material as the windshield on the Apollo spacecraft. The shield radiated heat to keep the patient warm without coverings that would irritate raw wounds. Both sheet and shield were among Richard Grossman's innovations.

A long tube was snaked down through Pryor's nose and into his stomach to empty it until his gastrointestinal system, turned off by the trauma of the burns, was ready to function again. In addition, Pryor was under electronic surveillance more intense than anything he had experienced during a career of performing in front of movie and television cameras. He was wired in numerous places to monitors keeping track of his heart rate, blood pressure, temperature and urine output. He was closely watched on a television scanning screen by nurses, technicians and doctors. And he had a round-the-clock audience: a nurse assigned solely to him.

When all this was readied, when all the equipment was in place, all the human skills and compassion brought into play, what were Pryor's chances of survival? "Fifty percent," the doctors told him with grim honesty. "We'll make it," Pryor replied.

Remembering, Richard Grossman shakes his head in admiration. "His will to live was remarkable," he says. "He came so very, very close to death. But he realized that God had given him a second chance, and boy, did he reach out and take it."

Pryor himself remembers praying repeatedly. "Nobody ever considers burning up," he says now. "And then, all of a sudden, there you are, burning up. You don't call on the Bank of America to help you; you don't call on nobody but God . . . "

Throughout the next critical weeks, there was plenty of reason to call for divine assistance. The morning after the fire, the doctors were already at work on treatments that would minimize scarring for Pryor—they still were anything but sure he would live, but if he did, they wanted him to look as normal as possible. There are too many burn victims whose miraculously saved lives often seem more a burden than a blessing because of deforming scars. In the case of a public figure like Pryor, facial deformity could mean the loss of his career and the familiar world of show business. That Pryor was black was also a source of some concern, because blacks are generally thought to scar more conspicuously than whites, developing raised welts called *keloids* along scar lines. The Grossman brothers, however, believe that healing ability depends more on an individual's particular pigmentation than on broad racial characteristics. As for Pryor: "In a burn ward," he says, "nobody's white or black. Everybody's pink."

Twice a day he eased his pink body into a warm whirlpool bath of water and Clorox. This treatment reduces the chances of heavy scarring by removing dead skin; it also helps kill pseudomonas. While he was in the whirlpool, Pryor was taught to remove his own dressings so that they could be changed—another Grossman innovation. Ordinarily, dressings changes are almost unendurably painful for burn patients, but having patients remove the bandages themselves while the raw area is under water helps significantly. Pryor still winces remembering the dressing changes, but he made them.

Once a day, Pryor entered a hyperbaric chamber—a high-pressure oxygen chamber that looks like a Plexiglass version of an iron lung, except that in the hyperbaric chamber, the patient's head is inside rather than outside the machine. The chamber, in which Pryor stayed for about an hour at a time, bombards the body with oxygen, promoting healing and minimizing scarring. Later, the chamber would be used to heal the unburned portions of Pryor's body that became donor sites from which skin for grafts was taken.

Incredibly, just three days after Pryor was brought to the burn center more dead than alive, he began to visit other patients. Despite the intensity of his pain and the difficulty of moving, he insisted on getting out of bed. Leaning on the arm of his friend, football player–movie star Jim Brown, he would walk into other patients' rooms to make a joke or say a prayer. "He was wonderful," says Jack Grossman. "He was an inspiration to others—especially the children." Pryor attributes much of this extraordinary display of courage to the fact that Brown was with him. "For three hard weeks, he was there," Pryor says. "When I went to sleep, he was there. When I woke up, he was there. I kept saying to myself, 'I can't give in to the pain. Not in front of Jim Brown.'"

Fighting burn infections takes an enormous amount of energy: Patients as badly burned as Pryor commonly lose 20 to 30 pounds in the struggle. So on the third day, the Grossmans removed the nose tube that had emptied Pryor's stomach and hooked him up to another nose tube that constantly dripped calories into his stomach while he walked, while he slept, while he ate meals by mouth. If he used up 5,000 calories, they were replaced—and then some—with 6,000.

So far, so good, but serious questions remained. Pryor's lungs had been damaged by smoke inhalation and needed help; the doctors forced air into them using a technique called Intermittent Positive Pressure Breathing. His weakening kidneys had to be restored to normal function, and the doctors set about treating them by altering the balance of electrolytes—sodium and potassium—in his body fluids. An ear surgeon was called in; Pryor's ears had actually been aflame, and damage to the eardrums was suspected—but not found. Very slowly, the chances that the actor might survive began to edge in his favor. As the days passed, it seemed more and more possible that he would make it after all.

But what shape would he be in? In third-degree burns, the body develops an *eschar*, a deep scab that must be surgically removed in a procedure known as *debridement*. If there is healthy *granulated tissue* with adequate blood supply under the eschar, a skin graft can be performed. If not, there is nothing to do but wait. In their first tests, the doctors found that Pryor was not yet ready for a graft. That meant more endless days of whirlpool baths and trips to the hyperbaric chamber. Finally, three days later, the doctors tried again: They brought Pryor back to surgery and put him to sleep. This time, when they removed the eschar, they found healthy, bleeding tissue underneath. The skin graft could proceed.

Very delicately, the surgeons removed a sheet of skin about as thin as a wet paper tissue from Pryor's hips and thighs. Then they attached it with tiny metal clips to the new blood-rich tissue on one burned area of his body. (The blood, which feeds the skin graft, also acts as a glue to hold it in place.) Finally, they wrapped Pryor in antiseptic dressings and fluff gauzes, and brought him back to his room. The next two days were a living hell—despite painkillers, Pryor was in agony. After 48 hours, they put him back into the whirlpool and the hyperbaric chamber, and started changing his dressings daily. Once the tiny blood vessels in the healthy tissue began to incorporate themselves into the grafted skin, the graft was labeled a success. Then the whole process was started again on another part of the body. (It was impossible to graft over all of Pryor's burns at once because different areas developed healthy tissue under the eschar at different rates.) All told, Pryor went through five operations—two debridements and three grafts.

And through it all, whenever he could walk, Pryor would clench his teeth, ignore his pain, grasp his ever-present IV pole and totter down the hall to visit other patients. "Look at me," he'd tell newcomers, terrified at their prospects, "I've had my grafts. I'm almost ready to go home. If I can do it, you can."

Later, he had more to say. "I'm grateful for the fire; it saved my life. I believe that in about three months I would have been dead. I was just going down inside. Now I feel born again."

Six and a half weeks after he was rushed nearly dead to the burn center, Pryor went home—incredibly, alive and, even more incredibly, well. Three weeks after that, he was given a tight elastic compression T-shirt to help flatten his body scars. In a month, he was back to his normal routine, and in three months he was at work on the set of "Bustin' Loose."

"He looks great," says Jack Grossman. "He does have significant scars, but fourtunately, they're on his chest and neck. His face, thank God, has healed remarkably."

Adds Richard Grossman, "He has scars that some people would hide with turtleneck collars. But he's not ashamed. He feels very fortunate that he's here."

In the time that has passed since then, Richard Pryor has not forgotten his debt to his doctors: He held a benefit premiere of his movie, "Some Kind of Hero" (filmed after his recovery), to raise money for the Grossmans' burn center. With that money and an interest-free loan from the Humana Corporation, Richard Grossman and a team of doctors from Toronto are performing experiments aimed at cloning the skin of severely burned patients. The preliminary results are very good, and if the technique continues to show results, it will mean that patients without enough unburned skin for ordinary skin grafts can receive grafts of their own cloned skin. It will be invaluable to burn victims, and Pyror is pleased to have contributed to it.

But Pryor's feelings about the Grossmans do not end there. He once expressed them in a letter:

"You possess the greatest gift of all—the gift to make others want to live. God bless you, and I thank you for helping me in my new life. May you do for others what you did for me."

SAMURAI SCREW-UP[2]

On screen and in life, John Belushi played the fool. He was 33 when he died of an overdose at the Château Marmont in 1982. By then, gross overeating had swollen his 5´ 7´´ frame to 222 pounds, and he was strung out from his now legendary drug binges. The rapacity and restlessness of Hollywood were epitomized in him. His comedy partner Dan Aykroyd described

[2]Reprint of an article by John Lahr, author of books on stage and film. Review of *Wired: The Short Life and Fast Times of John Belushi*, by Bob Woodward. *The New Republic*. p 37–40. Ag. 6, '84. Copyright © 1984 by *The New Republic*. Reprinted by permission.

Belushi's frenzy as "a state of trance and venom," an apt phrase for that vindictive triumph society calls stardom. From Belushi's earliest days as a comic with Chicago's Second City in 1971, his greed as an actor was as obvious as his talent. "Fight, scream, refuse to do things," he told a writer for "Saturday Night Live," which vaulted him to national celebrity. "Demand things, be an asshole." Belushi was. Among Belushi's fondest misconceptions was that he was "addicted to life." On the contrary, confusing excitement with experience and freedom with fame, he had become addicted to death. . . .

[Belushi] wanted to be extraordinary. He became instead a kind of caricature of "bigness." He sought from the public the love that he couldn't win from his parents. It was a mug's game; but, then, being an endearing mug was Belushi's stock-in-trade. Instead of banishing the tyranny of early parental figures, celebrity merely replaced it with an even more tyrannical authority figure: the public. "You *need* drugs," Belushi explained to his minder, hired to keep him from taking drugs, about the pressures of success. "You've got to be on top, got to store up everything." Of course, with drugs, as Belushi's chaotic life attested, experience didn't widen; it shrunk.

"Don't you have any self-respect?" says a straight-arrow collegian in *Animal House* (1978) to Belushi who, as Bluto, fills his face with cream cakes and then splats them over the tweedbag, exclaiming "I'm a zit!" In *Animal House*, Bluto is always throwing a show: pissing on feet, leering up co-eds' dresses, smashing guitars and beer bottles, butting heads, getting in food fights. He is adamantly anti-intellectual. On screen, Belushi's slapstick slovenliness was a gold mine; offstage, it was a nightmare. The benders, the sudden disappearances, the tirades, the passings-out, the spending sprees (one chauffeur was kept on twenty-four-hour call while Belushi ran up an $800 limousine bill on a drug binge), the squalid clutter, all had an extravagance in real life that far exceeded Belushi's lovable pigpen image on screen. No wonder that when John Guare was writing *Moon Over Miami* for Belushi and Aykroyd (the film Belushi was about to do for Louis Malle when Belushi died), Guare named Belushi's character Shelley Slutsky. The script was so near the knuckle that Aykroyd was worried about Belushi's reaction. Guare had seen the Belushi whirlwind in action.

Guare recounts to Woodward his meeting with Aykroyd and Belushi at their Dominick Street bar in New York which had set-ups for two and where they liked to entertain their friends. Belushi played The Dead Kennedy's "Too Drunk to Fuck" on the jukebox and proclaimed in his obtuse way that the reason why the song couldn't be played on the radio was what was wrong with America. His insisted they slam dance, which meant running across the room into each other at full speed. Guare, who is 6′3″, knocked Belushi down with a shoulder block. Belushi looked up and said: "You dance very well." The event left Guare with a deeper insight into Belushi than the Woodward biography reports. "Belushi had no private identity to retreat to," he says. "He was like that jukebox. I'm sorry we didn't work together. What kind of grief can you feel for this epic level of self-destruction?"

"It's worse winning," Jack Dempsey once said, "than losing." Belushi knew the feeling. He had always conceived of himself as a renegade outsider. He was obsessed with Brando and Bogart and worked up imitations of them. As as actor, he had girded himself for a life of struggle and rejection. But celebrity changed all that. Within three years of starting out on his career, Belushi found himself pushing at an open door. The success of "Saturday Night Live" made him a kind of household god before he'd hardly had time to explore his talent or his craft.

Belushi was asked (and declined) to be Grand Marshal of the Mardi Gras. Paul McCartney paid Belushi $6,000 to do his Joe Cocker imitation at his birthday party. As the Blues Brothers, he and Aykroyd cut a record; but unlike Belushi's high school band, who also made a record and painted it gold as a joke, The Blues Brothers' album found a wide audience. Belushi's curious screen charisma, at once shy and bold, made him bankable; and film studios lined up to offer him multimillion dollar deals. Every dream was coming true—and it was boring. "When you're a star," Belushi said derisively, "you're directed. People do it for you." Going to the edge with drugs was a way to test his incredible luck and make life interesting. "You put more pressure on yourself to make everything that much harder because work is no longer challenging," he explained. "You say, 'Well, I'll get screwed up and then it'll be a real challenge.' So stupid—I've often wondered why people do these things. You're so much happier if you don't, but I guess happiness is not a state you want to be in all the time." It was another of Belushi's delusions. Drugs didn't make him a rebel, just an epic consumer. He spent between $40,000 and $75,000 a month, most of it going up his nose. He was not, as Artaud called actors, "an athlete of the heart." He was just a mess.

"My characters say it's okay to screw up," Belushi told *Newsweek* after his success in *Animal House* had made him "an expert" on comedy. "People don't have to be perfect. They don't have to be real smart. They don't have to follow the rules. They can have fun. Most movies today make people feel inadequate. I don't do that." But Belushi himself was far from noncompetitive. He may have fought the star image, but not the star ethic. He was obsessed with measuring and maintaining the difference between himself and others. "I make more money in movies than you, *boy*," he said to Chevy Chase, a remark for which he later apologized. And when Paramount guaranteed Belushi $1.85 million, 7 to 12 percent of the gross, and a $2,500 weekly allowance, while he was writing a clunker that eventually was titled *Noble Rot*, Belushi almost walked away from the deal because Jack Nicholson got more. "How come Nicholson gets this," he told his business manager. "I should be getting this!" Fame was Belushi's ticket to ride roughshod over everyone, a trap he mistook for freedom. "Success," he told a punk musician he was trying to promote in the film industry, "means you can get up and leave when you want." In Belushi's case, the imperialism of the star's personality extended not just to trying to take full credit for the screenplay of *Noble Rot* that he'd co-written, or to hiring and firing people at whim, but to offering to pay his wife's employer $60,000 *not* to hire her so she'd be free to take care of him.

"What can be going on inside this person to make him so unhappy?" Judy Belushi wrote in her diary of what she euphemistically called "John Trouble." She had seen her high school sweetheart become a monster, the charm of his terrific energy turn into demented desire. She had tried to get Belushi's manager and accountant to stop giving him cash for dope. But they were in business, and Belushi was their gravy train. Belushi would tyrannize their offices until money was forthcoming. And if it took Dexamyl to keep Belushi awake after a bender for a $40,000 looping session, so be it—anything to keep the performing workhorse on the job. Belushi worried about himself as an artist, but the studios and his managers saw him as a unit. When news of his death filtered down the corridors of Paramount, the bosses initially thought it was their deal, and not Belushi, that had collapsed. At the time of his death, Paramount was trying to switch Belushi from the botched *Noble Rot* to the commercial schlock of *The Joy of Sex*. Belushi worried to his friends that Hollywood was trivializing his talent; but he's accomplished that all by himself.

No one, not even Belushi, quite knew what he'd lost until it was gone. "'Saturday Night Live' took a lot out of our souls," Belushi said. Relationships, especially his marriage, were a shambles; normality was a memory; and worst of all, his once-generous nature had been sacrificed to the brutal self-aggrandizement of stardom. Once, while shooting *The Blues Brothers* (1980), Belushi refused to come out of his trailer. The film was way behind schedule and millions over budget. The film's director John Landis stalked into the trailer and found Belushi sitting comatose at a table with a mound of cocaine piled in front of him. In a fury, Landis swept up the cocaine and flushed in down the john. He turned to see Belushi coming at him. In self-defense, Landis punched his star. Belushi began to cry. "I'm so ashamed," he said. "So, so, ashamed. . . . " Although it's misused in the narrative of *Wired*, the moment is the book's most poignant. Belushi had lost his goodness and he knew it. Dope was for Belushi what fast cars were for Clifford Odets's fictional golden boy, the boxer Joe Bonaparte, who dies in a crash, his "accidental" death a revenge on his keepers and his corrupted integrity. "We're off the earth—unconnected," Bonaparte says of speed. "We don't have time to think." For Belushi, speedballing, free-basing, and finally heroin, kept guilt and the pain of lost goodness at a distance, until, of course, they killed him.

Belushi's comic legacy is small and uneven. He was just beginning, although he fondly thought of himself as as master. "No one can tell me about two things—comedy and music," he said. As his films show, he had a lot to learn. With the laid-back and lanky Aykroyd, Belushi had a comic silhouette of immense but unrealized potential. The wit and aggression of his memorable cameos on "Saturday Night Live" didn't translate to the big screen, which wanted its laughter easy to swallow for mass consumption. On film, Belushi left a memory of moments, especially the food fight in *Animal House* and the rock concert in *The Blues Brothers*, where Belushi's gorgeous energy and his pain coalesce in fun.

Wired is perhaps a fitting epitaph to Belushi's short and shapeless life: the overlong in praise of the overpaid. Woodward, like Belushi, stays staunchly on the surface of life, has no point of view, sees no larger picture. As a biographer, Woodward refuses to interpret the facts and people around him. But the facts are clear enough. Belushi was an archetypal greedhead. He dreamed of wanting; and everything he wanted was worthless.

AGAIN, DEATH IN THE FAMILY[3]

The brothers and cousins walked slowly up the gentle slope from the gray hearse to the house called Hickory Hill, with shirt sleeves rolled up and heads bowed as they carried the walnut casket. The golden spring Virginia day was silent, but the scene recalled other bright sad afternoons when bands played brassy dirges, and a nation cried along with the family mourners. This time the fallen Kennedy was David, 28 years old, who had tossed the ancestral promise into a bottomless well of drugs and despair. But as they had done over the decades for David's father, Robert, and John Fitzgerald Kennedy before him, the clan members rallied together and faced death with dignity, nobility, even a hard-edged elegance. The Kennedys have always approached death, like life, with a certain style.

[3]Reprint of an article by Pete Axthelm, staff writer. *Newsweek*. p 50–54. My. 7, '84. Copyright © 1984 by *Newsweek*, Inc. All rights reserved. Reprinted by permission.

Once David had seemed a suitable heir to the style. He was good-looking and sensitive and easy to love. He was the life of parties and the quarterback on football teams. "A bundle of charisma," said a family friend. "If he wasn't the most popular kid in the group, you knew he could be by the next week." When the weeks ran out last Wednesday, David's body was found by a hotel front-desk secretary. He was lying dead, alone, between the two beds in his $250-a-day suite in the verdant and tasteful Brazilian Court Hotel in Palm Beach. There was a small amount of cocaine in the room, and medical examiners found traces of cocaine in his body. The physical cause of death was not immediately determined. The cosmic cause may have had something to do with style.

Love and Hate: Like several members of the young generation of Kennedys, David endured a persistent love-hate relationship with the family image. There was always the tug of the Camelot rafting parties and touch-football games, the allure of the easy access to the best prep schools, the most fashionable discos and, almost inevitably, Harvard. But there were almost times when he preferred to ride the rails or bum around the streets of New York where nobody knew he was a Kennedy. There were many enticing flings with family friends, drug counselors and other surrogate fathers selected either by the young man or his mother, Ethel. But there was always the searing memory of the night in 1968 when the 12-year-old favorite son watched on television as Sirhan Sirhan's bullets snuffed out the real father he adored.

A new book called "Young Kennedys," excerpted in the May Playboy, offers some particularly savage pop psychology on the failures of Ethel Kennedy and the troubles of three of her 11 offspring—David, Bobby Jr. and Joe. David was reportedly bitter and upset about the magazine piece, feeling that he had been falsely befriended and then exploited. If so, it was just one of many cruel tricks to which the innocent and self-destructive youth fell victim.

A more relevant text was written long before the New Frontier, by the old-fashioned novelist William Faulkner in 1929. In "The Sound and The Fury," the tragic hero was another doomed Harvard innocent named Quentin Compson. Scion of an Old

South family with pretensions to image and style of its own, Quentin wandered about Cambridge under his own burden of fragile and impossible idealism, his own sense of irretrievable loss. In black folklore, Quentin thought on the way to his suicide, "a drowned man's shadow was watching him in the water all the time. It twinkled and glinted, like breathing. . . . The displacement of water is equal to the something of something. Reducto absurdum of all human experience . . . "

The shadow haunting David Kennedy was the bloody head of his father swimming up on a TV screen from that mobbed corridor of a Los Angeles hotel. The glint came in glassine bags, shiny syringes and clinking ice cubes in the vodka and grapefruit juice. The reducto absurdum was found between the neatly arranged twin beds of a Palm Beach hotel room. "I personally believe that David was subject to too much in the way of emotional blows at a very tender period in his life," his uncle Sargent Shriver said last week. A family friend and Hyannis Port neighbor, Larry Newman, put it more directly: "David died when his father died. He was never really right after that."

Many have found it irresistible to leap from that tragic starting point toward some inexorable Kennedy curse. But sad reality indicates that hardly any far-flung American family can expect to keep all its offspring free from the velvet traps of easy living and hard drugs. The truth is that most young Kennedys—even those who dabbled in drugs like Bobby Jr. or crashed into disaster like the jeep accident that paralyzed a woman friend of Joe's—have endured and often prevailed over whatever dark destinies assassins had sketched for them. So it seems unfair to surmise that David represents Camelot gone wrong. Perhaps it is more accurate to suggest that he never quite got Camelot right.

Bravado: "In all the years since Bobby died," recalls Newman, "I never saw David without a distant look in his eyes. He was a morose, unhappy boy. He put on a bravado to cover that up, and some took that as arrogance. But David wasn't arrogant. He was troubled." Many Kennedys worked off their troubles in the athletic, competitive atmosphere of the clan gatherings. But even when he was in the middle of such whirling activities, David seemed to be gazing into a private space.

"Anything the Kennedys have ever done is for the Kennedy image," says one family friend. "Too often the kids were just props in the play. It wasn't so much that something might be bad for David Kennedy, but that it was explained as being bad for the Kennedy family." Surrounded by the frenetic activity, the high-minded good works and the free-spirited good times, most members of a remarkable family could accept love as a given. But poor David could take nothing for granted. "Playing football doesn't mean you love someone," said the same friend. "And you can hire all the bodyguards in the world, but you can't hire someone to love a kid and give him the attention he needs."

Gradually David's life took the shape of a desperate quest for something that those around him seemed to have found without trying. He was an honor student at the Middlesex School in Concord, Mass., graduating in the top third of his class. He spent various summers at a Blackfoot Indian reservation in Montana, with Cesar Chavez among the struggling farm workers of California and as a copy boy on the Nashville Tennessean. On the surface it appeared the stuff of a vigorous and inquisitive student; a few friends saw a bleaker side to his restlessness.

"He was the most decadent person I had ever seen," recalls a woman who knew him when he was in Nashville. "He used that quality to his advantage with women, who felt that they could be the ones to save him. He was very interested in writing and history, but he was already heavy into drugs then. Every time I saw him he was stoned on marijuana."

Dropping Out: In 1974 David followed family tradition to Harvard, majoring in history. By spring he decided he needed a semester off. He returned for a year, then dropped out in 1977. Reviewing that break with the Kennedy style, one can almost hear another echo of the death-seeking Quentin Compson: "he every man is the arbiter of his own virtues but let no man prescribe for another mans wellbeing and I temporary . . ."

I temporary: that was David, careering between summer jobs and aborted semesters, briefly loved women and half-formed dreams. One foray took him to Ft. Lauderdale, to work for family friend and flamboyant businessman John Jay Hooker, whom he knew from Nashville. But David never did work on that aimless journey. He slept until the early afternoons, whiled away the days around Hooker's pool and marshaled his energy only to organize a junket to a Rolling Stones concert in Memphis that summer. He was 20 then, but he daydreamed like a small boy, repeatedly telling the story of how his father had once rescued him from a treacherous undertow in the Malibu, surf. And how, late that very night, he had watched his father die.

"You got the feeling," says a friend from those times, "that Ethel kept sending him around to all of the old family friends in hopes that one night somebody would sit down and have the talk with him that would make the difference." Instead, there was only a gathering despair. Even when he tracked his gloom across his arm with needles, David seemed to wear it as a badge of honor. "His father's death scarred him," says one woman friend. "And he seemed attracted to the pain he felt."

Sometimes the anguish seemed the only reality in a blurred world. "When you lose so many people that you love, what kind of message does that deliver?" asks a friend. "He couldn't count on anything, and he was afraid to love. But when he shot that heroin into his veins, he felt, 'I *know* what this is going to do to me.' It was guaranteed feeling." And a temporary one.

'Twinkle': David's drug problem became an ugly headline in 1979, when he was mugged while trying to buy cocaine in a "shooting gallery" in Harlem. Soon after, he entered a drug-rehabilitation program in Sacramento, Calif. But the round-the-clock counselors apparently couldn't provide the magical "talk" that he needed, and he dropped out and moved into a singles apartment complex with a girlfriend from New York. That July he was arrested for drunken driving. The family contact who represented him as he paid the $380 fine, attorney Michael Sands, remembers him well: "A delightful young man with the twinkle in his eye that Bobby Kennedy had." For David, it was a rare flirtation with the family style.

By 1982 he was still trying to hold on. He wanted to re-enter Harvard, and as a condition he had to hold a steady job for six months. Again family friends were there; Atlantic Monthly publisher Mortimer Zuckerman hired him to work with senior editor C. Michael Curtis. "He was very sensitive, articulate and witty," says a former co-worker at the magazine, Maureen Foley. "I don't think he compared himself with his brothers and sisters and cousins. I think he knew he was a different kind of person. And he had an urgent desire to prove himself and find himself."

His problems were just as urgent. "He was clearly struggling with his drinking," says editor Curtis. "He sometimes would appear at work in a daze, not speaking clearly, his shirt outside his pants. From time to time he would fall asleep at his desk." David left the Atlantic in May of 1983, enrolled in summer school at Harvard, then completed the fall semester. He did not register again for the spring.

Cocaine: During the drift toward the end, there were still signs of hope, hints of style. Even the return to Harvard seemed encouraging. David could still light up the family gatherings when he arrived unexpectedly at the Cape—or when he visited 93-year-old matriarch Rose Kennedy in Palm Beach. But the last trip south was fueled with many double vodkas and concluded with cocaine and Demeral.

Inevitably, the incident sent rewrite men scurrying through libraries, compiling the sad list of misfortunes that some would add up to a family curse. There were the assassinations of Jack and Bobby, the planecrash deaths of sister Kathleen and brother Joe Jr., the drowning of Mary Jo Kopechne with Ted at Chappaquiddick. There was also the bravery of Ted Kennedy Jr. in the face of the cancer that claimed his leg.

But indications are that David Anthony Kennedy never sought a place in such a litany, in life or in death. At the funeral, a pale blue mass card was embossed with a poem that had been presented to Ethel Kennedy at the time of her husband's assassination. It was a passage from John Donne's Holy Sonnet X, "Death be not proud." David had written it out himself in his 12-year-old hand and bordered it with swirling decorations. It was sensitive and touching. It was his own style.

FROM CARS TO COCAINE[4]

John Zachary De Lorean had it all. At 47, he looked like a matinee idol and earned more than $500,000 a year as a top man at the General Motors Corp.—with a clear shot at the No. 2 spot. His wife was a stunningly beautiful model, they had beautiful homes, and beautiful child and they ran with the beautiful people. When De Lorean went for a spin, he chose from his personal fleet of 22 trucks, cars and motorcycles, and when he golfed, it might be with the likes of Arnold Palmer. But in 1973 impatient De Lorean suddenly left the GM job, and within a year he had embarked on what he considered his dream and his destiny: to create his own motorcar company. Last week De Lorean's dream came to an abrupt end. Just seven hours after the British government closed down his ailing company, John De Lorean was arrested and charged with conspiracy to traffic cocaine.

De Lorean, 57, was seized by the FBI as he haggled with undercover agents in what was to be the final stage of a drug deal that could have made him up to $60 million. The next day he was hustled in handcuffs to federal court in Los Angeles for arraignment on charges of conspiracy to possess narcotics with intent to distribute. Ashen, unshaven, his silver hair rumpled, he first said nothing and stared blankly ahead. But when his wife, Cristina Ferrare, arrived from New York, he embraced her and they spoke softly, holding hands throughout the rest of the proceedings.

Assistant U.S. attorney James Walsh argued for a staggering $20 million bail for De Lorean. "This man is recognized as a genius, a visionary," Walsh told Magistrate Volney Brown. "But one does not create an industry on the backs of cocaine users and heroin addicts." Walsh said he could produce a videotape of the millionaire automaker cradling a packet of cocaine in his lap and saying, shortly before he was arrested: "This is better than gold. This comes in the nick of time."

[4]Reprint of an article by Tom Nicholson, staff writer. *Newsweek*. p 36–40. N. 1, '82.

In response, defense attorney Bernard Minsky argued that De Lorean was "really a victim more than anything else." After De Lorean entered a plea of not guilty, Magistrate Brown ordered him held on $5 million bail. He set $20 million bail for one of De Lorean's alleged accomplices, William Morgan Hetrick, 50, operator of an airplane-repair service and a suspected big-time dope importer who is considered a high "flight risk." A Hetrick colleague, Stephen Arrington, 34, was held on $250,000 bail.

According to authorities, De Lorean was caught in a net cast last March. An anonymous tipster phoned the Ventura County Police Department near Los Angeles and said he had overheard two men discussing the transport of large sums of money. Officers began by following one of the men involved in the conversation. He led them to three or four others—and they, in turn, led to William Hetrick, operator of Morgan Aviation, the repair service.

Hetrick already was under investigation by the Customs Service and the Internal Revenue Service. They were curious about large sums of money brought across the U.S. border by his wife and about big deposits the Hetricks were making in various banks. By midsummer, federal investigators determined that all of the men turned up by the Ventura County police were couriers for Hetrick. According to the investigators, they would pick up packages of cash at various locations in the Los Angeles area and fly to Miami or Ft. Lauderdale, then take the cash to Hetrick's pleasure boat, the "Island Fling," docked at Lauderdale's Bahia Mar Wharf. The boat was known to have made trips to the Florida Keys and Cayman Islands, both transfer points for South American cocaine.

Meanwhile, the authorities said, De Lorean, his company edging ever closer to bankruptcy, contacted a man he believed to be in the drug business—but who was in fact an informant for the federal Drug Enforcement Administration (DEA). The informant told De Lorean he had ties to Hetrick, whom, the DEA says, De Lorean had known for some time.

Capital: Investigators claim that De Lorean met at the Loews L'Enfant Plaza Hotel in Washington with an informant indentified only as "CI" (for "cooperating individual") and with DEA agent John Valestra, who was posing as "John Vicenza," a drug distributor. According to affidavits submitted at De Lorean's arraignment, "De Lorean and the CI discussed the importation and distribution of heroin from Thailand and cocaine from South America as a means of generating large amounts of capital to be put into the De Lorean Motor Co." De Lorean agreed to furnish $1.8 million in cash and Vicenza $3.2 million to buy 220 pounds of cocaine.

That was on Sept. 4. On Sept. 28, the government claims, a final deal was struck. Hetrick had been brought in as a courier and DEA undercover agent Benedict J. Tisa was introduced as a dealer. According to government documents, Hetrick agreed to furnish the cocaine, which would be marketed by the CI. "Vicenza" told De Lorean that it would take "about five weeks" before De Lorean would net any profit—but that it could reach $60 million. In return, "Vicenza" would own 50 percent of De Lorean Motor Co.

On Oct. 18 Hetrick contacted Tisa to tell him he would arrive that day from Florida. Later that day, the government alleges, Hetrick arranged for Stephen Arrington to meet near Los Angeles with Tisa to exchange 55 pounds of cocaine for an initial payment of $1.8 million. Arrington produced the coke—and was promptly arrested. Hetrick was nabbed a few hours later.

Last Monday, in an interview with the British Broadcasting Corp., De Lorean confidently announced that he had found the money to save the firm. "We're planning to keep this company alive no matter what happens," he said. "And we have the funding in place." He declined to say where he had found the money. The next day De Lorean flew into Los Angeles, unaware of Hetrick's arrest and apparently prepared to complete the cocaine deal.

Why would a man of high intelligence and enormous wealth, with a loving wife and children and a generally good reputation turn to dealing in narcotics? The most charitable explanation his friends and associates could come up with was that De Lorean was simply blindly obsessed with saving his company. "It was a desperate act by a desperate man," said Mike Knepper, a former public-relations man for De Lorean Motor Co. Added Keith Fischer, a former president of Avrett, Free & Fischer, which once served as DMC's advertising agency: "De Lorean would move heaven and earth to save his company. It was an extension of himself and his ego."

But a less charitable view was offered by some former colleagues in Detroit, where De Lorean was once an automotive golden boy. They claim De Lorean had long been guilty of cutting ethical—if not legal—corners. Thomas B. Adams, chairman of Campbell-Ewald Co., which handled the Chevrolet advertising account when De Lorean headed that GM division, recalled that while running Chevrolet, De Lorean ordered Campbell-Ewald to print up large color posters of himself and his adopted son, Zachary, then sent them out as Christmas cards at company expense. Veteran Detroit newsmen remember that when De Lorean left GM he first became president of the National Alliance of Businessmen and told Johnny Carson and other interviewers he was doing it as a public service with no financial reward. In fact, GM paid him a $200,000 salary. "John lied all the time," said Waldo McNaught, a retired public-relations executive who worked with him at GM.

The son of a Detroit factory worker, De Lorean was a self-described street kid. He worked his way through college by playing the saxophone in dance bands. After stints at Chrysler Corp. and the old Packard Motor Car Co.—during which he earned graduate degrees in engineering and business administration—he joined GM's Pontiac Division as an engineer. There his mentor was Semon E. (Bunkie) Knudsen, then the division's general manager. The young De Lorean quickly became chief engineer and the succeeded Knudsen.

Under his leadership in the late 1960s, Pontiac sales soared, and De Lorean was rewarded with the leadership of Chevrolet. As at Pontiac, De Lorean increased profits with a savvy combination of sales, engineering and marketing pizzazz. He was named a group vice president of GM, in overall charge of all domestic car and truck divisions.

Clucking: It was not a happy marriage for either GM or De Lorean. He was uncomfortable in his high-level post in the stuffy GM building, preferring the hands-on job of a divisional general manager. And top GM brass were growing increasingly uncomfortable with the unconventional De Lorean. He grew his hair long, wore designer clothes to the office, divorced his wife and started dating show-business personalities like Ursula Andress and Nancy Sinatra. Nor did the criticism subside when he settled down in suburban Bloomfield Hills with his second wife, Kelly Harmon, daugher of ex-Michigan football great Tom Harmon and a woman half De Lorean's age. Four years later De Lorean left GM.

It was bad enough that De Lorean scorned GM; he compounded that sin by cooperating on an unfriendly book about the company. It was titled "On a Clear Day You Can See General Motors," and in it, he painted the company as a slow-moving, sometimes unethical behemoth that had no room for even a "token hippie" like himself.

But by then De Lorean was immersed in De Lorean Motor Cars Ltd.—a project that was probably doomed from the start. Financing was the first problem: private investors were wary. So De Lorean concentrated, instead, on getting government backing. He finally persuaded Great Britain to help him build a plant in job-hungry Northern Ireland. That decision has so far cost Britain $135 million. De Lorean raised other funds by requiring his American dealers to put up $25,000 apiece.

De Lorean made some early serious engineering, styling and marketing mistakes. He decided on a stainless-steel sports car with gull-wing doors, priced at $25,000. The gull-wing doors were a manufacturing nightmare, the stainless steel was drab and the $25,000 price tag was too much for potential buyers who could afford another top-of-the-line sports car.

Worse yet, De Lorean oversold himself. While his own analysts said there was a potential for only 3,000 or 4,000 sales annually, he directed the Belfast plant to produce 20,000 a year. Coming from giant GM, said J. Bruce McWilliams, former De Lorean marketing vice president in America, "he couldn't gear himself down to such piddling numbers."

When the cars were introduced a year ago, sales were encouraging. With great fanfare, Johnny Carson, Sammy Davis Jr. and others among De Lorean's showbiz friends helped generate interest by shelling out $25,000 for the car. But the recession was coming on.

As problems accelerated, De Lorean Motor Co. turned into an industrial Dunkirk. Worried about $18 million it had put up for export financing, Bank of America moved to repossess the company's inventory on the East and West coasts. A frantic De Lorean sent out a squad of armed men to get the cars first, according to Bank of America, and they managed to whisk 15 of them to De Lorean's estate in Bedminster, N.J. By late March De Lorean Motor Co. owed $6 million to more than 300 creditors, and the main sales office on the West Coast was foundering. Basic supplies like stamps, envelopes and coffee had run out. When the company wanted to show cars at a Los Angeles auto show, it had to borrow them from dealers—and decorate the display with potted plants it brought from its tattered office.

A deadly blow came in February, when the British government put the company into receivership. Ben Bidwell, a former Ford vice president and now president of Hertz Corp. recalled an encounter with De Lorean at that time. "I happened to be on the Concorde coming back from Europe the day after the roof fell in," Bidwell told *Newsweek* automotive editor James C. Jones last week. "In came John. He sat down and I remarked on the story I'd just read about his company, and he said . . . 'I'll get it fixed. No sweat.'" Added Bidwell, after hearing of De Lorean's arrest: "The old phrase 'he marches to a different drummer' applies more to him than to any man I've ever known."

Fallout: Until he can meet his $5 million bail—$250,000 of it in cash—John De Lorean will not be marching anywhere. And there was continuing fallout from the automaker's arrest: The Detroit News produced a copyrighted interview dated Aug. 2 in which De Lorean talked of selling his 10 percent share of the San Diego Chargers after it was found a number of the team's players were using drugs. "I thought it was too important to the youth of America," he said. "They looked at those guys as a bunch of heroes and they were turning the whole world into dopeheads."

In Great Britain, Parliament's Public Accounts Committee launched an investigation of the government's involvement with De Lorean. "There has been a scandalous lack of attention to the background of the people entrusted with taxpayers' money," charged M.P. Michael Crylls, chairman of the House of Commons Industry Committee. The one happy note was sounded in De Lorean salesrooms. "I've had more calls [in one day] than I've probably had in the last six weeks," exulted Grand Rapids, Mich., dealer Dan Pfeiffer. "It's been phenomenal." John De Lorean will at least enjoy hearing that.

Bibliography

An asterisk (*) preceding a reference indicates that the article or part of it has been reprinted in this book.

Books and Pamphlets

Anderson, Patrick. High in America: the true story behind NORML and the politics of marijuana. Viking. '81.

*Commission of the Institute of Medicine. Marijuana and health: report of a study. National Academy Press. '82.

*Glantz, Meyer D. Correlates and consequences of marijuana use. U.S. Department of Health and Human Services. '84.

Goldman, Bob. Death in the locker room; steroids and sports. Icarus Press. '84.

Himmelstein, Jerome L. The strange case of marijuana: politics and ideology of drug control in America. Greenwood Press. '83.

Hofman, Frederick G. A handbook on drug and alcohol abuse: the biomedical aspects. Oxford University Press. '83.

Jones-Witter, Patricia & Weldon. Drugs and society. Wadsworth. '83.

Kaplan, John. The hardest drug: heroin and public policy. University of Chicago Press. '83.

Lee, David. Cocaine handbook: an essential reference. And/Or Press. '81.

Liska, Ken. Drugs and the human body. Macmillan. '81.

Luongo, Ernest. Neurotransmitters, drugs, and stress. Lakeview Press. '84.

Oakley, Ray. Drugs, society, and human behavior. Mosby. '83.

O'Brien, Robert and Cohen, Sidney. The encyclopedia of drug abuse. Facts on File. '84.

Schlaadt, Richard G. and Shannon, Peter T. Drugs of choice: current perspectives on drug use. Prentice-Hall. '82.

Stone, Nannette, et al. Cocaine: seduction and solution. C.N. Potter. '84.

Trebach, Arnold S. The heroin solution. Yale University Press. '82.

Periodicals

America. 148:458–9. Je. 11, '83. Drugs and crime. Thomas J. Reese.

Business Week. p 37. F. 18, '85. Companies are starting to sniff out cocaine users. Joan M. O'Connell and Bob Arnold.

Christian Science Monitor. p 24. Jl. 7, '82. The cocaine threat. Editorial.

Christian Science Monitor. p 25. D. 15, '83. Profiles of the major illicit drugs.

Christian Science Monitor. p. 14. Ap. 5, '85. Why cocaine? John Hughes.

Consumer Research Magazine. 64:17. Jl. '81. Facts for parents about marijuana. Michael Castleman.

Consumer Research Magazine. 65:31–33. Mr. '82. Marijuana: the chemical effects. Gabriel G. Nahas.

Current Health. 9:17. Mr. '83. Evaluating long-term marijuana risks.

Department of State Bulletin. 84:29–34. N. '84. The campaign against drugs: the international dimension. George Shultz.

*Department of State Bulletin. 85:50–53. Ja. '85. International campaign against drug trafficking. Jon R. Thomas.

*Discover. 6:16–21. Mr. '85. Coke: the random killer. Gina Maranto.

*Drug Enforcement. 6–9. Fall '82. International initiatives to control coca production and cocaine trafficking. Dominick L. DiCarlo.

Drug Enforcement. 10–12. Fall '82. Health hazards of cocaine. Sidney Cohen.

Esquire. 100:77–80+. O. '83. Cocaine: you can bank on it. Howard Kohn.

Esquire. 101:23. Ap. '84. Out of control; we're a nation of drug users. Anthony Brandt.

Essence. 14:54. S. '83. Cocaine: a deadly blow.

Essence. 15:68–70, 136–37. Ag. '84. The truth about marijuana. Bebe Moore Campbell.

FDA Consumer. 18:12–15. S. '84. Anabolic steroids: pumping trouble. Annabel Hecht.

Harper's. 264:29–39. Ja. '82. The informant. John Rothchild.

Harper's. 265:18. D. '82. Boycott cocaine. David Owen.

Harper's. 267:27. S. '83. Poppy tours. Robert P. Kearney.

*Health. 54–59, 62. S. '82. Reconstructing Richard Pryor. Micki Siegel.

Health. 8. Ja. '85. Cocaine con. Gabe Mirkin.

Los Angeles Times. p C1. D. 26 '82. The new Hollywood connection: cocaine anonymous.

Los Angeles Times. p V1. F. 1, '83. Middle-class drug abusers' new trend: cocaine and heroin.

Los Angeles Times. p III 1. D. 24, '83. Cocaine in sports: why?

Maclean's. 95:36. Jl. 12, '82. Drawing the line on cocaine abuse. Hal Quinn.

Maclean's. 96:6+. Jl. 4, '83. The politics of pot. J. Van Dusen.

Maclean's. 96:36–38. S. 5, '83. The doping of amateur sports.

Maclean's. 96:60. N. 14, '83. The athletes and steroids.

Maclean's. 98:49. Ap. 1, '85. A continental drug war. Chris Neal.

Mademoiselle. 89:140–41+. Je. '83. Cocaine: mainstream, middle-class—and moving in fast. J. Bode.

Mademoiselle. 91:176–77+. Mr. '85. Cocaine: a pretty poison. Alan Weitz.

Mother Earth News. 138. My–Je. '81. The health effects of marijuana. Michael Castleman.

Mother Jones. 7:34. Ap. '82. The sweet smoke of success: guess what's become of California's no. 1 cash crop? Steve Chapple.

Nation. 235:99. Ag. 7, '82. "Tea" time again. Editorial.

*Nation. 238:186–96+. F. 18, '84. The Miami connection. Penny Lernoux.

Nation. 238:734–45+. Je. 16, '84. The minister who had to die. Penny Lernoux.

National Geographic. 107:142–89. F. '85. The poppy. Peter T. White.

National Review. 35:485–9+. Ap. 29, '83. Pot-talk: is decriminalization advisable? Richard Vigilante and Richard C. Cowan.

*New Republic. 190:37–40. Ag. 6, '84. Samurai screw-up. John Lahr.

New Republic. 191:16–18. D. 10, '84. Fraud international. Judith Harris.

New Republic. 192:5–6. F. 25, '85. Heroin and cowardice. Editorial.

New York Times. p A 1. O. 31, '82. Pervasive use of cocaine is reported in Hollywood. Robert Lindsey and Aljean Harmetz.

New York Times. p A 13. Je. 1, '83. 1,000 calls a day for cocaine hotline.

New York Times. p A 2. My. 18, '84. U. S. said to be losing war on cocaine flights.

New York Times. p A 1+. S. 9, '84. A world of drugs: America as target. (part 1). Part 2: p A 1+. S. 10 '84. Part 3: p A 1+. S. 11, '84. Part 4: p A 1+ S. 12, '84. Part 5: p A 1+ S. 13, '84. Part 6: p A 1+. S. 13, '84.

New York Times. p A 1. O. 18, '84. Extensive use of drugs before the 7th grade found in New York.

New York Times. p A 22. N. 28, '84. Panel is told cocaine abuse has reached epidemic level.

New York Times. p C 18. F. 18, '85. Women and cocaine: a growing problem. Nadine Brozan.

*New York Times Magazine. p 108–12. D. 11, '83. The big business of illicit drugs. Mathea Falco.

Newsweek. 99:89. Mr. 8, '82. The hazards of marijuana. Matt Clark.

Newsweek. 100:36–38+. O. 25, '82. Guns, grass—and money. Tom Morganthau.

*Newsweek. 100:36–40. N. 1, '82. From cars to cocaine. Tom Nicholson, et al.

Newsweek. 102:52–53. Jl. 25, '83. Cocaine crisis in the NFL. Pete Axthelm.

Newsweek. 102:36–41. S. 5, '83. Olympian drug scandal. Charles Leerhsen.

*Newsweek. 103:50+. My. 7, '84. Again, death in the family. Pete Axthelm, et al.

Newsweek. 103:48. My. 14, '84. The cocaine assassination. Bill Hewitt.

Newsweek. 103:62–63. Je. 25, '84. The Asian connection. Elaine Shannon.

Newsweek. 104:30. O. 8, '84. California's war against pot. Tom Morganthau.

Newsweek. 105:14–23. F. 25, '85. The evil empire. Harry Anderson.

*Newsweek. 105:28–30+. Mr. 18, '85. Drug wars: murder in Mexico. Harry Anderson.

Omni. 7:29. Ja. '85. Cocaine fires. Ronald K. Siegel.

Psychology Today. 17:36–44. O. '83. The chemistry of craving. Harvey Milkman and Stanley Sunderwirth.

Psychology Today. 19:20. Ja. '85. The lady is addictive. Sam A. Rosenfeld.

Reader's Digest. 121:98–102. Jl. '82. Havana's drug-smuggling connection. Nathan M. Adams.

Reader's Digest. 122:89–96+. Mr. '83. Inside the cocaine wars. Nathan M. Adams.

Reader's Digest. 125:35. D. '84. A cruel deception. David F. Musto.

Rolling Stone. 20–1+. J. 7, '83. The young, the rich and heroin. A. Haden-Guest.

Science. 215:1488–89. Mr. 19, '82. Marijuana "justifies serious concern." T. H. Maugh.

Science. 217:228–29. Jl. 16, '82. Frank Peress takes exception to NAS panel recommendations on marijuana. J. Walsh.

Science News. 124:55. Jl. 23, '83. Pot-smokers may be imperiled by paraquat-spraying program. L. Garmon.
Science News. 126:37–38. Jl. 21, '84. Cocaine smoking may cause lung damage. B. Bower.
Science News. 126:38. Jl. 21, '84. Steroids heft heart risks in iron pumpers. D. Franklin.
*Scientific American. 246:128+. Mr. '82. Cocaine. Craig Van Dyke and Robert Byck.
*Society. 20:67–80. Ja.–F. '83. Marijuana policy and drug mythology. Louis Lasagna and Gardner Lindzey.
Sporting News. 192:12. D. 12, '81. Baseball needs drug crackdown. Dick Young.
Sports Illustrated. 56:66–72+. Je. 14, '82. I'm not worth a damn. Don Reese.
Sports Illustrated. 57:24–26+. Ag. 9, '82. A test with nothing but tough questions. Douglas S. Looney.
Sports Illustrated. 59:62–66. Ag. 1, '83. The steroid predicament. Terry Todd.
Sports Illustrated. 60:36–38+. My. 28, '84. Taking steps to solve the drug dilemma. Jim Kaplan.
Time. 119:73. Mr. 8, '82. Another sort of smoke.
Time. 120:15. Ag. 9, '82. Grass was never greener. Anastasia Toufexis.
Time. 120:49. Ag. 9, '82. Coke and no smile. Tom Callahan.
Time. 120:30–38. N. 1, '82. The bottom line . . . busted. John S. DeMott.
Time. 121:32. Ja. 17, '83. Battle of the warlords. George Russell.
Time. 121:21. Mr. 28, '83. Belushi's death.
Time. 121:22–31. Ap. 11, '83. Crashing on cocaine. Kurt Anderson.
Time. 122:70. S. 5, '83. The big Caracas drug bust. Janice Castro.
Time. 125:26–33+. F. 25, '85. Fighting the cocaine wars. Pico Iyer.
UNESCO Courier. 35:4–34. Ja. '82. The drug dilemma.
USA Today. 112:4. O. '83. Treating drug-dependent women. Beth G. Reed.
USA Today 112:10–11. F. '84. Great risk to young athletes.
*U. S. News & World Report. 91:63–64. O. 12, '81. Marijuana: a U. S. farm crop that's booming. John S. Lang.
*U. S. News & World Report. 92:27–29. Mr. 22, '82. Cocaine spreads its deadly net. John S. Lang.
U. S. News & World Report. 93:54–55. O. 4, '82. Feds vs. drug runners: game gets trickier. Orr Kelly.

U. S. News & World Report. 94:59. My. 16, '83. Is show biz pushing drugs? the big debate. Alvin P. Sanoff.

U. S. News & World Report. 95:8. Ag. 8, '83. Behing the drug crackdown in pro sports.

U. S. News & World Report. 95:10. S. 5, '83. Why next Olympics may be drug-free.

U. S. News & World Report. 95:64–65. S. 12, '83. How drugs threaten to ruin pro sports. Alvin P. Sanoff.

U. S. News & World Report. 97:65–66. N. 19, '84. The deadly path of today's PCP epidemic. William L. Chaze.

*U. S. News & World Report. 98:52–57. Mr. 25, '85. Flood of drugs—a losing battle. Susanna McBee.

Wall Street Journal. Sect. 2, p. 34. Mr. 21, '84. Cocaine valued at $1.2 billion reported seized in Colombia.

Washington Post. Sect. A, p. 16. Jl. 16, '84. "Freebasing" of cocaine is reported severely damaging to users' lungs.

*World Press Review. 30:43. F. '83. The cocaine society. Guy Sitbon.

"PARTY
HARDY"